MECHANICS' INSTITUTE
~ MECHANICS' ~
MERCANTILE LIBRARY

Mortgage and Mortgage-Backed Securities Markets

Harvard Business School Press Series
in Financial Services Management
Series Editor: Samuel L. Hayes III

Mortgage and Mortgage-Backed Securities Markets

Frank J. Fabozzi
Franco Modigliani

HARVARD BUSINESS SCHOOL PRESS
Boston, Massachusetts

MECHANICS' INSTITUTE

96   95   94   93   92   5   4   3   2   1

Library of Congress Cataloging-in-Publication Data

Fabozzi, Frank J.
    Mortgage and mortgage-backed securities markets / Frank J.
Fabozzi, Franco Modigliani.
        p.   cm.
    Includes bibliographical references and index.   ISBN 0-87584-322-0 (pbk.)
    1. Mortgage-backed securities—United States.   1. Mortgages—
United States.   I. Modigliani, Franco.   II. Title
HG5095.F33   1992
332.7'2'0973—dc20   91-40849
                                                                          CIP

The paper used in this publication meets the requirements of the
American National Standard for Permanence of Paper for Printed Library
Materials Z-39-49-1984.

Contents

Acknowledgments   vii
1. Introduction   1
2. The Development of the Secondary Mortgage Market   15
3. Mortgage Origination   39
4. Mortgage Servicing and Insurance   61
5. The Traditional Mortgage   81
6. The Mismatch Problem and the Creation of Variable-Rate Mortgages   99
7. The Tilt Problem and the Creation of Other Mortgage Instruments   117
8. Features of Passthrough Securities   145
9. Price and Yield Conventions for Passthroughs   169
10. Factors Affecting Prepayment Behavior   197
11. Derivative Products: CMO and Stripped MBS   217
12. Review of Fixed-Income Analysis   249
13. Methodologies For Valuing Mortgage-Backed Securities   271
14. The Future of Asset Securitization   311
Index   329

Acknowledgments

We are indebted to many individuals who provided direct or indirect assistance in this project. The following people read earlier drafts of the manuscript and provided insightful comments that helped us significantly improve the final product: Anand Bhattacharya (Prudential Securities), Michael Ferri (George Mason University), Hal Hinkle (Goldman, Sachs), Frank Jones (The Guardian), Adolfo Marzol (Chase Home Mortgage Corporation), Frank Ramirez (MMAR Group), Scott Richard (Goldman, Sachs), and David Yuen (Franklin Resources Inc.). Students in the Investment Banking and Markets course at MIT read Chapters 8 through 13 and provided helpful comments. We benefited from Eric Silverman's research on the mortgage servicing industry in our writing of Chapter 4. Craig Wood (Olson Research) provided assistance in checking the analysis reported in Chapter 9.

We are grateful to Beth Preiss, editor-in-chief of *Secondary Mortgage Markets*, for giving us permission to reprint material and to use the Freddie Mac data base reported in that journal. We appreciate Andrew Carron (First Boston), Robert Kulason (Salomon Brothers), Paul Jablansky (Goldman, Sachs), and Gregory Parseghian (First Boston) for allowing us to use unpublished data prepared by their organizations. A special thanks to Scott Richard who permitted us to use examples demonstrating the application of OAS technology to CMO valuation in Chapter 13, and the joint research of Denise DiPasquale (Harvard University) on inflation-proof mortgages in our writing of Chapter 7.

Our production editor, Natalie Greenberg, efficiently assisted in many ways in moving this book through the production process. Chris Palaia provided helpful editorial comments.

Finally, we wish to thank our editor, Richard Luecke, for encouraging us to undertake this project and providing support at each phase.

January 1992   Frank J. Fabozzi
                                                         Franco Modigliani
                                                  Cambridge, Massachusetts

Mortgage and Mortgage-Backed Securities Markets

1

Introduction

While the American dream may be to own a home, the major portion of the funds to purchase one must be borrowed. The market where these funds are borrowed is called the mortgage market or, equivalently, the housing finance market. This sector of the debt market is by far the largest in the world, with an estimated size at the beginning of 1990 of roughly $3.5 trillion, an amount far exceeding the $1.9 trillion U.S. government securities market and $1.4 trillion corporate-bond market.

Public policy and private initiatives have sought to overcome the recurrent crises plaguing the housing finance market since the late 1960s. These crises can largely be traced to the interaction of a rising and fluctuating rate of inflation with two major institutional features that have characterized the financing of housing in the United States since World War II. These are (1) almost exclusive reliance on a mortgage instrument in which borrowers paid a fixed interest rate to finance the acquisition of their home; and (2) overwhelming dependence for mortgage funds on thrift institutions, primarily savings and loan associations, which secure the bulk of their funds through relatively short-term deposits.

In the 1970s and early 1980s, the focus of innovations was in the design of new mortgage instruments such as adjustable-rate mortgages and graduated-payment mortgages. These new designs attempted to overcome the unappealing features of the traditional fixed-rate mortgage from the perspective not only of borrowers, but also of lenders/

investors, thereby broadening the institutional base of potential investors. Although great strides have been made in designing mortgage instruments with greater economic appeal to borrowers, a mortgage design that can adequately cope with inflation has not been successfully marketed.

The liquidity of mortgages was enhanced with the creation of government agencies (Government National Mortgage Association, Federal Home Loan Mortgage Corporation, and Federal National Mortgage Association), which were charged by Congress to foster a secondary market. The major means of providing such liquidity was the creation of securities backed by a pool of mortgages and guaranteed by these agencies. The enhanced liquidity and reduced credit risk, coupled with a myriad of risk/return patterns offered by *mortgage-backed securities* (MBSs), further expanded the range of both U.S. and foreign (particularly, Japanese) institutional investors that were willing to invest in the mortgage market. As a result, the housing finance market that developed in the 1980s relies less on the savings and loan industry. Thus, the misfortunes of that industry will not have the dire consequences for the mortgage market that they would have had prior to the 1980s.

WHY STUDY THE MORTGAGE MARKET?

In addition to the importance of a well-functioning housing finance market and the importance for investors of understanding how to value mortgage-backed securities, there are other reasons for studying the mortgage market. First, a close examination of the development and current status of this market helps explain how the traditional method of financing assets by financial intermediaries will change in the future. The traditional method will be supplanted by a system in which individual assets will be pooled and used as collateral for the issuance of securities. This process, referred to as *asset securitization,* represents a transfer of the financial technology developed for the creation of mortgage-backed securities in the mortgage market to other loan markets such as credit card receivables, car loans, lease receivables, and senior bank loans. Moreover, the mortgage market clearly demonstrates how financial engineering can redirect cash flows from a pool of assets so as to create securities that more closely satisfy the asset/liability needs of institutional investors.

The second reason why the mortgage market is interesting is that it is a market in which the government or government-sponsored entities played an important function in providing credit guarantees for mortgage-backed securities. However, investment bankers and commercial bankers have used credit enhancements to structure mortgage-backed securities so that such securities receive high credit ratings without explicit or implicit government guarantees. The public policy question is then whether in the future the mortgage-backed securities market can be changed from a government-guaranteed market to a private market. In light of the projected cost of the savings and loan bailout, sentiment for making this change has increased.

Finally, a study of the mortgage market demonstrates how the frontiers of financial technology are being applied to the valuation of the assets traded in this market. The simplest product, the mortgage loan, is an instrument for which cash flow is unknown because the borrower/homeowner has an option to prepay part or all of the loan at any time. The uncertainty about when a borrower/homeowner will prepay a mortgage is called *prepayment risk,* and if it were not for this risk, the analysis of mortgages and mortgage-backed securities would be relatively straightforward. Investors have used option theory to determine whether they are adequately compensated for accepting the complex options embedded in mortgages and mortgage-backed securities. They have also applied econometric techniques to the forecasting of prepayments.

THE CREATION OF MORTGAGE-BACKED SECURITIES

In later chapters we will be discussing various mortgage-backed securities: passthrough securities, collateralized mortgage obligations, and stripped mortgage-backed securities. In this section, we will provide an overview of how these securities are created. Don't look for details here—these will be provided in later chapters. The investment characteristics and motivation for creating these instruments will also be discussed later in the book.

We will illustrate the creation of mortgage-backed securities using Figures 1-1 through 1-4. Figure 1-1 shows ten mortgage loans (each loan depicted as a home) and lists the cash flows from these loans. For the sake of simplicity, we will assume that the amount of each loan is $100,000 so that the aggregate value of all 10 loans is $1 million. The cash flows are monthly and consist of three components:

1. interest
2. scheduled principal repayment
3. payments in excess of the regularly scheduled principal repayment

How (1) and (2) are determined is explained in Chapter 5. The third component, payments in excess of the scheduled principal payment, is referred to as a *prepayment*. It is the amount and timing of this component of the cash flow from a mortgage that make the analysis of mortgages and mortgage-backed securities complicated. As we examine the way in which mortgage-backed securities are created, we will find that the total amount of prepayment risk does not change. The distribution of that risk among investors, however, can be altered.

An investor who owns one of the mortgage loans shown in Figure 1-1 faces prepayment risk. For an individual loan, it may be difficult to predict prepayments. If an individual investor purchased all ten loans, then the investor might be able to better predict prepayments. In fact, if there were 500 mortgage loans in Figure 1-1 rather than 10, the investor might be able to use historical prepayment experience to improve his or her predictions about prepayments. But an investor would have to invest $1 million to buy 10 loans and $50 million to buy 500 loans, assuming each loan is for $100,000.

Figure 1-1

Ten Mortgage Loans

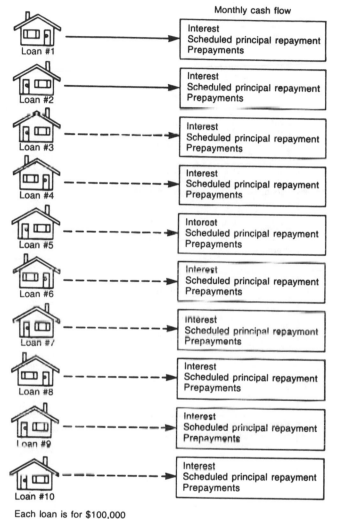

Each loan is for $100,000

Total loans: $1 million

Figure 1-2

Creation of a Passthrough Security

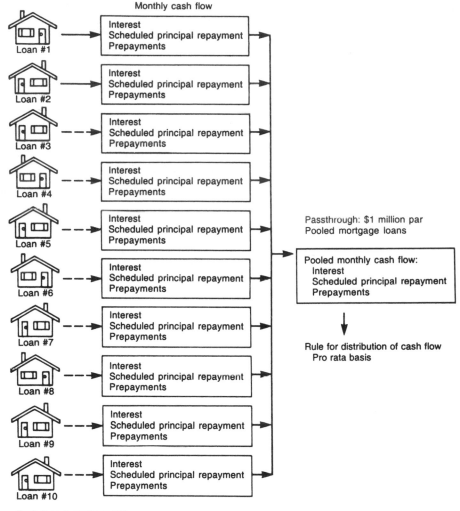

Each loan is for $100,000

Total loans: $1 million

Figure 1-3

Creation of a Collateralized Mortgage Obligation

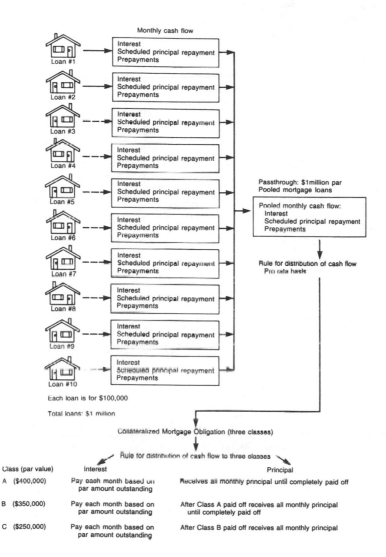

Each loan is for $100,000

Total loans: $1 million

Collateralized Mortgage Obligation (three classes)

Rule for distribution of cash flow to three classes

Class (par value)	Interest	Principal
A ($400,000)	Pay each month based on par amount outstanding	Receives all monthly principal until completely paid off
B ($350,000)	Pay each month based on par amount outstanding	After Class A paid off receives all monthly principal until completely paid off
C ($250,000)	Pay each month based on par amount outstanding	After Class B paid off receives all monthly principal

Figure 1-4

Creation of a Stripped Mortgage-Backed Security

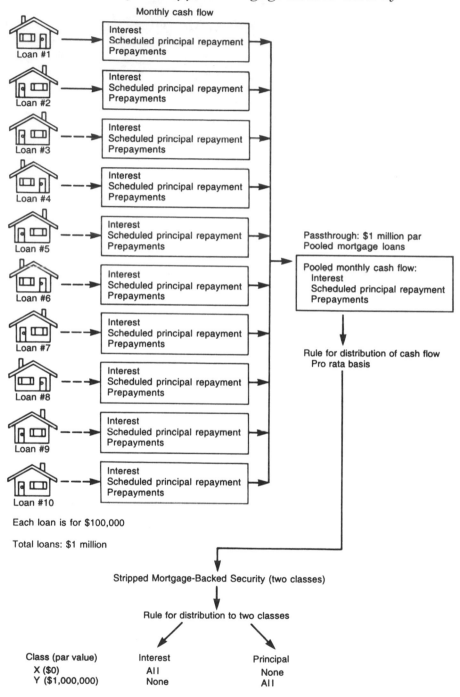

Monthly cash flow

Loan #1 — Interest / Scheduled principal repayment / Prepayments
Loan #2 — Interest / Scheduled principal repayment / Prepayments
Loan #3 — Interest / Scheduled principal repayment / Prepayments
Loan #4 — Interest / Scheduled principal repayment / Prepayments
Loan #5 — Interest / Scheduled principal repayment / Prepayments
Loan #6 — Interest / Scheduled principal repayment / Prepayments
Loan #7 — Interest / Scheduled principal repayment / Prepayments
Loan #8 — Interest / Scheduled principal repayment / Prepayments
Loan #9 — Interest / Scheduled principal repayment / Prepayments
Loan #10 — Interest / Scheduled principal repayment / Prepayments

Each loan is for $100,000

Total loans: $1 million

Passthrough: $1 million par
Pooled mortgage loans

Pooled monthly cash flow:
Interest
Scheduled principal repayment
Prepayments

Rule for distribution of cash flow
Pro rata basis

Stripped Mortgage-Backed Security (two classes)

Rule for distribution to two classes

Class (par value)	Interest	Principal
X ($0)	All	None
Y ($1,000,000)	None	All

Passthroughs

Suppose, instead, that some entity purchases all 10 loans in Figure 1-1 and pools them. The 10 loans can be used as collateral for the issuance of a security, with the cash flow from that security reflecting the cash flow from the 10 loans, as depicted in Figure 1-2. Suppose that 40 units of this security are issued. Thus, each unit is initially worth $25,000 ($1 million divided by 40). Each unit will be entitled to 2.5% (1/40) of the cash flow. The security created is called a *mortgage passthrough security,* or simply, a *passthrough.*

Let's see what has been accomplished by creating the passthrough. The total amount of prepayment risk has not changed. Now, however, with an amount of less than $1 million, the investor can be exposed to the total prepayment risk of all 10 loans rather than face the risk of an individual mortgage loan.

So far, this financial engineering has not resulted in the creation of a totally new instrument, since an individual investor could have accomplished the same outcome by purchasing all 10 loans. But buying a passthrough does enable an investor with less than $1 million to acquire a proportionate share of all 10 loans; as explained in later chapters, the marketability of a passthrough is also greater than that of individual loans. Moreover, by selling a passthrough the investor can dispose of all 10 loans simultaneously rather than having to dispose of each loan one by one. A passthrough can thus be viewed as a more transactionally efficient vehicle for investing in mortgages than is the purchasing of individual mortgages.

Mortgage loans that are included in a pool to create a passthrough are said to be *securitized.* The process of creating a passthrough is what we referred to earlier as securitization.

Collateralized Mortgage Obligations (CMOs)

An investor in a passthrough is still exposed to the total prepayment risk associated with the underlying pool of mortgage loans. Instruments can be created, however, in which investors do not share prepayment risk equally. Suppose that instead of distributing the monthly cash flow on a pro rata basis as in the case of a passthrough, the distribution of the principal (both scheduled and prepayments) is carried out on some prioritized basis. How this is done is illustrated in Figure 1-3.

Figure 1-3 shows the cash flow of our original 10 mortgage loans and the passthrough. Also shown are three classes of bonds, the par value of each class, and a set of rules indicating how the principal from the passthrough is to be distributed to each. Note the following. The sum of the par value of the three classes is equal to $1 million. Though not shown in the figure, for each of the three classes there will be units representing a proportionate interest in a class. For example, suppose that for Class A, which has a par value of $400,000, there are 50 units of Class A issued. Each unit would receive a proportionate share (2%) of what is received by Class A.

The rule for the distribution of principal shown in Figure 1-3 is that Class A will receive all principal (both scheduled and prepayments) until that class receives its entire par value of $400,000. Then, Class B receives all principal payments until it receives its par value of $350,000. After Class B is completely paid off, Class C receives principal payments. The rule for the distribution of cash flow in Figure 1-3 indicates that each of the three classes will receive interest based on the amount of par value outstanding.

The mortgage-backed security that has been created is called a *collateralized mortgage obligation*. The collateral for a loan may be either one or more passthroughs or a pool of mortgage loans that have not been securitized. The ultimate source for the CMO's cash flow is the pool of mortgage loans. The process of using passthroughs to create CMOs is called *resecuritization*.

Let's look at what has been accomplished. Once again, the total prepayment risk for the CMO is the same as the total prepayment risk for the 10 mortgage loans. However, the prepayment risk has been distributed among the three classes of the CMO. Class A absorbs prepayments first, then Class B, and then Class C. The result of this is that Class A will effectively have a shorter-term security than the other two classes; Class C will have the longest maturity. Certain institutional investors will be attracted to the different classes given the nature of their liability structure and the effective maturity of the CMO class. Moreover, the uncertainty about the maturity of each class of the CMO is far less than the uncertainty about the maturity of the passthrough.

Thus, by redirecting the cash flow from the underlying mortgage pool, classes of bonds have been created that satisfy the asset/liability objectives of certain institutional investors better than a passthrough. In theory, a CMO is not a new market instrument since it simply represents the redirecting of the cash flow. However, it is a more transactionally efficient instrument for distributing prepayment risk.

The CMO we depicted in Figure 1-3 has a simple set of rules for prioritizing the distribution of principal. Today, much more complicated CMO structures exist. The purpose is to provide certain CMO classes with less uncertainty about prepayment risk. However, this can occur only if the reduction in prepayment risk for such classes is absorbed by other classes in the CMO structure.

Stripped Mortgage-Backed Securities

Consider once again the 10 mortgage loans in Figure 1-1. In the CMO there was a set of rules for prioritizing the distribution of the principal payments among the various classes. In a stripped mortgage-backed security, the principal and interest are divided among two classes unequally. For example, one class may be entitled to receive all of the principal and the other class all of the interest. This is depicted in Figure 1-4. Since the collateral for a stripped mortgage-backed security is a passthrough, this is another example of resecuritization.

What may be confusing is why stripped mortgage-backed securities are created. We outlined the motivation for the creation of passthroughs and CMOs, but no motivation was given for a stripped mortgage-backed security. A detailed explanation is provided in Chapter 11. For now it is sufficient to say that the risk/return characteristics of these instruments make them attractive for purposes of hedging a portfolio of passthroughs and hedging other assets such as mortgage servicing rights, which we describe briefly below and in more detail in Chapter 4.

Mortgage Servicing Rights

The cash flow to investors in Figures 1-1 through 1-4 omitted an important component: a fee paid to service a mortgage loan. Unlike other capital market instruments, a loan must be serviced. If an investor in mortgage-backed securities were forced to maintain an administrative staff to service the underlying pool of mortgage loans, the appeal of these securities to institutional investors would diminish.

Fortunately, the servicing of mortgage loans can be separated from the investment in those loans. This is depicted in Figure 1-5 which is similar to Figure 1-2 but now shows that the cash flow is separated into two parts: (1) a servicing fee (a fixed percentage of the outstanding mortgage balance), and (2) the cash flow minus the servicing fee. The right to service the mortgage loan is an asset for which cash flow is uncertain because of the uncertainty about prepayments and the future cost associated with servicing a mortgage.

OVERVIEW OF THE BOOK

In Chapter 2, we describe the development of the secondary mortgage market. We describe how the market has been transformed from one that was totally dependent on local deposits in savings and loan associations, which were also the major investors, to a market that now has a broad base of investors in the United States and overseas.

In Chapter 3, we explain the mortgage origination process and the risks associated with it. The various strategies that can be employed to manage these risks are reviewed. After a mortgage loan is originated, it must be serviced. The investor in a mortgage loan is often different from the entity that services the mortgage. In Chapter 4, we describe the eco-

Figure 1-5

Cash Flow When Servicing Is Considered

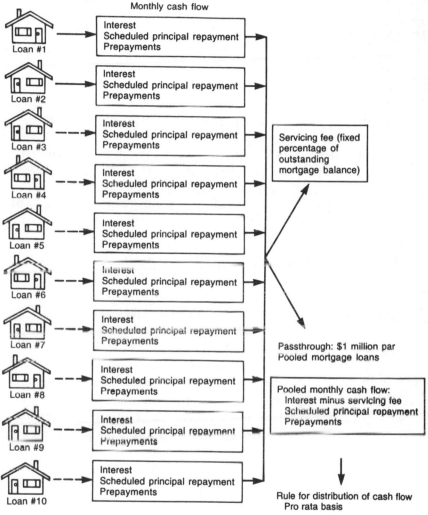

Each loan is for $100,000

Total loans: $1 million

nomics of the mortgage servicing and mortgage insurance industries.

Chapters 5, 6, and 7 describe alternative mortgage designs. We begin in Chapter 5 with an explanation of the traditional mortgage design, the fixed-rate level payment mortgage. The drawbacks of this mortgage are highlighted in terms of what is referred to as the "mismatch problem" and the "tilt problem." The former problem led to the creation of variable-rate mortgage designs, described in Chapter 6. Alternative mortgage designs such as the graduated-payment mortgage and the price-level adjustment mortgage were introduced to mitigate the tilt problem. However, these mortgage designs fail to protect borrowers and investors against inflation. In Chapter 7, we illustrate these various mortgage designs and describe a mortgage design, the dual-rate or MIT mortgage, that we believe provides a solution to the inflation problem.

Chapter 8 describes the various types of passthroughs and their investment characteristics. The conventions for determining prepayments and therefore a passthrough's cash flow, price, and yield are illustrated in Chapter 9. The factors affecting prepayments are explained in Chapter 10. The various types of CMOs and stripped mortgage-backed securities are the subject of Chapter 11.

In the first 11 chapters there is no attempt to analyze mortgage-backed securities. Chapter 13 explains the various technologies that have been employed to value mortgage-backed securities. Since these concepts rely on fundamental principles of fixed-income analysis, Chapter 12 provides a review of these principles.

We conclude this book with a discussion of the merits of asset securitization and its extensions to other loans in Chapter 14.

2

The Development of the Secondary Mortgage Market

The mortgage market is a collection of markets that includes a primary mortgage market, or origination market, and a secondary market in which mortgages trade. These two markets are related: the development of a strong secondary market was essential for the development of the robust primary market in the United States. Similarly, the secondary market is dependent on a consistent and healthy primary market for its product or raw material.

While we provide here a thumbnail sketch of the early mortgage market—to give the reader an appreciation of the need for a secondary mortgage market—the focus of this chapter is on the secondary mortgage market. That market includes the market for whole loans and the market for mortgage-backed securities. Our primary focus is on products backed by single-family mortgage loans. The secondary markets for mortgages backed by multifamily houses and commercial property are still in the early stages of development.

GOVERNMENT INTERVENTION IN THE HOUSING MARKET

A major goal of U.S. public policy is to provide adequate and affordable housing for U.S. citizens. Historically, the private sector has not been able to accomplish this goal without the intervention of the federal government. To understand the ways in which the government can intervene in the housing market, it is necessary to recognize the three groups participating in the housing market: (1) those who demand funds with which to purchase a home (i.e., borrowers), (2) those who supply funds by investing in mortgage loans or mortgage-related products (i.e., investors), and (3) those who supply housing (i.e., builders).[1] The amount of housing construction and the amount of funds demanded for the purchase of homes are determined by the combined actions of these three groups.

The U.S. government has influenced the behavior of all three groups by creating government agencies or government-sponsored entities that have done one or more of the following:

- insured or guaranteed mortgage loans against default, thus making mortgage funds available to certain segments of the population who would not otherwise have been able to acquire a home; moreover, government guarantees made such mortgage loans attractive to investors;
- introduced or promoted various types of mortgage designs that are more attractive to borrowers and investors;
- developed various mortgage-backed securities products such as passthroughs and collateralized obligations, and guaranteed those products against default risk so that a wider range of institutional investors would supply funds to the mortgage market;
- standardized mortgage loan terms and documentation as a result of the process of insuring/guaranteeing mortgage loans and securitizing them;
- provided liquidity to the mortgage market by buying mortgage loans;

---

[1] This description of the housing and mortgage market is provided in Roy C. Fair, "Disequilibrium in Housing Models," *Journal of Finance* (May 1972), pp. 207–221.

- provided credit facilities to certain lenders in the mortgage market; and
- granted loans at an interest rate below the prevailing market rate to encourage the construction of low-income housing.

Most of these functions are described in this chapter, as we discuss the role of the U.S. government in the development of the secondary mortgage market.

Government intervention has not come without a cost. Several policies, particularly those relating to savings and loan associations, were ill conceived and resulted in the problems we noted in Chapter 1. The issue facing public policy decision makers today is whether the private sector can now step in and adequately fulfill several of the functions that previously required government intervention.

LIMITATIONS OF THE EARLY MORTGAGE MARKET

In the first decades of the post–World War II period, the bulk of mortgage loans was originated and kept in the portfolios of depository institutions (and to a lesser extent, insurance companies). By 1950, depository institutions held nearly 50% of these loans, of which S&Ls held 20%; by the mid-1970s, the share of depository institutions had grown to 64%, of which S&Ls held 37%.

Thus, the supply of funds to the mortgage market was dependent on the ability of depository institutions, particularly S&Ls, to raise funds. Depository institutions, however, were encouraged by legislation and regulation to confine their deposit seeking and lending activities to their local market. Since they were constrained to obtain their funds from local citizens, a poor allocation of mortgage capital resources resulted, as some regions had an excess supply of funds and low rates and others experienced shortages and high rates.

Enter a new participant—the mortgage banker or, more accurately, the mortgage broker. Unlike thrift and commercial bankers, mortgage bankers did not provide funds from deposit taking. Instead, they originated mortgages and sold them, not only to life insurance companies, but also to thrifts in other parts of the country looking for mortgage investments. They provided a brokerage function, laying the foundation for a national market. Although the mortgage market operated this way through the late 1960s, it had a major flaw—it remained dependent on the availability of funds from thrifts and banks, either local or national.

The late 1960s was a period of high and fluctuating inflation and interest rates; disintermediation, induced by government-imposed interest rate ceilings on deposits, led to a reduction in the funds available to all depository institutions for investment in the mortgage market. Even if funds were available, the traditional fixed-rate mortgage loan in such an economic environment was an unattractive investment, particularly to depository institutions that were borrowing short term. To counter, or at least mitigate, this problem, a mortgage market that was not dependent on deposit-taking institutions was needed. This could be accomplished by developing a strong secondary mortgage market in which financial institutions, in addition to deposit-taking institutions and life insurance companies, would find it attractive to make investments that in turn provided funds to housing. To make mortgage loans more palatable to other financial institutions, new mortgage designs and security structures collateralized by mortgage loans had to be developed.

FOUNDATIONS FOR THE DEVELOPMENT OF THE SECONDARY MARKET

The foundations for the secondary mortgage market can be traced back to the Great Depression and resulting congressional legislation. Congress's response to the depression's adverse effects on financial markets was to establish several public-purpose agencies. The two entities that were established to provide credit facilities for depository institutions were the Federal Reserve for commercial banks and the Federal Home Loan Banks for thrifts.

Congress founded the Federal Housing Administration (FHA) through the National Housing Act of 1934. The FHA was authorized to provide programs to assist in constructing, acquiring, and/or rehabilitating single-family and multifamily properties. Following World War II, its role expanded to programs for urban renewal projects, hospitals, and nursing homes. To meet its policy objectives, the FHA did two things.[2] First, it reduced credit risk for investors by offering insurance against mortgage defaults. Not all mortgages could be insured, however. To be insured, the mortgage applicant had to satisfy the underwriting standards established by the FHA. The FHA was thus the first agency to standardize the mortgage design it insured. While this standardization may be taken for granted today, it was essential for the development of a secondary mortgage market.

Second, in the process of insuring mortgages, the FHA developed and promoted a mortgage design that would be more palatable to borrowers. Prior to the founding of the FHA, only balloon mortgages were available. In a balloon mortgage, the homeowner made only interest payments over the term of the mortgage; that is, no periodic payments were made to reduce the original loan balance. At the maturity date of the mortgage, usually between 5 and 10 years after the loan was obtained, the original loan balance had to be repaid, with the proceeds for repayment typically coming from yet another mortgage loan. This mortgage design increased the probability of default, since a homeowner, for a variety of reasons, might not have found a funding source to pay off the balloon payment due. The FHA developed and promoted the long-term, self-amortizing mortgage loan that we shall discuss in Chapter 5. This provided for continual repayment of the principal balance, making the balloon payment unnecessary.

Who was going to invest in these mortgages? Thrifts could, and they had, at that time, tax incentives to do so. But these investments would be illiquid in the absence of a market in which they could be traded. Congress thought of that, too. It created a government-sponsored agency, the Federal National Mortgage Association (FNMA) to provide liquidity. This agency, popularly known as "Fannie Mae," was charged with the responsibility for creating a liquid secondary market for

[2]The FHA was made part of the Department of Housing and Urban Development in 1965.

mortgages by primarily buying FHA mortgages. Unlike mortgage bankers, Fannie Mae was an investor in mortgages.

Despite the presence of Fannie Mae, the secondary mortgage market did not develop to any significant extent. During periods of tight money, Fannie Mae could do little to mitigate the problem because of the continued reliance on depository institutions to originate mortgage loans. In response to this problem, Congress divided Fannie Mae into two organizations in 1968: (1) the current Fannie Mae, and (2) the Government National Mortgage Association (popularly known as "Ginnie Mae"). Ginnie Mae's function was to use the "full faith and credit of the U.S. government" to support the FHA mortgage market, as well as the market for mortgage loans insured by two other government agencies, the Veterans Administration (VA) and the Farmers Home Administration (FmHA).[3]

Two years later in 1970, Congress authorized Fannie Mae to purchase conventional mortgage loans (i.e., those not insured by the FHA, VA, or FmHA) and created the Federal Home Loan Mortgage Corporation ("Freddie Mac") to provide support for conventional and FHA/VA/FmHA mortgage loans. While Fannie Mae and Freddie Mac are commonly referred to as "agencies" of the U.S. government, both are corporate instrumentalities of the U.S. government. The stock of these two entities trades on the New York Stock Exchange; therefore they are effectively quasi-private corporations. They do not receive a government subsidy or appropriation, and are taxed like any other corporation. Fannie Mae and Freddie Mac are more appropriately referred to as government-sponsored entities. The guarantee of a government-sponsored entity does not carry the full faith and credit of the U.S. government. In contrast, Ginnie Mae is a government-related agency because it is part of the Department of Housing and Urban Development. As such, its guarantee carries the full faith and credit of the U.S. government.

Ginnie Mae accomplished its objective by guaranteeing securities issued by private entities that pooled FHA, VA,

[3]The Veterans Administration began insuring qualified loans to veterans in 1944. The Farmers Home Administration was created in 1947 to provide rural housing and development funding at below-market interest rates; in that capacity it guarantees qualified loans.

and FmHA mortgages together, using the mortgages as collateral for the security sold. Freddie Mac and Fannie Mae purchased and pooled primarily conventional mortgages and then issued securities using the pool of mortgages as collateral. As we explained in Chapter 1, this process of converting individual mortgages into securities collateralized by mortgage pools is called securitization, and the securities thus created are known as passthroughs. The way in which these three government agencies guaranteed their securities will be discussed in Chapter 8. These passthroughs were then purchased by many types of investors who had previously shunned individual mortgages.

THE AGENCY MORTGAGE-BACKED SECURITIES MARKET

Table 2-1 shows the total amount of passthroughs issued or guaranteed by the three agencies, while Table 2-2 shows the origination of passthroughs by agency from 1984 to 1990. (Also shown in Table 2-2 is the same information for private issuers, whom we will discuss later in this chapter.)

Ginnie Mae mortgage-backed securities were first issued in 1968. As can be seen from Table 2-1, they are the largest type of passthroughs outstanding; however, as Table 2-2 clearly indicates, in 1989 and 1990, the annual issuance of Ginnie Mae passthroughs was less than that of Fannie Mae and Freddie Mac. Although Ginnie Mae guarantees these passthroughs, it does not issue them. That is the task of the lenders

Table 2-1

Outstanding Passthroughs by Agency as of September 1991

Agency	Outstanding ($ millions)
Ginnie Mae	$ 418,421
Freddie Mac	341,132
Fannie Mae	331,089
Total	$1,090,642

Source: Federal Reserve.

Table 2-2

Origination of Passthroughs by Agency, 1984–1990
($ millions)

Year	Ginnie Mae	Freddie Mac	Fannie Mae	Private Firms	Total
1984	28,097	18,684	13,546	6,273	66,600
1985	45,980	38,829	23,649	6,916	115,374
1986	101,433	100,198	60,566	13,163	275,360
1987	94,929	75,018	63,229	18,576	251,764
1988	55,248	39,777	54,878	20,699	170,667
1989	57,190	73,518	69,764	12,010	212,715
1990	64,651	73,815	96,695	14,341	249,502

Source: Adapted from *Secondary Mortgage Markets* (Summer 1991) by permission of Freddie Mac. All rights reserved.

it approves: thrifts, commercial banks, and mortgage bankers. Only mortgages insured or guaranteed by either the FHA, VA, or FmHA can be included in a mortgage pool guaranteed by Ginnie Mae. By guaranteeing the securities issued by approved lenders, Ginnie Mae permits these lenders to convert illiquid individual mortgages into liquid securities backed by the U.S. government.

This action accomplishes the goals set forth for Ginnie Mae by Congress: to supply funds to the FHA/VA/FmHA-insured mortgage market and to provide an active secondary market. The former objective is accomplished as more institutional investors are willing to invest in passthroughs, thereby providing funds to the housing finance market. The latter objective is accomplished in two ways: (1) the liquidity of individual mortgage loans is enhanced by the lenders' ability to sell their mortgage loans to other institutions that will securitize them; and (2) passthroughs are actively traded, thereby effectively improving the liquidity of mortgage loans.

The second-largest type of agency passthrough securities are those issued by Freddie Mac. The primary security issued by Freddie Mac is called a *participation certificate* (PC), first issued in 1971. Most of the pools of mortgages underlying Freddie Mac participation certificates consist of conventional mortgages (i.e., mortgages not backed by a government agency), although PCs with underlying pools consisting of FHA-insured and VA-guaranteed mortgages have been issued.

Freddie Mac has two programs by which it creates PCs: the *Cash Program* and the *Guarantor/Swap Program*. In the former program the individual mortgages that back the PC are those purchased from mortgage originators, then pooled by Freddie Mac and sold in the market or in daily auctions through its dealer network. Under the Conventional Guarantor/Swap Program, Freddie Mac allows originators to swap pooled mortgages for PCs in those same pools. For example, a thrift may have $50 million of mortgages. It can swap these mortgages for a Freddie Mac PC in which the underlying mortgage pool is the same $50 million in mortgage loans that the thrift swapped for the PC.

Both programs provide capital to the residential mortgage market and foster a secondary mortgage market. The Guarantor/Swap Program, started in 1984, was specifically designed by Freddie Mac to provide liquidity to the troubled thrift industry. This program allowed thrifts to swap mortgages that were trading below par (that is, with mortgage rates less than the mortgage rate prevailing in the market) without being forced to recognize an accounting loss for financial reporting purposes. The PC received by the thrift in exchange for the mortgage pool could then be either (1) held as an investment, (2) used as collateral for either short-term or long-term borrowing, or (3) sold. The Guarantor/Swap program was a huge success and is one of the reasons for the recent growth in PC issues. This can be seen in Table 2-3, which shows passthrough issuance by program from 1984 to 1990. The swap program clearly dominates.

Fannie Mae was created by Congress in 1938, but in its present form it is the youngest player in the agency passthrough securities market. While Fannie Mae has purchased mortgages and held them as investments since 1972, it was not until 1981 that Fannie Mae pooled these mortgages and issued its first mortgage passthroughs, called *mortgage-backed securities*. In late 1984, Fannie Mae became the first agency to issue passthroughs backed by a pool of adjustable-rate mortgage loans. Fannie Mae also has a swap program similar to that of Freddie Mac, providing liquidity to mortgage

Table 2-3

Freddie Mac Passthrough Origination for Cash and Swap Programs, 1984–1990 ($ millions)

Year	Cash Program	Swap Program
1984	3,349	15,335
1985	13,230	25,598
1986	41,799	58,399
1987	17,935	57,083
1988	11,049	28,728
1989	12,533	60,985
1990	16,095	57,720

Source: Adapted from *Secondary Mortgage Markets* (Summer 1991) by permission of Freddie Mac. All rights reserved.

originators such as thrifts. Origination for the cash and swap programs is shown in Table 2-4. The swap program is by far the more popular program.

Ginnie Mae, Freddie Mac, and Fannie Mae passthroughs are backed primarily by a pool of single-family (1-to-4 family) mortgages. Of the estimated $2.74 trillion of 1-to-4 family mortgage debt outstanding at the end of the first quarter of 1991, about $1.11 trillion, or 40%, had been securitized. In contrast, only 10% of the total multifamily mortgage debt outstanding of $303 billion had been securitized.[4] An important breakthrough in the development of the secondary market for multifamily mortgages came in 1984 when Fannie Mae created the first passthrough collateralized by multifamily mortgages through its swap program.[5] Three months later, Freddie Mac issued through its swap program a passthrough in which the underlying collateral was a pool of multifamily mortgages.[6] An important innovation introduced by Freddie Mac in July 1988 was a program in which the financial institution that sold a multifamily mortgage could do so with differ-

---

[4] *Secondary Mortgage Markets*, Summer 1991.
[5] In the transaction, Midwest Federal Savings and Loan of Minnesota swapped about $140 million in multifamily mortgages for a Fannie Mae MBS. Subsequently, these Fannie Mae MBSs were used to create a CMO.
[6] This transaction involved more than $800 million of multifamily mortgages swapped by Financial Corporation of America.

Table 2-4

Fannie Mae Passthrough Origination for Cash and Swap Programs, 1984–1990 ($ millions)

Year	Cash Program	Swap Program
1984	979	12,567
1985	1,319	22,330
1986	10,957	49,609
1987	5,214	58,015
1988	5,047	49,831
1989	3,036	66,728
1990	5,845	90,850

ent degrees of recourse obligation, rather than on a nonrecourse basis. The guarantee fee charged by Freddie Mac varied with the degree of recourse.

Despite the greater appeal of passthroughs to nontraditional mortgage investors, a large segment of the institutional investor community remained reluctant to invest in these securities. The investment characteristics that made these securities unattractive to such investors were mentioned in the previous chapter and will be discussed further in Chapter 8. In June 1983, Freddie Mac created a new type of mortgage-backed security, the collateralized mortgage obligation, designed to appeal to institutional investors with varying asset/liability objectives. As explained in Chapter 1, CMOs are created by redirecting the cash flow from the underlying mortgage pool to various bond classes based on some set of priority rules for the distribution of principal and interest. Table 2-5 shows the origination of CMOs by agency from 1984 to 1990. At the time of this writing, Ginnie Mae had not been involved in the CMO market; however, the possibility of its future involvement was under review.

To show the broader appeal of mortgage-backed securities, Table 2-6 gives the estimated proportion of these securities held by U.S. institutions. Less than 25% of these securities are held by thrifts. The increasing appeal of these securities for non-U.S. investors can be seen by looking at the

Table 2-5

Origination of CMOs by Agency, 1984–1990 ($ millions)

Year	Ginnie Mae	Freddie Mac	Fannie Mae	Private Firms	Total
1984	0	1,805	0	9,392	11,197
1985	0	2,905	0	12,973	15,878
1986	0	1,573	0	46,494	48,067
1987	0	0	916	58,137	59,053
1988	0	14,985	10,782	50,984	76,751
1989	0	39,731	44,043	16,730	100,504
1990	0	38,676	58,819	21,064	118,559

Note: Excludes state and local credit agencies.
Source: Adapted from *Secondary Mortgage Markets* (Summer 1991) by permission of Freddie Mac. All rights reserved.

Table 2-6

Percentage Distribution of Holdings of Mortgage-Backed Securities by U.S. Institutions

Thrifts	23.4%
Banks	21.0
Pension funds	9.7
Life insurance companies	14.4
Dealers, mutual funds, asset managers, and property and casualty ins. cos.	31.5

Source: Bear Stearns & Co., Inc.

distribution of the 1990 production of agency MBSs: Japanese investors purchased about 11.25% and European and U.K. investors purchased about 3.75%.[7]

The Effect of FIRREA

In 1989, as a result of the savings and loan crisis, Congress passed the Financial Institutions Reform, Recovery, and Enforcement Act (FIRREA). While there are numerous provisions in FIRREA that affect thrifts and how they are regulated,

[7]This information was provided by Bear Stearns & Co., Inc.

we will restrict our discussion here to only those provisions that affect the secondary mortgage market.

First, FIRREA gave the primary regulatory responsibility for Freddie Mac to the Department of Housing and Urban Development (HUD). Fannie Mae had already been under the supervision of HUD. Second, the law required thrifts to satisfy specific capital standards similar to those imposed on banks. By similar, we mean that it imposed risk-based capital guidelines, where "risk" means credit risk. These capital guidelines will adversely affect the issuance by thrifts of private passthroughs (to be discussed later) backed by single-family and multifamily mortgages. Third, FIRREA will affect areas of the mortgage market (such as low-income housing) that historically have not been well served by the existing secondary market.

Finally, as a result of the U.S. bailout of the savings and loan industry, Congress grew increasingly concerned with the potential cost of having to bail out government sponsored entities such as Freddie Mac and Fannie Mae. FIRREA mandated the General Accounting Office (GAO) and the Secretary of the Treasury to study the matter and prepare reports for Congress. Specifically, they were to investigate whether government-sponsored entities maintained appropriate capital levels given the risks associated with their activities. In addition, the Treasury was to assess the impact of the activities of government-sponsored agencies on federal borrowing.

Market Making

Table 2-7 shows the substantial trading activity of existing agency mortgage-backed securities. The top panel shows the dollar volume for the years 1984 to 1990; the lower panel shows the turnover (the ratio of dollar volume to the amount of issues outstanding). According to the Market Reports Division of the Federal Reserve Bank of New York, for the week ended May 15, 1991, daily average primary dealer transactions of agency MBSs were about $12.4 billion, $5.7 billion being transactions between primary dealers and brokers and $6.7 billion being transactions between primary dealers and customers. For U.S. government securities over the

Table 2-7

Trading of Existing Issues of Agency Mortgage-Backed Securities, 1984–1989*

Volume
($ millions)

Year	Ginnie Mae	Other**	Total
1984	646,682	222,587	869,269
1985	919,416	494,817	1,414,233
1986	1,451,063	1,259,586	2,710,649
1987	1,630,376	1,317,866	2,948,242
1988	1,261,288	1,184,980	2,446,208
1989	1,522,568	1,577,786	3,100,354

Turnover
(Ratio of volume to the amount of existing issues)

Year	Ginnie Mae	Other**	Total
1984	3.59	1.46	2.62
1985	4.33	2.44	3.41
1986	5.52	4.16	4.79
1987	5.13	3.29	4.10
1988	3.70	2.93	3.28
1989	4.13	3.15	3.57

*Volume data are estimates based on dealer transactions in U.S. government and federal agency securities as reported by the Federal Reserve Bank of New York.
**"Other" constitutes primarily Freddie Mac and Fannie Mae securities.
Source: Adapted from Secondary Mortgage Markets (Summer 1991) by permission of Freddie Mac. All rights reserved.

same week, the corresponding daily average primary dealer transactions were $136.9 billion, $83.7 billion, and $53.2 billion, respectively. Although the amount of secondary market transactions of agency mortgage-backed securities is substantial, it is still small in comparison with trading in U.S. government securities, which is the most actively traded cash market in the world.

Trading in the secondary market has been fostered by several factors. First, investment banking firms and commercial banks have committed capital to make markets in passthroughs and CMOs. Second, because of the improved liquidity of the market, institutional investors have been more willing to trade mortgage-backed securities actively. Such trading has allowed them either to capitalize on expectations about yield spread changes between these securities and other sectors of the bond market or to rebalance a portfolio based on the changing characteristics of their liabilities.

A measure of the liquidity of the market is the bid-ask spread; the narrower the spread, the better the liquidity. Bid-ask spreads on agency passthroughs are now typically between 1/32nd and 4/32nds.[8] (A 32nd is 1/32 of 1%.) The spread represents the risk of market making and the degree of effective competition.

The second half of the 1980s saw a sharp decline in bid-ask spreads for several reasons. First was the increased competition among U.S. investment banking firms, money center banks, and, more recently, foreign securities firms. Initially, dealer firms competed by offering a variety of services to clients in exchange for transactions. Examples of such services included the valuation of mortgage-backed securities, asset/liability analysis for commercial banks and thrifts, and research information. Today, the passthrough market is more of a commodity business.

Second, the development of a myriad of interest rate risk-control tools allowed dealer firms to reduce their capital risk effectively and inexpensively. This is not to say that there was not an extensive learning process involved with hedging positions—in early 1986 several dealer firms realized substantial losses both on their long passthrough position and on a short position in Treasury futures that they had tried to use to hedge their long position.

Standardized agreements to accommodate the nuances of the mortgage-backed securities market were developed to permit dealer firms to improve their market-making capabilities. More specifically, the repurchase agreement[9]

---

[8]These spreads are for TBA (to be announced) trades. A TBA trade is one in which the pool information is not known at the time of the the trade. This is discussed further in Chapter 8. Spreads higher than those given above may reflect services performed by the dealer firm on behalf of the customer.

[9]In a repurchase agreement (or "repo"), one party agrees to sell a security to a counterparty and, at some specified future date, to purchase from that counterparty an identical security at a predetermined price. Effectively, a repo is a collateralized loan transaction. The difference between the purchase price and sale price represents interest. The repo market is used by dealer firms to either finance their inventory position or cover their short position.

limited the flexibility of dealers in covering a short position so as to avoid the expensive cost of a fail[10] or to postpone delivery of a security to a future date. If the dealer uses a repurchase agreement in such cases,[11] the dealer firm is obligated to return the identical security. The *dollar roll agreement* (or simply, *dollar roll*) is a form of collateralized borrowing developed for the passthrough market. A dollar roll permits dealer firms greater flexibility in covering a short position by allowing a dealer firm to return "substantially identical" securities.[12]

THE PRIVATE MORTGAGE-BACKED SECURITIES MARKET

The mortgages that the agencies may purchase or guarantee in securitized form are restricted to those that meet their underwriting standards, which set limits such as the maximum size of the loan and the maximum ratio of the amount of the loan to the amount of the market value of the mortgaged property. Such mortgages are called *conforming mortgages*. Similarly, a mortgage that fails to satisfy the underwriting standard is called a *nonconforming mortgage*. Mortgage loans that are greater than the maximum permissible loan size are referred to as *jumbo loans*. Congress has periodically increased the maximum amount of the loan that may be included in passthroughs guaranteed by the three agencies, but it is still often below the typical average cost of a home in certain geographical areas.

The agencies did not do anything for the liquidity of nonconforming mortgages such as jumbo mortgages. The importance of the nonconforming mortgage market can be seen by the size of the jumbo loan market, estimated at $500 billion. In 1988, jumbos constituted about 25% (or $91 billion) of

---

[10] A fail results when the seller cannot make delivery of a security on the designated settlement date. A fail is costly because a buyer does not have to pay the seller any accrued interest beyond the designated settlement date.

[11] Technically, when a dealer borrows securities and lends funds, from the dealer's perspective the transaction is referred to as a reverse repurchase agreement.

[12] Dollar roll transactions are also discussed in Chapter 8.

newly originated mortgages.[13] This segment of the mortgage market had to be securitized by the private sector, with any such securities carrying no explicit or implicit U.S. government guarantee.

Privately issued—i.e., *conventional* or *private label*—passthroughs were first issued in 1977 by the Bank of America, but met with many impediments (discussed below) to widespread acceptance by investors. The government wanted to see the private sector market develop, not only to improve its liquidity, but because of concern with the huge potential liability of the U.S. government should the agencies have to make good on their guarantee in the event of massive homeowner defaults. One of the objectives of the Presidential Commission on Housing established in mid-1981 was to recommend a number of private sector alternatives.

The commission's report in April 1982 recommended the privatization of Fannie Mae and Freddie Mac and the development of private sector alternatives to the two government-sponsored entities. The commission pointed out three major problems to be solved before an efficient private sector market could be developed. First, private passthroughs were being crowded out by agency issues. Second, private issuers faced federal and state laws or regulations that either limited the demand for private label products, or resulted in security structures that were not cost-efficient for issuers. Moreover, these restrictions had no economic justification. For example, federal or state regulators would not permit such securities to be treated as "qualified" investments for the institutions they regulated. Tax rules regarding how a transaction must be structured in order to qualify as a nontaxable conduit resulted in needlessly expensive security structures. Finally, private issues lacked standardization, thereby limiting liquidity.

The development of the private passthrough market has been the result of government intervention to foster the growth of this sector, as well as initiatives undertaken by the private sector to structure passthroughs in a way that would

[13] Robert Gerber, "Introduction to the Private Label Pass-Through Market," in Frank J. Fabozzi, ed., *The Handbook of Mortgage-Backed Securities,* 3d ed. (Chicago: Probus Publishing, 1992).

enhance their credit quality. Government intervention is discussed in this chapter; credit enhancement devices developed by the private sector are discussed in Chapter 8.

Government Intervention

Several legislative acts and regulatory changes helped foster the development of the private mortgage-backed securities market. The Secondary Mortgage Market Enhancement Act of 1984 (SMMEA) included provisions to improve the marketability of mortgage-related securities earning a double-A quality rating or better from one of the nationally recognized commercial rating companies.[14] SMMEA declared such securities (which are referred to as SMMEA-qualified securities) to be legal investments for federally chartered banks and thrifts. It also made SMMEA-qualified securities permissible investments for state regulated financial institutions (depository institutions and insurance companies) that are permitted to invest in Treasury securities or federal agency securities. The SMMEA granted individual states the right to override this particular provision of the act by October 1991. The immediate effect of the SMMEA was to open the door to enormous pools of investment capital. By October 1991, however, 21 states have exercised their prerogative and overridden the portion of the act that applics to state regulated financial institutions, thereby reducing the funds that could be invested in the private sector market.[15] The Department of Labor, which has the responsibility of regulating pension funds, had made private passthroughs acceptable plan assets.

The peculiarities of the packaging of passthroughs made it difficult for issuers to comply with SEC registration regulations. The SEC requires that the prospectus contain pertinent information about the underlying pool of mortgages. However, in the creation of mortgage-backed securities, issuers sell the securities while they are assembling the underly-

---

[14] This is the reason why the private passthroughs are also referred to as AA passthroughs.

[15] The states are Alaska, Arkansas, Colorado, Connecticut, Delaware, Florida, Georgia, Illinois, Kansas, Maryland, Michigan, Missouri, Nebraska, New Hampshire, New York, North Carolina, Ohio, South Dakota, Utah, Virginia, and West Virginia. This was reported in Laureen Meservey, "Votes Are In on SMMEA Override," *Freddie Mac Reports* (December 1991), p. 4.

ing pool of mortgage loans. Thus, the final pool is unknown at the time of registration and cannot be indicated in the prospectus. SEC regulations prevented the registration of these "blind pools" and refused to allow such underwriting on a shelf-registration basis (Rule 415). In addition to the registration requirements, issuers had to contend with the requirements for periodic reporting after the MBS was issued. None of these rules applied to agency MBSs, since such securities are exempt from SEC registration. The increased cost associated with the inability to time issuances via the shelf registration mechanism, the lost flexibility to assemble pools prior to the offering, and the ongoing reporting requirements all made private issuance unattractive and impeded the development of the private label passthrough market.

Recognizing this, the SEC significantly modified the requirements for private passthrough issuers in 1983 by permitting the registration of securities backed by blind pools, as long as the issuer commits to obtain a specified quality rating and provides sufficient information about the potential pool in the prospectus. When the final pool is assembled, that information must be sent to investors. Private mortgage-backed security issuers can now also qualify for shelf registration, and the periodic reporting requirements are less stringent than for corporate issuers. The SMMEA exempted qualified SMMEA securities from state blue sky laws unless overridden by state statutes. By October 1991, eight states overrode this provision.[16]

The Tax Reform Act of 1986 made the structuring of private mortgage-related securities less costly from a tax perspective. An entity that issues a mortgage-backed security is simply acting as a conduit in passing interest payments received from homeowners through to the security holders, and thus it wants to make sure that any legal structure created to distribute those payments is not taxed. Under the tax law, the issuer is not treated as a taxable entity if the passthrough is issued through a legal structure known as a *grantor trust*. Therefore, the grantor trust arrangement is used by issuers of

---

[16]As reported in Meservey, ibid., the eight states are Arkansas, Indiana, Louisiana, Maryland, Minnesota, New Mexico, Oklahoma, and South Dakota.

passthroughs. However, there is a major disadvantage to the grantor trust arrangement: if there is more than one class of bonds, then the trust does not qualify as a nontaxable entity.

While structures could be designed to avoid adverse tax treatment, such structures were inefficient, considering that in the absence of the tax rule restricting multiple classes of bonds, the same collateral could be used to create securities with a higher price. Private issuers needed a new type of trust device so that mortgage-backed security structures with more than one class of bonds could be issued more efficiently. Such a multiple-class passthrough structure was needed for issuers to design passthroughs, such as the A/B structure discussed in Chapter 8, and privately issued CMOs.

The 1986 act expanded the types of structures that could be issued (if certain conditions were satisfied), without incurring a separate tax on the legal entity that distributes the cash flow. More specifically, the act introduced a new type of trust device called the *Real Estate Investment Conduit* (REMIC), so that mortgage-backed securities with multiple bondholder classes could be issued without any adverse tax consequences.

Finally, brokers and dealers could use agency passthroughs as collateral for margin transactions. Prior to 1983, private passthroughs were not marginable. In January 1983, the Federal Reserve Board rectified that situation by amending Regulation T to allow the same margin requirements as for over-the-counter nonconvertible bonds.

The Issuers

Private passthroughs have been issued by commercial banks, insurance companies, and savings institutions. Tables 2-2 and 2-5 show the origination of passthroughs and CMOs by private conduits, respectively. Private passthroughs made up only $14.3 billion of the $249.5 billion (or about 6%) of passthroughs originated in 1990, roughly the same percentage as in 1989. While private issuers were the major originators of CMOs from 1984 through 1988, their market share has declined since then.

Prior to 1990, the five private issuers that dominated the market included subsidiaries of one commercial bank (Citicorp), two investment banking firms (Salomon Brothers and Merrill Lynch), one savings institution (Home Savings), and one life insurance company (Travelers). Today, the two active issuers are Citicorp and General Electric. Citicorp has been by far the largest issuer of private label passthroughs.

The newest player in the private issuance market might become the Resolution Trust Corporation (RTC), which has worked with investment banking firms in creating private passthroughs backed by real estate loans from failed S&Ls. The complication is that their portfolio includes nonperforming loans or lower-quality loans that would not be acceptable collateral for obtaining a double-A credit rating. This problem has been resolved by designing rather complicated credit structures.

THE WHOLE LOAN SECONDARY MARKET

The securitization of mortgages played the critical role in improving liquidity in the mortgage market, as originators sold mortgage loans (called "whole loans") to the conduits or created their own securities with newly originated mortgages. However, there was still a need for a secondary market for trading whole loans among investors. This market could serve several functions.

First, even mortgage originators that had products qualified for sale to the conduits could sell them in the whole loan market. By packaging both conforming and nonconforming products for sale in the whole loan market, mortgage originators would receive a better price than by splitting up the two and selling them in their respective markets. Because they are less liquid, the yield of whole loans is typically 50 to 100 basis points higher than that of comparable coupon passthroughs.

Second, mortgage originators would also use this market to purchase whole loans to satisfy mandatory commitments (discussed in Chapter 3). Third, institutions that sought to rebalance their investment portfolio needed a market to do so. Depository institutions that sought adjustable-rate mortgages which they could not originate themselves would use this market.

Secondary Market Trading Services

While the whole loan secondary market continues to be a highly illiquid and fragmented market, the market has been improved by the participation of entities that provide various secondary market trading services.

Whole loan brokers provide a wide range of services, including the screening of potential counterparties to a transaction in terms of their financial capabilities and integrity. Other brokers work closely with their customers in negotiating the terms of bulk sales. For example, if a life insurance company wants to sell residential mortgages with a mortgage balance of $20 million, varying coupons and remaining lives, the price must be negotiated. This requires an in-depth analysis of the mortgage portfolio. The terms must be negotiated as well. For example, mortgages require servicing (collecting payments and so forth); the mortgages can be sold with the servicing released or retained. Brokers also provide various types of analysis such as optimal delivery analysis or pricing of servicing.

In the 1980s, private mortgage insurance companies (discussed in Chapter 4) expanded their traditional function to include various forms of services to secondary market participants. At one time, private mortgage insurers introduced buyers and sellers without direct compensation. Their compensation was indirect through the insuring of the mortgages. They now receive direct compensation for this service and other services. Examples include: (1) evaluating the credit quality of mortgage loans to ensure compliance with the buyer's underwriting standards, and (2) acting as a master servicer to the numerous entities that may be servicing the mortgage loans in a portfolio. The increased role of private mortgage insurance companies in secondary mortgage services has come at time when the need for private mortgage insurance has declined. As will be explained in Chapter 8, newly devised credit enhancement structures have diminished the need for such insurance.

Dealers

Dealers in a market provide liquidity by buying for and selling from their own inventory. Private entities are active as dealers in the whole loan market. The major dealers buy individual whole loans or bulk loans but usually do not sell individual whole loans to investors. Instead, they accumulate whole loan positions with the intent of doing one of two things with the inventory: (1) creating a capital market instrument (passthrough or CMO), or (2) in the case of private conduits, selling a package of whole loans to an institutional investor.

Typically, a dealer does not know how it will ultimately use the whole loans accumulated. Instead, the best use will depend on market conditions. The prices that dealers bid on whole loans are a worst-case scenario bid. By this we mean that the dealer determines the alternative for its accumulated position that will offer the lowest proceeds.

Dealers compete among themselves for whole loans, as well as with Fannie Mae, Freddie Mac, and institutional investors that wish to buy whole loans for their investment portfolio. Dealers are less aggressive in bidding on whole loans than institutional investors because they require a greater spread to generate a profit from originating capital market instruments or from the resale of packages of whole loans to their clients. In addition, unlike institutional investors that bid on whole loans and hold them in their portfolio, a dealer must hedge the price risk of the whole loan position.[17] Bidding will reflect the cost of hedging.

The bid-ask spread on whole loans varies. Typical spreads are around ten 32nds, with aggressive bidding reducing spreads to eight 32nds when collateral is needed. For whole loans with unusual collateral, spreads are much wider—the odder the collateral, the higher the spread. In such instances, bids are made by appointment only.

[17] Hedging will be discussed in Chapter 3.

CONCLUSION

As a result of government intervention, the liquidity of all sectors of the secondary mortgage market—agency MBSs, private label MBSs, and whole loans—has increased. The market for agency passthrough securities is now the second most liquid, long-term fixed-income market in the United States, the first being the U.S. Treasury securities market. Thus, the government has accomplished one of its goals. However, the dominance of agency securities has crowded out the private sector, whose growth the government seeks to encourage in order to reduce potential liabilities resulting from its implicit or explicit guarantees.

The greater liquidity, coupled with new mortgage designs and security structures, has resulted in increased participation by a greater number of nondepository financial institutions. This, in turn, has assured a supply of funds to the mortgage market sufficient to keep mortgage rates in line with rates in other sectors of the long-term debt market. As such, rates in the mortgage market have reflected supply and demand in the capital markets rather than the fortunes or misfortunes of thrifts.

3

Mortgage Origination

The process of linking borrowers who need financing to purchase a home with lenders (or investors) involves a myriad of functions. These functions include originating, servicing, and, if necessary, insuring mortgages. In this chapter and Chapter 4, we will discuss these functions, the participants that perform them, the revenues generated, and the risks associated with each function. Our focus in this chapter is on mortgage origination; in the next we cover servicing and insuring.

MORTGAGE ORIGINATORS

Mortgage originators include thrifts, commercial banks, mortgage bankers, life insurance companies, and pension funds. Table 3-1 shows total residential originations for each group for the years 1984 through 1990. Clearly, the three largest originators for all types of residential mortgages are thrifts, commercial banks, and mortgage bankers. These three groups originated $475 billion (or 98%) of the $485 billion of residential mortgages originated in 1990. Prior to 1990, thrifts were the largest originators, followed by commercial banks. In 1990, thrift origination declined; coupled with an increase in commercial bank origination, the share of thrift origination fell below that of commercial banks. Table 3-1 also shows that in 1990 mortgage bankers' share of origination was the largest. As noted in the table, however, comparison of this group's share in previous years is complicated by the change

Table 3-1

Total Residential Mortgage Loan Originations, 1984–1990
($ millions)

	Thrifts	Commercial Banks	Mortgage Bankers	Life Insurance Companies	Pension Funds	Federal Credit Agencies	State & Local Credit Agencies	Total
1984	124,085	45,406	48,032	2,292	32	5,630	5,804	231,281
1985	133,236	61,529	66,042	4,078	98	5,154	4,870	275,007
1986	229,950	115,789	138,800	7,537	123	4,415	8,308	504,922
1987	231,383	132,851	112,502	6,756	50	4,010	7,811	495,363
1988	209,422	108,783	89,833	7,063	166	4,013	2,444	421,724
1989	171,145	130,862	70,049	4,229	153	3,888	2,745	383,171
1990	147,509	160,325	166,689	2,778	122	4,539	2,796	484,758

Note: Residential mortgage loans include loans for the following types of property: conventional 1-to-4 family, conventional multifamily, FHA/VA 1-to-4 family, and FHA multifamily. Original source is the U.S. Department of Housing and Urban Development, Survey of Mortgage Lending Activity. Mortgage origination data beginning with the first quarter of 1990 are not comparable to previous data because of a change in HUD's survey methodology, the effect of which is to capture greater origination activity by mortgage bankers.
Source: Secondary Mortgage Markets (Summer 1991) by permission of Freddie Mac. All rights reserved.

in HUD's survey methodology. This change more than doubled the estimated origination of 1-to-4 family mortgages.

SOURCES OF REVENUE

Originators may generate income for themselves in one or more of the following ways. First, they typically charge an origination fee. This fee is expressed in terms of *points,* where each point represents 1% of the borrowed funds. For example, an origination fee of two points on a $100,000 mortgage represents $2,000. In addition, they may charge application fees and certain processing fees.

The second source of revenue is the profit that might be generated from selling a mortgage at a higher price than it originally cost. This profit is called *secondary marketing profit.* Of course, if mortgage rates rise, an originator will realize a loss when the mortgages are sold in the secondary market. Strategies to hedge against the risk of loss in such cases will be described later in this chapter. Finally, the mortgage originator may hold the mortgage in its investment portfolio.

Regulatory and, until 1986, tax considerations encouraged S&Ls to invest in mortgages and mortgage-backed securities. Because S&Ls have become more conscious of the problem of matching maturities and because the tax benefits have been reduced by the Tax Reform Act of 1986, S&Ls have tended to sell a good portion of what they originate and to become increasingly dependent on the fees generated from originating and servicing mortgages. Mortgage bankers that are not subsidiaries of thrifts or commercial banks typically do not invest in mortgages. Instead, they rely solely on origination fees.

THE ORIGINATION PROCESS

A potential homeowner who wants to borrow funds to purchase a home will apply for a loan from a mortgage originator. Upon completion of the application form (which provides financial information about the applicant) and the payment of an application fee, the mortgage originator will perform a credit evaluation of the applicant.

Credit Evaluation

This phase of the origination process can be subcontracted to another entity. Depository institutions should have a comparative advantage in carrying out this stage of the origination process.

The two primary factors in determining whether the funds will be lent are the *payment-to-income* (PTI) ratio and the *loan-to-value* (LTV) ratio.

The PTI is the ratio of monthly payments (both mortgage and real estate tax payments) to monthly income and is a measure of the ability of the applicant to make monthly payments. The smaller this ratio, the greater the likelihood that the applicant will be able meet the required payments. Some applicants may apply for a loan and request that no credit check be performed. If the lender is satisfied that collateral will be sufficient, the loan may be granted. A lower LTV will be required and a higher mortgage rate will be charged.

The difference between the purchase price of the property and the amount borrowed is the borrower's down payment. The LTV is the ratio of the amount of the loan to the market (or assessed) value of the property. The lower this ratio, the greater the protection the lender has if the applicant defaults and it therefore becomes necessary to repossess and sell the property. For example, if an applicant wants to borrow $150,000 on property with an assessed value of $200,000, the LTV is 75%. Suppose the applicant subsequently defaults on the mortgage loan. The lender can then repossess the property and sell it to recover the amount owed. But the amount that will be received by the lender depends on the market value of the property. In our example, even if conditions in the housing market are weak, the lender will still be able to recover the proceeds lent if the decline in the value of the property plus the costs of disposing of the property is no more than $50,000. In contrast, suppose that the applicant wants to borrow $180,000 for the same property. The LTV will then be 90%. If the property has to be sold by the lender because the applicant defaults, there is less protection for the lender.

We will have more to say about lending and lending risks later in this chapter.

Costs of Mortgage Origination

The origination process requires that, at a minimum, the originator work with the borrower, credit bureaus, appraisers, title insurers, and escrow agents or lawyers. In addition, if necessary, the originator may have to work with a mortgage insurer and investors. The process is labor intensive. According to Gregory Barmore, president and chairman of General Electric Capital Mortgage Insurance Corporation:

> . . . there is no denying that almost every loan made today requires a two-inch-thick pile of paper, the end result of about 500 different tasks done by 10 different

people. And it takes about 900 minutes—15 hours—
over four or five weeks to process that two-inch pile.[1]

In addition to the labor and computer systems costs,
the originator that does not plan to hold the mortgage loan as
an investment must also fund the loan until it is sold. The
carrying cost of a mortgage loan will depend on the shape of
the yield curve.

According to the Mortgage Bankers Association, the
average expense per loan (including personnel costs) in 1988
was $2,357.[2] The average revenue per loan was $1,113. Consequently, there was a net loss per loan of $1,244. This loss has
to be offset by gains from the sale of the loan in the secondary
market or recaptured by the present value of the mortgage-
backed security created.

Commitment Letter

If the lender decides to loan the funds, a commitment
letter will be sent to the applicant. This letter commits the
lender to loan funds to the applicant on the terms specified in
the agreement. The length of time of the commitment varies
between 30 and 60 days. At the time of the commitment letter, the lender may require that the applicant pay a commitment fee.

The commitment letter obligates the lender—not the
applicant—to perform. Any commitment fee that the applicant
may pay is lost if the applicant decides not to purchase the
property or if the applicant uses an alternative source of funds
to purchase the property. Effectively, a commitment letter is
an option sold by the lender and purchased by the applicant.

Setting the Contract (Mortgage Loan) Rate

At the time the application is submitted for approval,
the mortgage originator will give the applicant a choice of the

---

[1] Gregory T. Barmore, "The Roles of FHA and HUD in the 1990s," *Secondary Mortgage Markets* (Spring 1990), pp. 17–18.
[2] Of course, these are only estimates and are subject to the standard cost accounting problem of cost allocation.

type of mortgage. The various types of mortgages are discussed in Chapters 5, 6, and 7. Basically, the choice is between a fixed-rate mortgage and an adjustable-rate mortgage. In the case of a fixed-rate mortgage, the lender may give the applicant a choice of when the contract (that is, the mortgage loan) rate will be determined. The three choices may be:

1. *application date:* the time the loan application is submitted,
2. *commitment date:* the time a commitment letter is issued to the borrower, or
3. *closing date:* the date the property is purchased with the borrowed funds.

Notice that by selecting the application date, the applicant has effectively purchased an option on the contract rate for a price equal to the application fee. The length of this option is equal to the time between the date the application is submitted and the commitment date. Once the commitment letter is sent out and the applicant accepts by paying a commitment fee, the cost of the option becomes the commitment fee. It is important to understand these implicit options because, as we explain below, they expose the mortgage originator to different types of risk which must be protected against.

ALTERNATIVES FOR THE ORIGINATOR AFTER CLOSING

Once an originator has closed a mortgage loan, it has three choices as to what it can do with the individual mortgage loan:

1. hold it as an investment in its portfolio;
2. sell it in the secondary market;
3. warehouse it in order to aggregate a sufficient amount of mortgage loans to either (a) sell them as a package in the secondary mortgage market (since packages of mortgages offer better prices than individual mortgages), (b) sell them to conduits that will securitize them, or (c) securitize the mortgages.

If the first alternative is selected, the mortgage loan originator takes on the lending function, exposing itself to lending risk.

When an originator intends to sell the mortgage (the second alternative), it can obtain a commitment from the potential investor (buyer). As we explained in the previous chapters, two federally sponsored credit agencies and several private conduits buy mortgages. The contract rate that the originator sets on the loan will depend on the rate required by the investor who plans to purchase the mortgage loan. Conduits post rates at which they will purchase mortgage loans in their various programs. The rate posted, called the required net yield, is the yield at which the conduit agrees to buy the mortgage loan, less a servicing spread that is retained by the mortgage originator. The minimum required net yield will reflect conditions in the Treasury market. To that yield a premium is added to reflect each of the following:

1. the uncertainty associated with the cash flow of a mortgage-backed security and any perceived default risk;
2. the costs associated with the guarantees that the conduit has made. For example, in the case of Freddie Mac and Fannie Mae, this involves the costs associated with defaults (foreclosure costs and interest cost for timely payments that the conduit must make to the investor). In the case of private passthroughs, there is the cost of credit enhancement;
3. the required return on equity on the capital that the conduit must commit; and
4. the expected operational expenses.

From the minimum required net yield plus the premium to reflect (1) through (4) above is subtracted the value of the float that the conduit will realize in the delay of monthly payments to investors.[3]

Rates are reported on various services such as Telerate and Echo I Reuters (the Mortgage Bankers Association's

---

[3]This payment delay will be discussed in Chapter 8.

electronic mail system) and on dedicated telephone lines established by the conduit.

If the mortgages are warehoused for purposes of securitizing, then the mortgage origination is performing the securitization function. If the mortgages are warehoused for sale to conduits or nonconduit investors, then contract rates will be set based on investor requirements.

Rather than selling whole loans, a mortgage originator can sell participation interests in them. Conduits and nonconduit investors purchase such interests.

RISKS ASSOCIATED WITH MORTGAGE ORIGINATION

A mortgage originator's inventory of unsold loans (i.e., loan applications being processed and loan commitments made) is called its *pipeline,* and the associated risks are referred to as *pipeline risk.* There is also risk associated with warehousing closed mortgages in order to sell them in the secondary market or securitize them. This is called *warehousing risk.* The risks are shown on a flow chart in Figure 3-1.

Pipeline Risk

This risk can be decomposed into two types of risk: *price risk* and *fallout risk.*[4]

Price risk refers to the adverse effects on the value of the pipeline if mortgage rates rise. For example, if mortgage rates rise and the mortgage originator has made commitments at a lower rate, the mortgage originator will have to either sell the mortgages when they close at a lower value than the funds lent to homeowners or else retain the mortgages as a portfolio investment earning a below-market mortgage rate. The mortgage originator faces the same risk for mortgage applications in the pipeline in cases where the applicant has elected to fix the mortgage rate at the application date.

---

[4]There is also another type of pipeline risk, *counterparty risk.* This is the risk that the investor that agreed to purchase a mortgage loan at a predetermined rate will renege on its commitment. Counterparty risk is essentially credit risk, which the mortgage originator can try to protect against by thoroughly investigating the financial strength and integrity of the investor.

Figure 3-1

Flow Chart of Pipeline and Warehousing Risks

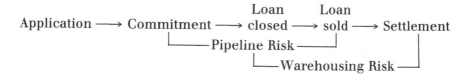

Note: In this figure the loan sold date refers to the sale of an individual mortgage loan. The settlement date refers to the sale of a package of loans or the securities that are collateralized by the loan.

Fallout risk is the risk that applicants or those that were issued commitment letters will not close (i.e., complete the transaction by purchasing the property with funds borrowed from the mortgage originator). The chief reason for potential borrowers to cancel their commitment or withdraw their mortgage application is a decline in mortgage rates; if rates decline sufficiently, it may become economic to obtain an alternative source of funds. Fallout risk is the result of the mortgage originator giving the potential borrower the right but not the obligation to close (that is, the right to cancel the agreement). As noted earlier, the mortgage originator has effectively sold the potential borrower an option. There are reasons other than a decline in mortgage rates that a potential borrower would choose to fall out of the pipeline. For example, there may have been an unfavorable engineering report or the purchase may have been based on a change in employment that has not materalized.

While the fallout risk faced by an originator is much like an option, there are some important differences. The most important one has to do with when an option is exercised. Specifically, the following two conditions must exist. First, if the economic value resulting from the exercise of the option is negative, then the option holder should not exercise the option. In option parlance, an out-of-the-money option should never be exercised. Second, if a positive economic value would result from the exercise of an option at the option's expiration date, the option should be exercised. That is, an option that is in the money at its expiration date should be exercised.

In the case of mortgage applications and commitments, potential borrowers effectively hold an out-of-the-money option if the prevailing mortgage rate is less than the contract rate that has been fixed on the loan. Although, from an option perspective, it would be inefficient to exercise the option and close on the mortgage loan, there are reasons why potential borrowers might do so. The potential borrower that does not take down the mortgage loan must begin the application process over again. This will result in a delay of closing which could have several disadvantages. For example, if the potential borrower has committed to sell his or her home by a certain date and must move out, there is the cost of temporary residence and storage costs until the new loan application is approved. In instances where a potential borrower effectively holds an in-the-money option (i.e., one with a prevailing mortgage rate greater than the contract rate on the loan), the option may not be exercised for the reasons we cited earlier. It is important to keep in mind that unlike a true option, to benefit from the intrinsic value of the option the potential borrower can only exercise it if he purchases the property with the borrowed funds.

The combination of price risk and fallout risk produces an asymmetric risk for pipeline risk with respect to a decline in interest rates. When interest rates rise, the value of the pipeline declines because the mortgages decline in value. However, when interest rates decline, the occurrence of fallout reduces the potential for selling the mortgages at a higher value. This situation reduces the effectiveness of any hedge that the originator may have in place relative to the price risk of the pipeline.[5] We will describe various instruments for hedging pipeline risk later.

Warehouse Risk

An originator that has warehoused mortgages does not face fallout risk, but only price risk. When interest rates increase, the warehoused mortgages will be sold in the secondary market at a lower price than was paid to the borrower.

---

[5]This gives an originator's pipeline a negative convexity characteristic, a characteristic of a callable security or a position in callable securities that we will explain in Chapter 12.

Or, if the warehoused mortgages are securitized, the securities will be sold at a lower price than the cost of acquiring the underlying pool of mortgage loans.

A mortgage originator with unclosed and warehoused mortgages has a total risk exposure that reflects the combination of pipeline risk and warehouse risk. And that raises the issue of how those risks can be managed.

HEDGING MORTGAGE ORIGINATION RISK

There are a variety of ways to hedge the risks associated with the origination function.[6] These include the use of delivery choices that conduits grant mortgage originators, exchange-traded interest rate control products, and over-the-counter interest rate control products. In this section we will review these alternatives and then provide an overview of the strategies that can be employed.

Broadly speaking, instruments used to hedge interest rate risk fall into three categories: futures contracts, forward contracts, and option-type contracts. The first two contracts can be used to protect against symmetric risk and the last to protect against asymmetric risk.[7] Futures contracts are created by exchanges; forward contracts are over-the-counter products created by dealer firms. The firm commitment or mandatory forward delivery alternatives that are available from conduits are effectively forward contracts. There are both exchange-traded options and over-the-counter options. Optional forward delivery alternatives available from conduits are effectively over-the-counter options.

Forward Contracts

Forward and futures contracts are agreements that require a party to the agreement to either buy or sell *some-*

---

[6]For a more detailed discussion of pipeline risk and the methods mortgage originators can use to protect against it, see John Scowcroft, Andrew S. Davidson, and Anand K. Bhattacharya, "Pipeline Risk Management," Chapter 33 in Frank J. Fabozzi, ed., *The Handbook of Mortgage-Backed Securities*, rev. ed. (Chicago: Probus Publishing, 1988), and Chapter 12 in Mark Pitts and Frank J. Fabozzi, *Interest Rate Futures and Options* (Chicago: Probus Publishing, 1989).

[7]Technically, forward/futures contracts can be used to synthetically create a hedging profile similar to an option contract. Such a strategy is referred to as dynamic hedging.

thing at a designated future date at a predetermined price. Forward contracts are customized agreements between two parties. For example, one party can agree to deliver to another party, two months from now, $1 million principal amount of 30-year mortgages with a contract rate of 9.5% in exchange for $1 million. The party that agrees to deliver the mortgages is a mortgage originator; the party that agrees to accept delivery is an investor or conduit.

Notice two important features of the forward contract. First, both parties are obligated to perform two months from now. Second, neither party compensates the other for entering into the agreement.

To see the risk associated with using forward contracts to protect against certain types of interest rate risk, let's look at what will happen if interest rates change. We will assume that the mortgage originator has in its pipeline the applications or commitments for $1 million of 30-year mortgage loans with a 9.5% contract rate. A decline in mortgage rates increases the value of the mortgages; a rise in mortgage rates decreases the value of the mortgages.

What will happen if, two months from now, mortgage rates rise to 11% and the closure rate (i.e., the percentage of applications in the pipeline that close) is 100%? If the mortgage originator has not hedged its pipeline, the mortgage loans will have to be sold in the secondary market for $882,923, resulting in a loss of $117,077.[8] However, if the mortgage originator has entered into the forward contract and agreed to deliver the mortgage loans for $1 million, there will be no loss.

Now let's see what will happen if, instead of rising, mortgage rates decline to 8% two months from now and the closure rate is 100%. The market value of the mortgage loans will be $1,145,934. Thus, by not hedging, the originator has realized a secondary marketing profit of $145,934. But this profit does not arise if a forward contract has been entered into, since the originator has agreed to deliver the loans in exchange for $1 million.

Even in the unhedged case, the secondary marketing

---

[8]In Chapter 4 we will show how the price of a mortgage is calculated.

profit will only arise if the closure rate is 100%. Suppose that the closure rate is 70%. Then if the position is unhedged, a profit of $102,153 (70% × $145,934) will be realized. However, if the forward contract is used to hedge, then there will actually be a loss. The reason is that while the mortgage originator can deliver $700,000 of 9.5%, 30-year mortgages from its pipeline to satisfy its obligation under the forward contract, it must purchase the balance in the secondary market.[9] Assuming mortgage rates decline to 8%, the cost of purchasing $300,000 principal value of 9.5%, 30-year mortgages will be $343,780. Thus, the mortgage originator will lose $43,780, because it will receive $300,000 for delivering these mortgages to satisfy the forward agreement, but must purchase them in the secondary market for $343,780. The lower the closure rate, the greater the loss.

This illustration highlights two key points concerning hedging with forward contracts. First, by hedging with forward contracts, an originator locks in a value for the mortgages in the pipeline. By doing so, the originator sacrifices the upside potential resulting from a decline in mortgage rates in exchange for an elimination of downside loss should mortgage rates rise. Second, this only holds if all potential borrowers in the pipeline close (i.e., the closure rate is 100%). If a decline in mortgage rates results in a less than 100% closure rate, a loss will result. This is a consequence of trying to hedge pipeline risk, which is asymmetric, with a forward contract that provides protection against symmetric risk.

Mandatory Delivery Contracts Available from Conduits

Forward contracts are effectively available from conduits. Although they do not call them forward contracts, conduits allow forward delivery of mortgages at a price established. Such delivery agreements are called *mandatory contracts*. As an example, in Freddie Mac's Cash Program, mandatory contracts are available for delivery periods of from

---

[9]Or, as explained later in this chapter, the originator can "pair off" the excess amount.

10 to 120 days.[10] The longer the delivery period, the lower the price Freddie Mac offers (i.e., the higher the required net yield). This reflects the greater interest rate risk to which Freddie Mac is exposed.

The risk faced by the originator is that it will fail, because of fallout, to originate the amount that it has committed to deliver. In such instances, the originator has two alternatives. It can buy mortgage loans in the secondary whole loan market and deliver them to the conduit, realizing a loss if mortgage rates have fallen. The alternative is to compensate the conduit for its hedging cost. This is done through a *pairoff fee*. For example, in the case of Freddie Mac mandatory contracts, there is currently a pairoff fee of 10 basis points[11] on the difference between the commitment amount and the actual amount delivered less a permitted purchase tolerance of 5%. For example, suppose an originator has committed to deliver $3 million of mortgages in 60 days, but only delivers $2.2 million. The tolerance permitted is $150,000 ($3 million times 5%). Therefore, the pairoff fee would be calculated as follows:

total commitment amount	$3,000,000
actual amount delivered	(2,200,000)
purchase tolerance	(150,000)
shortfall	$ 650,000
	× .001
pairoff fee	$ 650

Mortgage originators can select mandatory commitments from conduits on single loans or bulk loans (i.e., more than one mortgage loan).

---

[10]The mandatory contracts vary with the type of mortgage (i.e., fixed-rate, level-payment mortgage, adjustable-rate mortgage, graduated-payment mortgage, and so forth). We've simplified the discussion here. In addition to locking in a rate or price at which it can sell its product, a Freddie Mac mandatory contract protects the originator against a change in underwriting standards prior to delivery.

[11]A basis point is equal to .01% or .0001; 10 basis points equal .1%.

Futures Contracts

Futures contracts represent an alternative to using forward contracts to hedge symmetric risk. Futures contracts are exchange-traded products. They represent a firm legal agreement between a buyer (seller) and an established exchange or its clearinghouse. The buyer (seller) agrees to take (make) delivery of *something* at a specified price at a designated time. They are identical to forward contracts in their hedging outcome when mortgage rates rise or fall. That is, a properly implemented hedge can be used to lock in a value for mortgages such that an originator can not benefit from a favorable movement in mortgage rates.

There are three advantages of futures contracts relative to forward contracts. The first is that the mortgage originator is exposed to default or credit risk. Since a forward contract is an agreement between two parties, there is counterparty risk (that is, the risk that the counterparty will fail to perform). In such an instance, if mortgage rates have risen, the originator will realize a secondary marketing loss. Default risk is minimal for a futures contract. The second disadvantage is the lack of liquidity of forward contracts, which makes it difficult to reverse a hedged position. Since futures contracts are exchange-traded products, they have considerably greater liquidity, particularly those futures contracts that mortgage originators have used historically. Finally, another problem that arises for a mortgage originator marking its position to market for reporting purposes is the lack of adequate prices in the forward market. In contrast, futures prices are available at the end of each trading day.

There are disadvantages of futures contracts relative to forward contracts. The major one is that since futures contracts are standardized with respect to both the delivery date (i.e., most have contract settlement months of March, June, September, and December) and the underlying instrument, using them for hedging introduces what is called *cross-hedging risk*. This recalls our earlier statement that if properly used, they can accomplish the objective of locking in a value for mortgage loans. We will discuss this risk later. There is no cross-hedging risk with forward contracts because the agreement can be customized to suit the specific needs of the mortgage originator. Another disadvantage is that in using futures contracts a mortgage originator must post cash (or an acceptable interest-bearing security) when a futures position is initiated (i.e., initial futures margin). It must also be prepared each trading day to put up additional cash (i.e., variation margin) if the futures price rises.

The futures contracts most commonly used by mortgage originators are those based on Treasury securities. The two with the greatest liquidity are the Treasury bond and Treasury note futures contracts, both traded on the Chicago Board of Trade (CBOT). The other futures contract that has been used is the CBOT mortgage-backed futures contract. This contract is described in the appendix to Chapter 8.

The risks of hedging with futures contracts. Hedging with either futures or forward contracts involves the employment of a futures transaction as a temporary substitute for a transaction to be made in the cash market. The hedge position locks in a value for the cash position. As long as cash and futures prices move together, any loss realized on one position (whether cash or futures) will be offset by a profit on the other. When the profit and loss are equal, the hedge is called a *perfect hedge*.

In practice, hedging is not that simple. The amount of the loss or profit on a hedge will be determined by the relationship between the cash price and futures price when a hedge is placed and when it is lifted. The difference between the cash price and the futures price is called the *basis*. That is,

$$\text{basis} = \text{cash price} - \text{futures price}$$

If a futures contract is correctly priced, the difference between the cash price and futures price will equal the cost of carry. The hedger always takes the risk that the basis will change because of the market's mispricing of the futures contract relative to the cash price. This is called *basis risk*. Therefore, hedging involves the substitution of basis risk for price risk: the substitution of the risk that the basis will change for the risk that the cash price will change.

When a futures contract is used to hedge a mortgage originator's position and when the underlying instrument for the futures contract is not identical to the mortgages either in the pipeline or being warehoused, it is called a *cross-hedge*. Cross-hedging introduces another risk, the risk that the price movement of the underlying instrument of the futures contract may not accurately track the price movement of the mortgages. This is cross-hedging risk. Therefore, the effectiveness of a cross-hedge will be determined by:

1. the relationship between the cash price of the underlying instrument and its futures price when a hedge is placed and when it is lifted (i.e., basis risk);
2. the relationship between the market value of the mortgage position and the cash price of the instrument underlying the futures contract when the hedge is placed and when it is lifted (i.e., cross-hedging risk)

Holding aside basis risk, cross-hedging risk can be significant when using the Treasury bond and note futures contract. Although Treasury bond and note yields are highly correlated with mortgage rates, the correlation is not perfect. While the correlation is higher for mortgage-backed securities, suggesting that the CBOT mortgage-backed futures contract might be more suitable, this contract has less liquidity. Consequently, the mortgage originator faces trade-offs in selecting the futures contract to employ.

Options

An option is a contract in which the writer of the option grants the buyer of the option the *right*, but not the obligation, to purchase from or sell something to the writer (i.e., the underlying instrument) at a specified price within a specified period of time (or at a specified point in time). The writer, also referred to as the seller, grants this right to the buyer in exchange for a certain sum of money called the *option price* or *option premium*. The price at which the underlying instrument may be bought or sold is called the *exercise* or *strike price*. The date after which an option is void is called the *expiration date*.

When an option grants the buyer the right to purchase the underlying instrument from the writer (seller), it is called a *call option,* or *call.* When the option buyer has the right to sell the underlying instrument to the writer (seller), the option is called a *put option,* or *put.*

Unlike a forward or futures contract, an option gives the buyer the *right,* but not the obligation, to perform. The option writer (seller) *does* have the obligation to perform. In contrast, both the buyer and seller are obligated to perform in the case of a forward or futures contract. A second difference is that in a forward or futures contract, the buyer does not pay the seller to accept the obligation, whereas in the case of an option, the buyer pays the seller the option price.

Consequently, the risk/reward characteristics of an option differ from those of a forward and futures contract when used for hedging purposes. In a forward or futures contract, the buyer of the contract locks in a price for the underlying instrument at the settlement date. In contrast, an option's strike price establishes the worst possible price that the option buyer will have to accept regardless of how unfavorable the price movement. The option buyer, however, can benefit from a favorable price movement. The option price is the cost of being able to establish such a hedge.

Since mortgage originators wish to protect against a decline in the market value of their mortgage position, the appropriate option for them to purchase is a put option. To illustrate both the reason why a put option is used and the difference between using a put option and a forward contract, we will return to our earlier illustration, in which a mortgage originator seeks to hedge pipeline risk. Recall that the mortgage originator sought to protect an expected position consisting of $1 million principal value of mortgages with a 9.5% mortgage rate and 30 years to maturity two months from now. Suppose that a put option in which $1 million of 9.5%, 30-year mortgages with a strike price of $1 million can be purchased for $8,000. Again, let's consider the two scenarios for changes in mortgage rates (a rise to 11% and a decline to 8%) and let's assume that all potential borrowers close.

If mortgage rates rise to 11%, the mortgage originator

will exercise the option. This means that the mortgage originator can deliver the mortgages and receive $1 million. Effectively, the mortgage originator is receiving $992,000 because the cost of the put option is $8,000. If mortgage rates fall to 8%, the mortgages will have a market value of $1,145,934. The mortgage originator will let the put option expire and sell the mortgages in the secondary market, realizing a secondary marketing profit of $145,934 minus the $8,000 cost to purchase the option.

Comparing the put option position to the forward contract position, we see that if there is an unfavorable movement in mortgage rates, the mortgage originator would have fared better with the forward contract, since the purchase of a put option requires an outlay for the option price. However, if mortgage rates decline, the mortgage originator realizes the benefit of a favorable movement by having purchased the put option. Hedging with a forward contract means that no benefit is realized from a decline in mortgage rates. Also notice that since the mortgage originator will not exercise the option, a closure rate of less than 100% will not adversely affect the hedge.

When using a put option to hedge its position, a mortgage originator may have a choice of strike prices to select from. The higher the strike price, the higher the price the mortgage originator is setting as the minimum value at which it can sell its mortgages. However, the higher the strike price, the greater the cost of the option. Buying a put is often compared to purchasing insurance. Like insurance, the premium paid for the protection is nonrefundable and is paid before coverage begins. The degree to which mortgages are protected depends upon the option's strike price; thus, the strike price is often compared to the deductible on an insurance policy. The lower the deductible (that is, the higher the strike on the put), the greater the level of protection but the more that protection costs. Conversely, the higher the deductible (the lower the strike price on the put), the more the mortgage originator can lose; but the cost of the insurance is lower. No one strike price dominates any other in the sense of performing better at all possible mortgage rate levels. Consequently, it is not possible to say a priori that one strike price is necessarily the "best" strike price.

Exchange-traded versus OTC options. A mortgage originator has the choice of using exchange-traded options or OTC options. The same factors to consider when choosing between forward contracts and futures contracts are applicable in deciding whether to use either of these for hedging.

In the case of interest rate, exchange-traded options, there are two types of options. The first is an option on a fixed-income instrument, referred to as an option on a physical. The second is an option on a futures contract, more popularly referred to as a *futures option*. By far, futures options are the more liquid.[12] Consequently, a mortgage originator that wants to use an exchange-traded option will often use a futures option. The futures options that are used by mortgage originators are the option on the Treasury bond futures contract, the option on the Treasury note futures contract, and the option on the mortgage-backed security, all traded on the CBOT.

Futures options. A futures option gives the buyer the right to buy from or sell to the writer a designated futures contract at a designated price at any time during the life of the option. If the futures option is a call option, the buyer has the right to purchase one designated futures contract at the exercise price. That is, the buyer has the right to acquire a long futures position in the designated futures contract. If the call option is exercised by the buyer, the writer (seller) acquires a corresponding short position in the futures contract. A put option on a futures contract grants the buyer the right to sell one designated futures contract to the writer at the exercise price. That is, the option buyer has the right to acquire a short position in the designated futures contract. If the put option is exercised, the writer acquires a corresponding long position in the designated futures contract.

Upon exercise, the futures price for the futures contract will be set equal to the then-current futures price. For a

---

[12] There are three reasons why futures options are preferred to options on physicals in the fixed-income area. First, unlike options on fixed-income securities, futures options do not require payment for accrued interest to be made. Consequently, when a futures option is exercised, the call buyer and the put writer need not compensate the other party for accrued interest. Second, futures options are believed to be "cleaner instruments" because of the reduced likelihood of delivery squeezes. Finally, for the purpose of pricing any option, it is imperative to know at all times the price of the underlying instrument. Bond prices are not as readily available to options traders as futures prices.

call futures option, the option writer must pay the difference between the current futures price and the exercise price to the buyer of the option. In the case of a put futures option, the option writer must pay the option buyer the difference between the exercise price and the current futures price. Unlike an option on a cash market instrument in which exercise requires the exchange of dollars equal to the exercise price, the only cash that will be exchanged upon exercising a futures option is the difference between the exercise and current futures price.

Optional Delivery Contracts Available from Conduits

With an optional delivery contract available from a conduit, the mortgage originator is not obligated to deliver any of the contracted amount. For this right, the conduit charges a commitment fee. The commitment fee, which is effectively an option price, must be paid up front. Depending on the conduit and program, a delivery period of up to 240 days may be available.

Using option pricing theory, Kutner and Seifert have estimated the value of mortgage loan commitments.[13] They find that, for the period 1985 to 1987, Fannie Mae fixed-rate $100,000 mortgage loan commitments for 30 days ranged from $500 to $3,000, with an average value of $1,300. In a subsequent study, these two researchers showed how to incorporate this option value into the contract rate. They find that to recover the cost of granting this option to the borrower, the contract rate should be increased by roughly 8 to 44 basis points.[14]

Compound Options

Hedging the entire pipeline with put options would be very costly for a mortgage originator. To reduce the cost, a mortgage originator can make an estimate of the closure rate

---

[13] George W. Kutner and James A. Siefert, "The Valuation of Mortgage Loan Commitments Using Option Pricing Estimates," *The Journal of Real Estate Research* (Summer 1989), pp. 13–20.
[14] George W. Kutner and James A. Seifert, "A Note on the Valuation of Mortgage Loan Commitments: Incorporating the Commitment Cost in the Mortgage Rate," *The Journal of Real Estate Research* (Summer 1990), pp. 281–284.

and protect only those expected to close. An alternative is to buy from a dealer a compound option or split-fee option. Such a contract is an option on an option.

We will explain the elements of a compound option by using the example of a call option on a put option. This particular type of compound option, called a *caput*, is the one a mortgage originator would use to hedge pipeline risk. A caput gives the buyer of this option the right but not the obligation to require the writer of the compound option to sell the buyer a put option. A caput would specify the following terms:

1. The day on which the buyer of the compound option has the choice of either requiring the writer of the option to sell the buyer a put option or allowing the option to expire. This date is called the *extension date*.

2. The strike price and the expiration date of the put option that the buyer acquires from the writer. The expiration date of the put option is called the *notification date*.

The payment that the buyer makes to acquire the compound option is called the *front fee*. If the buyer exercises the call option in order to acquire the put option, a second payment is made to the writer of the option. That payment is called the *back fee*.

The time period until the notification date gives the mortgage originator the opportunity to reassess the status of the pipeline (i.e., to obtain a better estimate of the closure rate) and market conditions (i.e., the level of mortgage rates). For example, if mortgage rates rise, the mortgage originator will exercise the option at the notification date and pay the back fee. Should mortgage rates decline, then the mortgage originator can either (1) allow the option to expire and forfeit the front fee, or (2) pay the back fee if mortgage rates are expected to remain at their lower level and therefore benefit from exercise of the option at the notification date.[15]

[15]For a discussion of how compound options can be used to hedge pipeline risk, see Anand K. Bhattacharya, "Compound Options on Mortgage-Backed Securities," Chapter 22 in Frank J. Fabozzi, ed., *The Handbook of Fixed Income Options* (Chicago: Probus Publishing, 1988).

4

Mortgage Servicing and Insurance

In this chapter we continue with our discussion of the functions necessary to link borrowers and lenders (or investors) in the mortgage market. Chapter 3 focused on mortgage origination. Here our focus is on the servicing and insuring of mortgages. As in the previous chapter, we will discuss the participants that perform these functions, the revenues generated, and the risks faced in carrying out these functions.

MORTGAGE SERVICING

Every mortgage loan must be serviced. Servicing of a mortgage loan involves collecting monthly payments and forwarding proceeds to the owners of the loan; sending payment notices to mortgagors; reminding mortgagors when payments are overdue; maintaining records of principal balances; administering an escrow balance for real estate taxes and insurance purposes; initiating foreclosure proceedings if necessary; and furnishing tax information to mortgagors when applicable.

Servicers include bank-related entities, thrift-related entities, and mortgage bankers. As of 1989, the *American Banker* survey found that bank-related servicers had 43% of the market share and thrift-related servicers 20%. The market share of the latter has decreased since 1987—when it reached

29%—because thrifts have been forced to sell off servicing rights in an attempt to bolster capital to satisfy the risk-based capital guidelines imposed by FIRREA. While the market shares of bank-related and thrift-related thrifts have been affected by regulatory requirements, particularly those relating to capital requirements, there are direct capital constraints on mortgage bankers.

For reasons discussed later, profit margins from mortgage servicing have been declining. Economies of scale in the servicing of mortgages are critical. While there are hundreds of small mortgage servicing companies, a survey conducted in the first half of 1990 by *Inside Mortgage Finance* found that 30 mortgage servicers accounted for more than $500 billion in servicing volume (i.e., the amount of principal serviced).[1] Yet no one firm has more than 3% of the servicing market. Efforts have recently been made to consolidate operations through mergers and acquisitions, as well as through the increased purchase of mortgage servicing rights. For example, the 30 top mortgage servicers increased their servicing volume by 15% in the first six months of 1990.[2] Figure 4-1 shows the increased concentration of market share from 1982 to 1988 for the top 100 firms, top 25 firms, and top 10 firms.[3] More recent data show that the servicing volume of the top 100 firms tripled between 1983 to 1990.

Mortgage Servicing Rights Transfer Market

There is a secondary market for servicing rights (i.e., the market for the transfer of the right to service a mortgage loan). The sale of servicing rights must be approved by the investor in the loans, or in the case of a mortgage loan that has been securitized, by the conduit that has securitized it (i.e., GNMA, FNMA, FHLMC, or private conduit).

There are brokers and listing services specializing in the trading of servicing rights. The service transfer brokerage

---

[1] As reported in Guy D. Cecala, "Mortgage Servicing Is Where the Action Is," *United States Banker* (October 1990), p. 35.

[2] Ibid.

[3] Excluded from the servicing volume figures reported is servicing associated with mortgage loans retained by the servicer as a portfolio investment.

Figure 4-1

Market Share Concentration

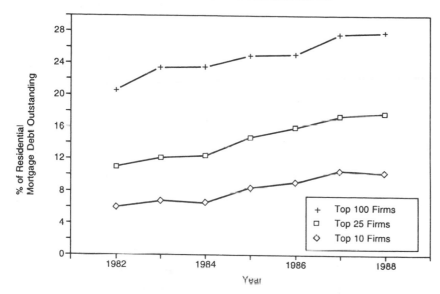

Source: Hal Hinkle, Steve Harris, and Dick Loggins, *Mortgage Servicing: Supply and Demand Trends and Prospects for Valuation* (New York: Mortgage Securities Research, Goldman, Sachs & Co., September 1989), p. 3.

industry includes major investment banking firms such as Merrill Lynch, Salomon Brothers, and Bear Stearns. But the industry seems to be fragmented, as is evidenced by its having been described in 1988 as a "cottage-industry, run mainly by middle-aged entrepreneurs from offices outside the big cities."[4]

Sales of Ginnie Mae servicing increased from $9 billion in 1983 to about $40 billion in 1990, with a peak of $65 billion in 1988.[5] Data on the volume of transfer of non–Ginnie Mae servicing rights are not readily available. One estimate is that in 1989, volume was $155 billion.[6] Ginnie Mae represented about a third of that volume.

Hinkle, Harris, and Loggins argue that the declining profitability of the mortgage banking industry between 1986

[4]"$150 Billion Industry," *United States Banker* (December 1988), p. 14.
[5]As reported by Ginnie Mae.
[6]Cecala, "Mortgage Servicing Is Where the Action Is," p. 38.

Table 4-1

Sellers and Buyers in the Transfer Servicing Rights Market

Sellers
Small and medium independent mortgage bankers
Federal Deposit Insurance Corporation/Resolution Trust Corporation managed
  thrifts
Capital deficient surviving thrifts
Office of the Comptroller of the Currency regulated banks

Buyers
Large independent mortgage bankers
Commercial banks
Capital sufficient servicing thrifts
New entrants

Source: Hinkle, Harris, and Loggins, *Mortgage Servicing*, p. 4.

and 1989 (the last year of their study) is the chief reason for the increased sales of servicing rights.[7] They note that the three activities of mortgage bankers have faced economic difficulty in at least one of the years: loan production in years 1986 through 1988, secondary marketing/warehousing in years 1987 through 1989, and loan servicing in the years 1987 and 1988. In addition, regulatory capital requirement changes and accounting changes have encouraged the sale of servicing rights by some players. Based on their analysis of these factors, Hinkle, Harris, and Loggins have classified the participants in the transfer servicing rights market as shown in Table 4-1.[8]

Revenue from Servicing

There are five sources of revenue from mortgage servicing. The primary source is the *servicing fee.* This fee is a fixed percentage of the outstanding mortgage balance. Consequently, the revenue of the servicing fee declines over time as the mortgage balance amortizes. When a mortgage is sold to a conduit, the conduit specifies a minimum servicing fee or a

[7]Hal Hinkle, Steve Harris, and Dick Loggins, *Mortgage Servicing: Supply and Demand Trends and Prospects for Valuation* (New York: Mortgage Securities Research, Goldman, Sachs, September 1989).
[8]For a further discussion, see ibid., pp. 4–9.

range for the fee. For example, Ginnie Mae has two programs, I and II, which we discuss in Chapter 8. The servicing fee in the Ginnie Mae I program is 44 basis points; for the Ginnie Mae II it can vary from 44 to 144 basis points. For Fannie Mae and Freddie Mac, it can range from 25 to over 200 basis points for fixed-rate mortgages. In the case of private label pass-throughs, it can range from 25 to over 100 basis points. When the servicing fee is considered outside of a normal range, the amount is referred to as *excess servicing*. Under certain circumstances, the potential revenue generated from excess servicing can be sold. The reason for the variance in servicing fees even by the same conduit is the difference in the cost of servicing a particular type of mortgage design. For example, the cost of servicing an adjustable-rate mortgage (discussed in Chapter 6) is generally greater than a fixed-rate mortgage since the former requires the periodic recalculation of the rate, and notification of the borrower and investor of the new rate.

The second source of servicing income arises from the interest that can be earned by the servicer from the escrow balance (or, as it is called in some states, the impound balance) that the borrower often maintains with the servicer. The interest that can be earned depends on the level of short-term interest rates. It is also dependent on the loan type and the state where the property is located, since certain loan types require the collection of tax and insurance impounds and certain states mandate a statutory interest rate the servicer must pay the homeowner on the impound or escrow balances. The third source of revenue is the float earned on the monthly mortgage payment. This opportunity arises because of the delay permitted between the time the servicer receives the payment and the time that the payment must be sent to the investor.

Fourth, there are several sources of ancillary income. First, a late fee is charged by the servicer if the payment is not made on a timely basis; it usually consists of 4% to 5% of the payment due. If a payment is due on the first of the month, the last date for payment to be received without the imposition of a late fee is the fifteenth of the month. When a servicer receives a late fee, it loses the float from investing the monthly payment. As explained below, the servicer may also have to advance the monthly mortgage payment to the conduit or investor. Second, many servicers receive commissions from cross-selling their borrowers credit life and other insurance products. Third, fees can also be generated from the sale of mailing lists.

Finally, there are other benefits of servicing rights for servicers that are also lenders. They can view their portfolio of borrowers as a potential source for other loans such as second mortgages, automobile loans, and credit cards.

Costs Associated with Servicing

The periodic costs of servicing mortgage loans are predominately the cost of labor and computer systems. Estimates of the average total annual servicing cost per loan in 1988 range from $149 to $162. The lower of the two figures is from KPMG Peat Marwick's Mortgage Servicing Performance Study; the higher figure is from a study by the Mortgage Bankers Association of America.

Table 4-2 provides more detailed information from the latter study showing the components of the cost and how these costs vary by the size of the mortgage servicing portfolio.

Table 4-2

1988 Average Servicing Costs by Size of Servicing Portfolio
($ millions)

Cost component	Less than $500	$500 to $999	$1,000 to $3,999	$4,000 or more	Average
Total direct expenses	$117.40	$115.96	$ 84.08	$ 85.82	$ 87.55
Provision for loan losses	3.60	15.72	9.66	36.99	27.39
Amortized cost of purchased mortgage servicing	24.23	26.93	33.21	55.83	47.14
Total avg. servicing costs	$145.23	$158.61	$126.95	$178.64	$162.08
No. of firms reporting	35	23	38	18	114

Source: The Mortgage Bankers Association of America, *Mortgage Banking* (February 1990).

The three components of cost are total direct expenses, provision for loan losses, and amortized cost of purchased mortgage servicing. By far, total direct expenses constitute the largest component. As can be seen, for servicing portfolios of less than $1 billion the total direct cost is greater than for servicing portfolios of $1 billion and greater—roughly $116 versus $85. This suggests that there are economies of scale with respect to this component of cost. However, total average servicing cost does not decline as the servicing portfolio increases because of the greater provision for loan losses and amortization of the cost of purchased mortgage servicing for the two larger servicing portfolio classes in the table.

Some servicers have specialized in certain types of mortgage loans such as FHA/VA loans. While the company may originate various types of mortgage loans, it may sell its servicing rights in the secondary market for those mortgage loans in which it does not specialize.

Less obvious are three potential costs associated with servicing. We alluded to one of these earlier: advances of the mortgage payment that the servicer may have to make to the conduit or investor. When advances must be made, the servicer loses the use of those funds. A second potential cost is that associated with the incremental servicing expense, which arises when a loan becomes delinquent or goes into foreclosure. Finally, when servicing rights are originated or purchased, the buyer is legally responsible to the investor for the representations and warranties made at the time of origination. Consequently, there is the potential cost of pursuing any claims by investors. Because of this, investors or conduits require approval when servicing is being transferred. If the purchaser of servicing rights does not satisfy the credit requirements of investors or servicers, all servicing may not be transferred. Instead, the servicing will be split (as will the servicing fee) between two servicers.

Risks Associated with Servicing

In the early years of a portfolio the major source of revenue is usually the servicing fee. Since that fee is a percentage of the outstanding mortgage balance, payments made in excess of the monthly mortgage payment (called pre-payments) reduce future revenue. A payoff of a mortgage loan by repayment or foreclosure makes the servicing of that loan worthless. Consequently, the value of the servicing rights depends upon prepayments, which, as we explain in Chapter 10, are related to the level of interest rates and foreclosures. As interest rates decline below the contract rate on the mortgage loan, the likelihood of a borrower prepaying all or a portion of his or her loan increases. A rise in the level of interest rates will reduce prepayments.

What this means is that the value of servicing rights depends in a complicated way on the level of interest rates. More specifically, there are two opposite effects on the ex-pected cash flow when interest rates change. The expected cash flow is equal to the expected mortgage balance times the servicing fee, minus the expected servicing cost. A fall (rise) in interest rates will decrease (increase) the expected future cash flow; a fall (rise) in interest rates will increase (decrease) the present value of that cash flow. In typical ranges for inter-est rates, the dollar value of the servicing fee will move in the same direction as the change in interest. Consequently, unlike typical fixed-rate coupon securities (whose price moves in the direction opposite to that of the change in interest rates), the value of the servicing rights tends to move in the same direction. This is magnified by the effects on the other revenue sources as discussed below.

Hedging the value of servicing rights against pre-payments is not simple. The usual capital market instruments and derivatives used to hedge fixed-income securities cannot effectively hedge the value of servicing rights. As we explain in Chapter 11, mortgage-backed derivatives securities that can be used for this purpose have been created.

In addition to the servicing fee, a change in interest rates will affect the revenue earned on the escrow balances. The effect, however, will not be symmetric. When interest rates rise, higher revenue will be generated; however, when interest rates fall, two adverse consequences will occur. First, lower interest revenue will be earned. If rates fall by a sufficient amount, some mortgage loans will be paid off, requiring the payout to the borrower of the escrowed balance. Therefore, no interest revenue will be earned on these loans. Similarly, interest earned on the monthly mortgage payment float will be in the same direction as the change in interest rates.

A change in interest rates will also affect the opportunity cost of any advances that must be made to conduits or investors. A decline in interest rates will reduce the opportunity cost; a rise in interest rates will do the opposite.

In addition to risk due to prepayments, there is inflation risk. The cost of servicing will rise over time because of inflation. Moreover, a servicer must continue to service a mortgage despite the decline in the servicing fee that occurs as amortization reduces the mortgage balance over time. Higher costs because of inflation and lower servicing fee because of amortization reduce the profitability of servicing a loan over time.

MORTGAGE INSURANCE

There are two types of mortgage-related insurance. The first type is originated by the lender to insure against default by the borrower and is called *mortgage insurance* or *private mortgage insurance*. It is usually required by lenders on loans with loan-to-value ratios greater than 80%. The amount insured will be some percentage of the loan and may decline as the LTV ratio declines. While the insurance is required by the lender, the cost of the insurance is borne by the borrower, usually through a higher contract rate. This type of insurance can be obtained from a mortgage insurance company or, if the borrower qualifies, from the Federal Housing Administration or Veterans Administration.

The second type of mortgage-related insurance is acquired by the borrower, usually with a life insurance company, and is typically called *credit life*. Unlike mortgage insurance, this type is not required by the lender. The policy provides for a continuation of mortgage payments after the death of the insured person, which allows the survivors to continue living in the house. Since the insurance coverage decreases as the mortgage balance declines, this type of mortgage insurance is simply a term policy.

Both types of insurance have a beneficial effect on the creditworthiness of the borrower, but the first type is more important from the lender's perspective. Mortgage insurance is sought by the lender when the borrower is viewed as being capable of meeting the monthly mortgage payments, but does not have enough funds for a large down payment. For example, suppose a borrower seeks financing of $100,000 to purchase a single-family residence for $110,000, thus making a down payment of $10,000. The LTV ratio is 91%, exceeding the uninsured maximum LTV of 80%. Even if the lender's credit analysis indicates that the borrower's payment-to-income ratio is acceptable, the mortgage loan cannot be extended. However, if a private mortgage insurance company insures a portion of the loan, then the lender is afforded protection. Mortgage insurance companies will write policies to insure a maximum of 20% of loans with a LTV ranging from 80% to 90%, and a maximum of 25% of loans with an LTV ranging from 90% to 95%. The lender is still exposed to default by the borrower on the noninsured portion of the mortgage loan; in the case of private mortgage insurers, the lender is also exposed to the risk that the insurer will default.

To illustrate what will happen if a borrower covered by private mortgage insurance defaults, suppose that in our previous example, mortgage insurance is obtained for $15,000, and a default occurs when the market value of the property is $94,000 and the outstanding mortgage balance is $98,000. The mortgage insurer has two choices. It can simply pay the claim by giving the lender $15,000, thereby fulfilling its insurance obligation. The lender then has $15,000 plus the mortgaged property with a value of $94,000, producing a total value of $104,000 and a profit of $6,000. A more economical alternative for the mortgage insurer would be to pay off the mortgage balance of $98,000 and take title to the property. It can then sell the property for $94,000, realizing a loss of $4,000. This loss, however, is less than the $15,000 loss that would result by paying the claim.

Mortgage insurance can also be obtained for pools of mortgage loans that collateralize mortgage-backed securities issued by private conduits. This form of credit enhancement is discussed in Chapter 8.

The Mortgage Insurance Industry

The mortgage insurance industry took off in the 1970s and continued to grow until the early 1980s. The share of private mortgage insurance, relative to the total mortgage market, grew from 15% in the 1970s to 30% in 1983–1984.[9]

In the 1970s and in 1980, the mortgage insurance industry was extremely profitable. However, for the remainder of the 1980s, profitability declined and underwriting losses were realized. According to Moody's Investor's Service, in 1979 mortgage insurers' total losses were only $39 million, representing 13% of premiums earned. By 1982, total losses increased to $210 million, representing 60% of premiums earned and producing an underwriting loss of about $40 million. By 1985, the industry as a whole had losses that exceeded premiums, with a total loss in excess of $1 billion. As a result, between 1985 and mid-1988 almost half the industry stopped writing mortgage insurance.

The underwriting losses that were realized in 1982 and 1983 were due in part to the default rate that resulted from the 1981–1982 recession. Even following the recession, there were increased claims and underwriting losses for a variety of reasons, including: (1) underpricing of mortgage insurance, (2) lax or fraudulent underwriting standards by mortgage originators, and (3) localized economic problems (such as in certain parts of Texas, Louisiana, and Oklahoma, for example). The upheaval this has caused in the industry is summarized in Table 4-3.

In addition, premiums from insuring mortgage pools for enhancing private mortgage-backed securities declined as private conduits used alternative vehicles for credit enhance-

[9] Bill Simpson, "Private Mortgage Insurance on the Rebound," *Secondary Mortgage Markets* (Spring 1989), p. 7.

Table 4-3

Upheaval in the Mortgage Insurance Industry

Date	Company	Approximate Market Share (percentage)	Event
Early 1985	MGIC	30	Transformed into WMAC; 80% re-insured in the European markets; capital released in conjunction with Baldwin United liquidation; new MGIC began operations.
Fall 1985	TICOR	20	Stopped writing new business after acknowledging $180 million exposure to EPIC default.
Spring 1986	TICOR	—	Placed in conservatorship by California Insurance Department and renamed TMIC Insurance Company, Inc. (TMIC).
1986	IMI	5	Stopped writing new business; began running off its book of business.
January 1988	VEREX	20	Stopped writing new business; began running off its book of business.
April 1988	TMIC	—	California placed company in liquidation—canceled coverage on 200,000 insured loans.

Source: Bill Simpson, "Private Mortgage Insurance on the Rebound," *Secondary Mortgage Markets* (Spring 1989), p. 8, by permission of Freddie Mac. All rights reserved.

ment. To counter this loss of business, mortgage insurers have increased their activities in the secondary marketing trading services we described in Chapter 3.

Default Risks Associated with Mortgage Insurance Underwriting

The upheavals of the industry discussed above are linked with the various sources of default risk to which insurers are exposed. These underwriting sources can be classified into the following broad categories: (1) normal (or actuarial) risks, (2) originator underwriting risks, (3) national economic risks, and (4) local economic risks. Below we summarize these risks and discuss the measures taken to manage them.

Normal risks. Insurers expect that a certain percentage of the borrowers will default because of unique circumstances not directly attributable to any of the other categories of default risk discussed below. A loss of employment in a period of rising national and local employment rates would be one example. Death or prolonged illness of the primary wage earner of the borrowing family would be another.

Originator underwriting risk. At one time, mortgage originators such as banks and thrifts would retain the mortgage loan in their portfolio. As a consequence, they kept underwriting standards tight. Since local lending was common, lenders were familiar with economic and real estate market conditions in their geographical area. However, as mortgage bankers, as well as banks and thrifts, began originating mortgages with the intention of selling them in the secondary market, some either became lax in their underwriting standards or in certain instances deliberately misrepresented information to mortgage insurers and investors about the borrower and/or property. Moreover, national mortgage originators were not as familiar with local real estate markets as local lenders.

To manage this type of default risk, mortgage insurers have become less reliant on the credit analysis of mortgage originators. Instead, they have established their own credit analysis departments and have undertaken more extensive quality control programs. They use this information to assess and analyze performance, continually revising their underwriting standards. For example, when analysis of claims with different types of mortgage designs showed that claims on adjustable-rate mortgages were greater than on fixed-rate mortgages, mortgage insurers changed insurance rates to reflect the greater default risk.

In the case of mortgage insurance policies written for mortgage loans in which fraudulent or misleading information is suspected, mortgage insurers have been more aggressive in fighting claims submitted by investors. Since the investor is not necessarily the mortgage originator, this means that investors may suffer losses because of fraudulent practices of which they were unaware. However, investors have a claim on the mortgage originator and servicer for any misrepresentations and warranties that it makes in the sale of the whole loan.

National economic risks. Default rates are positively related to national economic conditions. As national unemployment levels increase, claims increase. The extreme case of national economic risk is catastrophic risk, in which an economic depression and substantial nationwide decline in property values results in a surge of claims.

Local economic risks. Even when the national economy is thriving, regions within the United States may suffer high levels of unemployment and depressed property values. Some mortgage insurers have handled this problem simply, by not writing policies in problem regions or potential problem regions. Others have responded by controlling this risk through geographical diversification of policies, coupled with differential rates, to reflect the geographical location of the property.[10]

Studies of Default

There have been several studies of mortgage loan defaults. The measure of default used in these studies is the *conditional default rate,* which is the probability that a mortgage loan will default this year. Alternatively, the conditional default rate is the percentage of mortgage loans that exist at the beginning of the year and default sometime during the year. It is a conditional measure because it expresses the probability of default given that a mortgage loan has survived to this year.[11] Measuring default in this way is better than measuring it in terms of the percentage of mortgage loans that were originated and subsequently defaulted, because the conditional default rate relates defaults to a particular point in time and to a particular set of economic conditions.

One of the first extensive statistical studies of conditional default rates was by Peters, Pinkus, and Askin.[12] Their data base included 503,000 conventional fixed-rate, 1-to-4

---

[10] Another reason for differential rates by region—more specifically by state—is the effect of state laws on foreclosure costs. This effect is discussed later in the chapter.

[11] In other fields, conditional rates or probabilities are referred to as hazard rates.

[12] Helen F. Peters, Scott M. Pinkus, and David J. Askin, "Default: The Last Resort," *Secondary Mortgage Markets* (August 1984), pp. 16–22.

Figure 4-2

Estimated Default Rates by Loan-to-Value Ratio

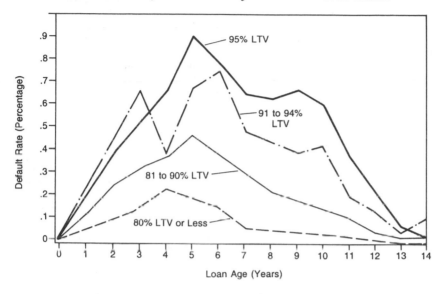

Loan Age (Years)

Note: Estimated using a proportional hazard model and Freddie Mac data on single-family, fixed-rate loans.
Source: Robert Van Order, "The Hazards of Default," *Secondary Mortgage Markets* (Fall 1990), p. 30, by permission of Freddie Mac. All rights reserved.

family, owner-occupied mortgage loans sold to Freddie Mac between 1973 and 1980. Of the sample mortgage loans, only about 1,000 (0.2%) defaulted during the study period. In a more recent study, Van Order examined 725,000 conventional, fixed rate single family mortgage loans originated from 1973 to 1983 and purchased by Freddie Mac.[13] The default experience of these mortgage loans was investigated through the middle of 1990.

One of the key characteristics of a mortgage loan that affects defaults is the LTV ratio at origination. The higher the LTV or, equivalently, the less equity the borrower has in the property, the higher the probability of default. This can be seen from Figure 4-2, which shows Van Order's findings for

[13]Robert Van Order, "The Hazards of Default," *Secondary Mortgage Markets* (Fall 1990), pp. 29–32.

Table 4-4

Simulations of Cumulative Default Probability within 10 Years of Origination (Percentage)

Origination Year	Loan-to-Value Ratio			
	80% or Less	81 to 90%	91 to 94%	95%
1976	.08	.31	.45	.63
1977	.15	.59	.86	1.23
1978	.39	1.53	2.23	3.16
1979	.73	2.87	4.16	5.89
1980	1.36	5.31	7.70	10.89
1981	1.86	7.26	10.51	14.85
1982	1.57	6.15	8.92	12.60
1983	1.03	4.02	5.84	8.26

Note: Estimated assuming a prepayment rate of 6% per year using a proportional hazard model and Freddie Mac data on single-family, fixed-rate loans.
Source: Robert Van Order, "The Hazards of Default," *Secondary Mortgage Markets* (Fall 1990), p. 31, by permission of Freddie Mac. All rights reserved.

the default rate by LTV.[14] In addition to the LTV, Van Order found that the origination year was significant in explaining defaults, with 1976 and 1981 being the worst years. Table 4-4 shows his simulation results for 10-year cumulative default probabilities by origination year, classified by original LTV.

The empirical results also suggest that there is a seasoning effect for default rates, i.e., default rates tend to decline as mortgage loans become seasoned.[15] The reason for the seasoning effect on default rates is twofold. First, since a borrower typically knows shortly after moving into a home whether or not he or she can afford to make the mortgage payments, default rates are higher in the earlier years. Second, the longer a borrower remains in a home, the lower the LTV ratio (i.e., the greater the equity in the home), and therefore the incentive to default declines.

Van Order also examined several characteristics of the borrower, which he hypothesized would affect default

[14]This was also found by Peters, Pinkus, and Askin, "Default: The Last Resort," and by Scott Brown et al. for FHA/VA loans as well as conventional loans (*Analysis of Mortgage Servicing Portfolios* [New York: Financial Strategies Group, Prudential-Bache Capital Funding, December 1990]).
[15]For conventional mortgage loans, the maximum default rate appears to be three to four years after origination. For FHA/VA mortgage loans, it seems to be two to three years after origination. See Brown et al., *Analysis of Mortgage Servicing Portfolios*, p. 8.

rates. For example, as explained in the previous chapter, the payment-to-income ratio is a measure of the burden of the mortgage payments. It is expected that the higher the PTI at origination, the greater the probability of default. Van Order found that the probability of default increased only slightly as this burden grew larger. As he notes, this conclusion is only tentative because his sample did not include many observations with high PTIs. None of the other borrower characteristics appeared to affect default rates significantly.

State Foreclosure Laws and Default Losses

State foreclosure laws significantly affect default losses. These state laws differ in three primary ways: (1) foreclosure procedures, (2) statutory right of redemption, and (3) deficiency judgment.[16] Foreclosure procedures can be either judicial or nonjudicial. The former is done under court supervision, which slows down the process of selling the property. This delay increases the losses associated with a foreclosure because of the opportunity loss on funds that could be reinvested, additional taxes and insurance that must be paid, and legal expenses. Moreover, the property value might decline in the interim because of lack of maintenance or a downturn in property values. In a nonjudicial foreclosure,[17] a sale can be made faster because there is no court proceeding; therefore, the costs associated with foreclosure are reduced. There are 23 states that permit only judicial foreclosure.[18]

A statutory right of redemption is a right granted to the borrower to redeem the property by paying any deficiencies, including legal expenses, for a specified period *after* a foreclosure;[19] 29 states now grant this right to borrowers.[20] If this right allows the borrower to occupy the property after

---

[16] Terrence M. Clauretie and Thomas N. Herzog, "How State Laws Affect Foreclosure Costs," *Secondary Mortgage Markets* (Spring 1989), pp. 26–27.

[17] Such foreclosure procedures are also called power of sale procedures, foreclosures by advertisement, or a trustee's sale.

[18] Clauretie and Herzog, "How State Laws Affect Foreclosure Costs," p. 26.

[19] An equitable right of redemption gives the borrower the right to redeem the property by paying all deficiencies and legal costs *before* a foreclosure. This right is granted to borrowers in all states.

[20] Clauretie and Herzog, "How State Laws Affect Foreclosure Costs," p. 26.

foreclosure, there is the standard moral hazard problem—the property may deteriorate, and potential buyers may be reluctatant to bid on property where moral hazard exists. This will result in lower bid prices being received.

A deficiency judgment allows the lender to recover any deficiencies from the borrower's personal assets. While the costs of recovery and the limited personal assets of the borrower may make it uneconomic for the lender to pursue this right, its existence may discourage a default in some instances. This would occur in cases where the borrower has the capacity to pay and sufficient personal assets to satisfy any judgment, but where property value has declined so that no equity remains in the property (i.e., the LTV is 1 or higher). Only six states do not allow deficiency judgments.[21]

An empirical study by Clauretie and Herzog, based on data from private mortgage insurance and FHA claims, investigated the effect of state laws on losses.[22] A statistical analysis of the data found that losses are significantly lower in states with nonjudicial foreclosure procedures and a deficiency judgment right;[23] losses are greater where states grant a statutory right of redemption. These researchers found that on a $100,000 loan, lenders are exposed to potential additional losses of $500 to $1,000 if a property is located in a state with only a judicial foreclosure process and statutory right of redemption.

CONCLUSION

Unlike a bond, a loan requires servicing. Investors that are willing to invest in a loan are usually reluctant, or may not be permitted, to engage in servicing activities. The presence of firms willing to service loans without committing funds to invest in those loans enhances the secondary market for loans. The development of mortgage derivative securities,

---

[21] Ibid., p. 27.
[22] Ibid., pp. 27–28.
[23] The deficiency judgment was not found to be statistically significant for the FHA data. The low default rates in California in the study period and the fact that California was one of only six states that did not have a deficiency judgment may have caused this result.

which we will discuss in Chapter 11, should help servicers better manage the major risks associated with this business. Moreover, in the future, the attractiveness of this business might be enhanced by the ability to securitize servicing fees. There have been recent attempts to do so;[24] however, to date we are not aware of any asset-backed securities that have been collateralized by mortgage servicing fees.

Mortgage insurers provide another function that enhances the secondary market by reducing default risk. The experience of the mortgage insurance industry since the early 1980s should help it structure its operations and establish pricing policy so as to generate a fair return on capital in the 1990s.

---

[24]Independence One Mortgage Corporation proposed the creation of an asset-backed security collateralized by the servicing fees on FHA/VA mortgages. The proposal was rejected by the Securities and Exchange Commission on the basis that servicing rights do not represent an ownership interest in the mortgages. For a further discussion of this topic, see Jerry DeMuth, "Look for Securities Backed by Fees," *Servicing Management* (April 1990), p. 5, and Eric S. Silverman, *Identifying and Managing Risk in the Mortgage Servicing Industry*, master's thesis, Sloan School of Management, MIT, May 1991, pp. 53–55.

5

The Traditional Mortgage

In this chapter and the two to follow, we describe the various mortgage instruments. There are numerous types of fixed-rate mortgages. Our primary focus in this chapter is on the level-payment, fixed-rate mortgage introduced in the 1930s. We refer to this mortgage design as the *traditional mortgage* and begin this chapter with some historical background about its origins. The chapter concludes by pointing out the weakness of this mortgage design, thereby setting the foundation for alternative mortgage designs, which we cover in the two chapters that follow. In the appendix to this chapter, we discuss a reverse mortgage, a mortgage design that allows the homeowner to capitalize on the increase in equity in his or her home without having to sell the property.

SOME HISTORICAL BACKGROUND

Since the Great Depression, both the design of mortgages and the origin of the funds that finance them have undergone revolutionary changes and have been affected by spectacular innovations. Until that time, mortgages were not fully amortized, as they are now (see below), but were balloon instruments in which the principal was not amortized, or only partially amortized at maturity, leaving the debtor with the problem of refinancing the balance. Sometimes the bank also had the right to ask for repayment of the outstanding balance on demand or upon relatively short notice, even if the mortgager was fulfilling his or her obligation.

This system of mortgage financing proved disastrous during the Great Depression, and contributed to both its depth and personal distress, as banks, afflicted by losses on their loans and by depositors' withdrawals, found it necessary to liquidate their mortgage loans at a time when debtors found it impossible to refinance.

This experience led, in the middle of the 1930s, to the widespread adoption of a much superior instrument called the fixed-rate, level-payment, fully amortized mortgage (for short, level-payment mortgage). This adoption was encouraged by the newly created Federal Housing Administration, which had been assigned to provide affordable insurance to protect the lender's claim against nonperformance by the borrower. This insurance was desirable not only for the lender but also for the borrower, for whom insurance usually led to better terms. The FHA specified what kind of mortgages it was prepared to insure, and one of its requirements was that it had to be a level-payment mortgage.

THE LEVEL-PAYMENT MORTGAGE

The basic idea behind the design of the level-payment or traditional mortgage, is that the borrower pays interest and repays principal in equal installments over an agreed-upon period of time, called the maturity or term of the mortgage. Thus at the end of the term, the loan has been fully amortized.

The interest rate is generally above the risk-free interest rate, in particular the yield on a Treasury security of comparable maturity, the spread reflecting the higher costs of collection, the costs associated with default that are not eliminated despite the collateral, poorer liquidity, and the uncertainty concerning the timing of the cash flow (which we explain later). The frequency of payment is typically monthly[1] and the prevailing term of the mortgage is 20 to 30 years;

[1] Recently there have been some mortgage loans with biweekly mortgage payments.

however, in recent years an increasing number of 15-year mortgages have been originated.

Each monthly mortgage payment for a level-payment mortgage is due on the first of each month and consists of:

1. interest of 1/12th of the fixed annual interest rate times the amount of the outstanding mortgage balance at the beginning of the previous month, and
2. a repayment of a portion of the outstanding mortgage balance (principal).

The difference between the monthly mortgage payment and the portion of the payment that represents interest equals the amount that is applied to reduce the outstanding mortgage balance. The monthly mortgage payment is designed so that after the last scheduled monthly payment of the loan is made, the amount of the outstanding mortgage balance is zero (i.e., the mortgage is fully repaid).

To illustrate a level payment fixed-rate mortgage, consider a 30-year (360-month), $100,000 mortgage with a 9.5% mortgage rate. The monthly mortgage payment would be $840.85. The formula for calculating the monthly mortgage payment is given later.

Table 5-1 shows how each monthly mortgage payment is divided between interest and repayment of principal. At the beginning of month 1, the mortgage balance is $100,000, the amount of the original loan. The mortgage payment for month 1 includes interest on the $100,000 borrowed for the month. Since the interest rate is 9.5%, the monthly interest rate is 0.0079167 (.095 divided by 12). Interest for month 1 is therefore $791.67 ($100,000 times 0.0079167). The $49.18 difference between the monthly mortgage payment of $840.85 and the interest of $791.67 is the portion of the monthly mortgage payment that represents repayment of principal. This $49.18 in month 1 reduces the mortgage balance.

The mortgage balance at the end of month 1 (beginning of month 2) is then $99,950.81 ($100,000 minus $49.19). The interest for the second monthly mortgage payment is $791.28, the monthly interest rate (0.0079167) times the mort-

Table 5-1

Amortization Schedule for a Level-Payment, Fixed-Rate Mortgage

Mortgage loan: $100,000
Mortgage rate: 9.5%
Monthly payment: $840.85
Term of loan: 30 years (360 months)

Month	Beginning Mortgage Balance	Monthly Mortgage Payment	Interest for Month	Principal Repayment	Ending Mortgage Balance
1	$100,000.00	$840.85	$791.67	$ 49.19	$99,950.81
2	99,950.81	840.85	791.28	49.58	99,901.24
3	99,901.24	840.85	790.88	49.97	99,851.27
4	99,851.27	840.85	790.49	50.37	99,800.90
5	99,800.90	840.85	790.09	50.76	99,750.14
6	99,750.14	840.85	789.69	51.17	99,698.97
7	99,698.97	840.85	789.28	51.57	99,647.40
8	99,647.40	840.85	788.88	51.98	99,595.42
9	99,595.42	840.85	788.46	52.39	99,543.03
10	99,543.03	840.85	788.05	52.81	99,490.23
...	...	...	...	...	...
...	...	...	...	...	...
...	...	...	...	...	...
98	$ 99,862.54	840.85	735.16	105.69	92,756.85
99	92,756.85	840.85	734.33	106.53	92,650.32
100	92,650.32	840.85	733.48	107.37	92,542.95
101	92,542.95	840.85	732.63	108.22	92,434.72
102	92,434.72	840.85	731.77	109.08	92,325.64
103	92,325.64	840.85	730.91	109.94	92,215.70
104	92,215.70	840.85	730.04	110.81	92,104.89
105	92,104.89	840.85	729.16	111.69	91,993.20
106	91,993.20	840.85	728.28	112.57	91,880.62
...	...	...	...	...	...
...	...	...	...	...	...
...	...	...	...	...	...
209	74,177.40	840.85	587.24	253.62	73,923.78
210	73,923.78	840.85	585.23	255.62	73,668.16
211	73,668.16	840.85	583.21	257.65	73,410.51
212	73,410.51	840.85	581.17	259.69	73,150.82
...	...	...	...	...	...
...	...	...	...	...	...
...	...	...	...	...	...
354	5,703.93	840.85	45.16	795.70	4,908.23
355	4,908.23	840.85	38.86	802.00	4,106.24
356	4,106.24	840.85	32.51	808.35	3,297.89
357	3,297.89	840.85	26.11	814.75	2,483.14
358	2,483.14	840.85	19.66	821.20	1,661.95
359	1,661.95	840.85	13.16	827.70	834.25
360	834.25	840.85	6.60	834.25	0.00

gage balance at the beginning of month 2 ($99,950.81). The difference between the $840.85 monthly mortgage payment and the $791.28 interest is $49.57, representing the amount of the mortgage balance paid off with that monthly mortgage payment.[2] Notice that the last monthly mortgage payment is sufficient to pay off the remaining mortgage balance. When a loan repayment schedule is structured so that the payments made by the borrower will completely pay off the interest and principal, the loan is said to be *self-amortizing*. Table 5-1 is thus an example of an *amortization schedule*.

As Table 5-1 clearly shows, *the portion of the monthly mortgage payment applied to interest declines each month and the portion applied to reducing the mortgage balance increases.* The reason for this is that as the mortgage balance is reduced with each monthly mortgage payment, the interest on the mortgage balance declines. Since the monthly mortgage payment is fixed, a larger part of the monthly payment is applied to reduce the principal in each subsequent month.

In contrast, a mortgage loan in which the monthly payments are sufficient to pay only interest is a *balloon mortgage*. With this mortgage, only interest is paid over the life of the mortgage; no payments are made to reduce the original mortgage balance. At the end of the term of the mortgage, the original principal must be paid (this is the so-called balloon payment). For example, suppose that $100,000 is borrowed to purchase a home and that the term of the mortgage is seven years and the mortgage rate is 9.5%. The annual dollar interest for each of the seven years will be $9,500. The monthly mortgage payment will then be $791.67 ($9,500 divided by 12). At the end of the seventh year, the homeowner must repay the principal of $100,000.

MATHEMATICS OF LEVEL-PAYMENT MORTGAGES

Investors in mortgages must be able to calculate the scheduled cash flow associated with a particular mortgage, and servicers of mortgages must be able to calculate the

---

[2]Because Table 5-1 was computer generated, rounding resulted in the value of $49.48 shown in the table.

scheduled servicing fee that will be earned. Moreover, when we examine pools of mortgage loans, it will be necessary to determine the cash flow from the pool. In this section we present formulas for calculating the cash flow associated with traditional mortgages. The formulas we present here will be extended to passthroughs in Chapter 9.

The Monthly Mortgage Payment

To compute the monthly mortgage payment for a level-payment mortgage requires the application of the formula for the present value of an ordinary annuity formula which is

$$PV = A \frac{1 - (1 + i)^{-n}}{i}$$

where

$$
\begin{aligned}
A &= \text{amount of the annuity (\$);} \\
n &= \text{number of periods;} \\
PV &= \text{present value of an annuity (\$);} \\
i &= \text{periodic interest rate.}
\end{aligned}
$$

We can redefine the terms in the above formula for a level payment mortgage as follows:

$$MB_0 = MP \frac{1 - (1 + i)^{-n}}{i}$$

where

$$
\begin{aligned}
MP   &= \text{monthly mortgage payment (\$);} \\
n   &= \text{number of months;} \\
MB_0 &= \text{original mortgage balance (\$);} \\
i   &= \text{simple monthly interest rate (annual interest} \\
     &\quad\ \text{rate/12).}
\end{aligned}
$$

Solving for the monthly mortgage payment (MP) gives

$$MP = \frac{MB_0}{\left[\dfrac{1 - (1 + i)^{-n}}{i}\right]}$$

Alternatively, this can be expressed in a simplified form as follows:

$$MP = MB_0 \left[\frac{[i(1+i)^n]}{[(1+i)^n - 1]}\right]$$

The term in brackets is called the *payment factor* or *annuity factor*. It is the monthly payment for a $1 mortgage loan with an interest rate of i and a term of n months.

To illustrate how the formula is applied, we'll use the $100,000, 30-year, 9.5% mortgage that we discussed above.

$n = 360$;
$MB_0 = \$100,000$;
$i = .0079167 \ (=.095/12)$.

The monthly mortgage payment is then

$$MP = \$100,000 \left[\frac{.0079167\,(1.0079107)^{360}}{(1.0079167)^{360} - 1}\right]$$

$$= \$100,000 \left[\frac{.0079167\,(17.095)}{17.095 - 1}\right]$$

$$- \$100,000\,[.0084085]$$

$$= \$840.85.$$

This agrees with the monthly mortgage payment we used in Table 5-1. The payment factor or annuity factor is .0084085.

The Mortgage Balance and Interest for Each Month

It is not necessary to construct an amortization schedule such as Table 5-1 in order to determine the remaining mortgage balance for any month. The following formula can be used:

$$MP_t = MB_0 \left[\frac{[(1+i)^n - (1+i)^t]}{[(1+i)^n - 1]} \right]$$

where

MB_t = mortgage balance after t months ($);
n = original number of months of mortgage;
MB_0 = the original mortgage balance ($);
i = simple monthly interest rate (annual interest rate/12).

For the mortgage in Table 5-1, the mortgage balance after the 210th month is:

t = 210;
n = 360;
MB_0 = $100,000;
i = .0079167.

$$MB_{210} = \$100,000 \left[\frac{[(1.0079167)^{360} - (1.0079167)^{210}]}{[(1.0079167)^{360} - 1]} \right]$$

$$= \$73,668.$$

This agrees with the ending mortgage balance for month 210 shown in Table 5-1.

The following formula can be used to determine the amount of the scheduled principal repayment in month t:

$$P_t = MB_0 \left[\frac{[i(1+i)^{t-1}]}{[(1+i)^n - 1]} \right]$$

where

P_t = scheduled principal repayment for month t.

The scheduled principal repayment for the 210th

month for the mortgage in Table 5-1 is

$$\$100,000 \left[\frac{[.0079167\,(1.0079167)^{210-1}]}{[(1.0079167)^{360} - 1]} \right]$$

$$= \$100,000 \left[\frac{[.0079167\,(5{,}19696)]}{[17.095 - 1]} \right]$$

$$= \$255.62.$$

Once again, this agrees with Table 5-1.

To compute the interest paid for month t, the following formula can be used:

$$I_t = MB_0 \left[\frac{i\,[(1 + i)^n - (1 + i)^{t-1}]}{[(1+i)^n - 1]} \right]$$

where

I_t = interest for month t.

For the 210th month, the interest for the mortgage in Table 5-1 is

$$I_{210} = \$100,000 \left[\frac{.0079167\,[(1.0079167)^{360} - (1.0079167)^{210-1}]}{[(1.0079167)^{360} - 1]} \right]$$

$$= \$100,000 \left[\frac{.0079167\,(17.095 - 5.19696)}{(17.095 - 1)} \right]$$

$$= \$585.23.$$

Cash Flow with Servicing Fee

An investor that acquires a mortgage may service the mortgage or sell the right to service the mortgage. In the former case, the investor's cash flow is the entire cash flow from the mortgage. In the latter case it is the cash flow net of the servicing fee. The monthly cash flow from the mortgage can therefore be decomposed into three parts:

1. the servicing fee,
2. the interest payment net of the servicing fee, and
3. the scheduled principal repayment.

Consider once again the 30-year mortgage loan for $100,000 with a mortgage rate of 9.5%. Suppose the servicing fee is 0.5% per year. Table 5-2 shows the cash flow for the mortgage with this servicing fee. The monthly mortgage payment is unchanged. The amount of the principal repayment is the same as in Table 5-2. The difference is that the interest is reduced by the amount of the servicing fee. The servicing fee, just like the interest, declines each month because the mortgage balance declines.

PREPAYMENTS AND CASH FLOW UNCERTAINTY

In our illustration of the cash flow from a level-payment mortgage, we assumed that the homeowner would not prepay any portion of the mortgage balance prior to the scheduled due date. But some homeowners do pay off all or part of their mortgage balance prior to the maturity date. As we noted earlier, payments made in excess of the scheduled principal repayments are called prepayments.

Prepayments occur for one of several reasons. First, homeowners prepay the entire mortgage when they sell their home. The sale of a home may occur for such reasons as a change of employment that necessitates moving, the purchase of a more expensive home ("trading up"), or a divorce in which the settlement requires sale of the marital residence. Second, as we explained earlier in this chapter, in the American system the borrower has the right to pay off all or part of the mortgage balance at any time. Effectively, someone who invests in a mortgage has granted the borrower an option to prepay the mortgage, and the borrower will have an incentive to do so if market rates fall below the rate in his own contract. Third, in the case of homeowners who cannot meet their mort-

Table 5-2

Cash Flow for a Mortgage with Servicing Fee

Mortgage loan: $100,000
Mortgage rate: 9.5%
Servicing fee: 0.5%
Monthly payment: $840.85
Term of loan: 30 years (360 months)

Month	Beginning Mortgage Balance	Monthly Mortgage Payment	Net Interest for Month	Servicing Fee	Principal Repayment	Ending Mortgage Balance
1	$100,000.00	$840.85	$750.00	$41.67	$ 49.19	$99,950.81
2	99,950.81	840.85	749.63	41.65	49.58	99,901.24
3	99,901.24	840.85	749.26	41.63	49.97	99,851.27
4	99,851.27	840.85	748.88	41.60	50.37	99,800.90
5	99,800.90	840.85	748.51	41.58	50.76	99,750.14
6	99,750.14	840.85	748.13	41.56	51.17	99,698.97
7	99,698.97	840.85	747.74	41.54	51.57	99,647.40
8	99,647.40	840.85	747.36	41.52	51.98	99,595.42
9	99,595.42	840.85	746.97	41.50	52.39	99,543.03
10	99,543.03	840.85	746.57	41.48	52.81	99,490.23
...	...	...	...	...	...	...
...	...	...	...	...	...	...
...	...	...	...	...	...	...
98	$ 92,862.54	840.85	696.47	38.69	105.69	92,756.85
99	92,756.85	840.85	695.68	38.65	106.53	92,650.32
100	92,650.32	840.85	694.88	38.60	107.37	92,542.95
101	92,542.95	840.85	694.07	38.56	108.22	92,434.72
102	92,434.72	840.85	693.26	38.51	109.08	92,325.64
103	92,325.64	840.85	692.44	38.47	109.94	92,215.70
104	92,215.70	840.85	691.62	38.42	110.81	92,104.89
105	92,104.89	840.85	690.79	38.38	111.69	91,993.20
106	91,993.20	840.85	689.95	38.33	112.57	91,880.62
...	...	...	...	...	...	...
...	...	...	...	...	...	...
...	...	...	...	...	...	...
209	74,177.40	840.85	556.33	30.91	253.62	73,923.78
210	73,923.78	840.85	554.43	30.80	255.62	73,668.16
211	73,668.16	840.85	552.51	30.70	257.65	73,410.51
212	73,410.51	840.85	550.58	30.59	259.69	73,150.82
...	...	...	...	...	...	...
...	...	...	...	...	...	...
...	...	...	...	...	...	...
354	5,703.93	840.85	42.78	2.38	795.70	4,908.23
355	4,908.23	840.85	36.81	2.05	802.00	4,106.24
356	4,106.24	840.85	30.80	1.71	808.35	3,297.89
357	3,297.89	840.85	24.73	1.37	814.75	2,483.14
358	2,483.14	840.85	18.62	1.03	821.20	1,661.95
359	1,661.95	840.85	12.46	0.69	827.70	834.25

gage obligations, the property is repossessed and sold. The proceeds from the sale are used to pay off the mortgage in the case of a conventional mortgage. For an insured mortgage, the insurer will pay off the mortgage balance. Finally, if property is destroyed by fire or another insured catastrophe occurs, the insurance proceeds are used to pay off the mortgage.

The effect of prepayments is that the cash flow from a mortgage is not known with certainty. This is true not only for level-payment mortgages but for all the mortgages we discuss in this book.

Because of the critical importance of prepayments in the valuation of mortgages and mortgage-backed securities, we discuss prepayment behavior in more detail in Chapter 10.

THE LEVEL-PAYMENT MORTGAGE BEFORE THE 1970s

The level-payment mortgage was initially a great success. It contributed to the recovery of housing after the Great Depression, and continued to perform a valuable role in financing residential real estate in the first two decades of the postwar period until the inception of the era of high inflation, just before the mid-1970s.

In this golden period, the organization that played the central role in providing mortgage loans was the thrift institution, and especially savings and loan associations. There are several reasons for this, the first of which has to do with differentiated interest rates offered on deposits. One of the financial reforms introduced in the early days of the New Deal was the imposition of deposit ceilings. These included a mandatory ceiling of zero interest on demand deposits—then held only at commercial banks—and the authorization of the Federal Reserve Bank to impose and regulate ceiling rates on savings and related deposits (Regulation Q). The justification for this regulation was basically that, in its absence, banks would be induced to outbid each other for deposits, to the point of impairing the financial security of depositors—indeed, it was believed that the lack of a ceiling had probably contributed to the collapse of the banking system during the depression. The important point, however, is that regulation did *not* extend to the thrift institutions.

As the economy emerged buoyantly from the war, there was a large demand for housing and mortgages, especially in view of the low construction rate of the previous two decades. At the same time, the Federal Reserve Bank kept interest rate ceilings at below-market levels. That gave the S&Ls, unencumbered by ceilings, an opportunity to attract deposits and to grow heftily by outbidding banks and still earning a comfortable margin. The growth was facilitated by favorable tax legislation, which was inspired by the notion that S&Ls were to be the pillar of the housing market, as well as provide an attractive, highly liquid investment for the middle and upper income classes. S&Ls accepted deposits that were universally regarded as demand liabilities, although in theory notice was required before withdrawal. At the same time they were making mortgage loans of 20- to 30-year maturities, and were further required to give the borrowers the right to prepay the loan at their option. This is equivalent to giving the borrowers a valuable option in case interest rates should fall. At the same time the lender had no recourse if they rose.

Nobody seemed to appreciate, at the time, the highly speculative and risky position these institutions were taking by borrowing short and lending long; in essence they were taking on a commitment to make 20- to 30-year loans at the current long-term market rate, which they would have to cover later by attracting deposits at prevailing short-term market rates. Nevertheless, they were regarded as very solid and had no difficulty securing deposits. The result was an explosive growth of S&L financing of housing, as can be seen from Table 5-3. Beginning with 1950, the share of mortgages held by savings institutions grew from 32% to 47% in the short space of 14 years. As one would expect, the explosion was in large measure at the expense of commercial banks, which were losing in the competition for funds, and of insurance companies, for which the competition of S&Ls was reducing the attractiveness of mortgages as an investment. Thereafter, with the emerging problems of the S&Ls, the share of savings institutions first stabilized and then in the 1970s began to de-

Table 5-3

*Share of Mortgages Held by Main Financial Intermediaries,
1950–1988*

	1950	1964	1977	1988
Total of all holders	73	306	1,000	3,260
Share held by:				
Commercial banks	18	14	18	21
Savings institutions, primarily S&Ls	32	47	46	30
Insurance	22	20	11	8
Mortgage pools	0	3	6	25
All of the above	72	84	81	84

Sources: Board of Governors of the Federal Reserve System, *Flow of Funds in the United States 1939–1953*. Other years, Board of Governors, *Flow of Funds·Accounts: Financial Assets and Liabilities.*

cline, mostly because of the secondary market benefits from the explosive growth of mortgage pools and passthrough securities.

The earliest signs of trouble came in the 1960s. First the Federal Reserve, perhaps concerned with the shrinkage of its domain, the banking system, started cautiously to lift the interest rate ceilings, and to allow innovations such as certificates of deposit, which provided a partial means of circumventing ceiling regulations. Then in the mid-1960s, short-term rates began to rise quickly, first because of the economic boom, and later because of the budget deficit induced by the Vietnam War. The rise in short rates squeezed the profits of the unhedged S&Ls and threatened to play havoc with an industry essential to housing. The reaction of the authorities was to attempt to protect the S&Ls from the market by extending to them the ceilings previously applying to banks. But S&Ls were allowed to keep some advantage by being granted a ceiling rate somewhat higher than that of banks. Thus began the disruptive practice of generalized ceilings that came to an end in the 1980s.

The ceilings were only a short-term palliative, which helped shield the S&Ls from their immediate competitors by allowing them to offer depositors interest rates matching the higher market rates. But the ceiling could not solve the S&Ls'

basic problem: holding low yielding long-term assets in an environment of much higher short-term market rates. By administering ceilings based upon what S&Ls could pay depositors rather than what market rates dictated, banking regulators opened the door to disintermediation—that is, the transfer of funds by investors from low-paying depository institutions to direct investment in final lending and other intermediaries. Higher market rates, spurred by inflation and the impact of anti-inflationary policies, channelled funds by the billions away from traditional depository institutions. Disintermediation was further encouraged by financial innovations such as the money market funds designed to circumvent the interest ceilings. These provided services similar to those of depository institutions, while offering market rates. Disintermediation and low growth of the thrift institutions were reflected in repeated financial difficulties in the housing market. And these problems were magnified by serious shortcomings of the level-payment mortgage in the presence of inflation.

In Chapters 6 and 7, we will explain how this situation motivated the development of alternative mortgage instruments.

APPENDIX
REVERSE MORTGAGES

A major investment made by many families is their home. During periods of high inflation and rising home prices, a significant portion of the wealth of some families will be their home. A study conducted in the late 1970s found that for the elderly the average home equity represented more than two-thirds of the assets they held.[3]

Traditionally, the only way the elderly can capture the increase in the equity of their home (which reflects reduction of the principal and home value appreciation) in order to meet current expenditures is to either sell their home or obtain a second mortgage. The reverse mortgage was designed to give the elderly a third alternative.

[3]Joseph Friedman and Jane Sjogren, *The Assets of the Elderly as They Retire* (Cambridge, MA: Abt Associates, 1980).

With a reverse mortgage, the homeowner receives monthly payments from the lender over the mortgage's life. The homeowner's equity in the property declines each month by an amount equal to the monthly payment. Effectively, the lender is making a monthly loan to the homeowner, the property being the collateral for the loan. Unlike a traditional mortgage, the lender's investment in a reverse mortgage is only the monthly mortgage payments. Nevertheless, the lender faces certain risks, which we discuss below.

To illustrate a reverse mortgage, suppose that an individual purchased a home for $40,000 25 years ago and that the mortgage loan is fully repaid at this time. Suppose also that the market value of the property is $180,000; therefore the homeowner's equity is now $180,000. The homeowner can obtain a 10-year reverse mortgage for, say, $120,000. Assuming a borrowing rate of 10%, the homeowner will receive $586 each month for the next 10 years. Correspondingly, each month the homeowner's equity in the property will decline by $586.

In our illustration, the mortgage rate was fixed over the loan's life. This need not be the case. It can be an adjustable interest rate with restrictions on how the rate may change during each period and over the mortgage's life. (The adjustable-rate mortgage design is the subject of Chapter 6.) Though the life of the loan in our illustration was fixed, reverse mortgages may have an indefinite life, permitting the borrower to receive monthly payments while living in the home. In such instances, an upper limit to the total amount that can be loaned will be imposed by the lender. There are even reverse mortgages with a shared appreciation feature, a feature described in the appendix to Chapter 7.[4]

Today there are no restrictions imposed on lending institutions in the use of the reverse mortgage design. In 1979, federally chartered S&Ls were permitted to make such loans; in 1982, federal legislation removed state barriers. Yet the amount of reverse mortgages originated has been small. It has been estimated that only 3,000 reverse mortgages were

---

[4]Thomas P. Boehm and Michael C. Ehrhardt, "How Risky Are Reverse Mortgages?" (Knoxville: Finance Department, The University of Tennessee, December 1990), p. 8.

originated in the 1980s, 2,000 by a single private lender and the balance by state and local government units or nonprofit agencies.[5]

One might expect this market to grow as the proportion of elderly homeowners in the United States increases. Demand and supply for such mortgage designs will depend on whether the risks associated with this mortgage design for lenders and borrowers can be reduced, as well as on the development of a secondary mortgage market.

Lenders face three major risks.[6] First, as in the traditional mortgage, they face prepayment risk. More specifically, when interest rates decline, the loan may be repaid, forcing the lender to reinvest at a lower interest rate. In the case of a fixed-rate reverse mortgage, when interest rates rise, the lender is forced to continue the loan at a less than market interest rate. The second risk has to do with the repayment of the loan. In the case of a fixed life, the property will have to be sold to repay the loan unless other funds are available. However, if the homeowner continues to live in the home, the lender will have to extend the term of the loan (without making additional monthly payments) until the property is sold. Thus, even in a fixed-life reverse mortgage, there is uncertainty about when the loan will be repaid. The third risk is related to the second. During any period of extension of a fixed-life reverse mortgage or in the case of a reverse mortgage where the loan period is indefinite, there is the possibility that the property will decline in value below the amount loaned.

From the borrower's perspective, in a fixed-life reverse mortgage that does not permit extension, there is the problem of repaying the loan. This may necessitate the eventual sale of the property to obtain the proceeds needed.

State agencies and nonprofit agencies were the first to establish programs to try to reduce the risks associated with reverse mortgages. Examples of the earliest programs are

[5] Judith V. May and Edward J. Szymanoski, Jr., "Reverse Mortgages: Risk Reduction Strategies," *Secondary Mortgage Markets* (Spring 1989), p. 16.
[6] The interest rate risk associated with reverse mortgages is analyzed in Michael C. Ehrhardt and Thomas P. Boehm, "Reverse Mortgages and Interest Rate Risk," *Financial Institutions Center Working Paper Series,* No. 5 (Knoxville: Finance Department, University of Tennessee, 1990).

those established by the San Francisco Development Fund and the state housing finance agencies in Rhode Island and Connecticut.[7] In May 1989, HUD began a demonstration program to foster the development of this mortgage design by allowing FHA insurance for up to 2,500 reverse mortgages.[8] The FHA has standardized the features of the reverse mortgages that may be insured. Freddie Mac and Fannie Mae have agreed to purchase FHA-insured reverse mortgages, thereby helping to foster the secondary market. However, the securitization of such loans represents an enormous challenge because of their negative cash flow characteristics and the small amount of such mortgages available for pooling.[9]

[7] For a discussion of these and other programs and how they seek to reduce lender and borrower risks, see May and Szymanoski, "Reverse Mortgages: Risk Reduction Strategies."

[8] The program is described in "Home Equity Conversion Mortgage Insurance Demonstration: Proposed Rules," *Federal Register,* vol. 53, no. 206, October 25, 1988.

[9] For a more detailed discussion of the problems of developing a secondary mortgage market, see Maurice D. Weinrobe, *Reverse Mortgages: Problems and Prospects for a Secondary Market and an Examination of Mortgage Guarantee Insurance* (Madison, WI: National Center for Home Equity Conversion, 1989).

6

The Mismatch Problem
and the Creation of
Variable-Rate Mortgages

The traditional mortgage (the fixed-rate, level-payment, fully amortized mortgage) suffers from two basic and very serious shortcomings. These may be labeled the "mismatch" problem and the "tilt" problem. The mismatch problem made traditional mortgages unattractive to investors during times of significant inflation and led to the development of the variable-rate mortgage or, as it is more popularly referred to, the adjustable-rate mortgage design. The tilting problem led to the development of other types of mortgage instruments that we will describe in Chapter 7.

THE MISMATCH PROBLEM

The mismatch problem, which we alluded to at the end of Chapter 5, has existed in the United States during most of the postwar period, because mortgages—a very long-term asset—have largely been financed by institutions that obtained their funds through deposits primarily, if not entirely, of a short-term nature. These institutions were engaging in the highly speculative activity of borrowing short and lending very long. Speculation on the term structure of interest rates is a losing proposition if interest rates rise, as is bound to happen in the presence of significant inflation (Fisher's Law).[1] The institution will be earning the mortgage rate, but to attract the deposits needed to finance the loan, it will have to pay the current higher market rate; considering that the intermediation margin, or spread, is modest (100 to 200 basis points), it will not take much inflation or much of a rise in interest rates before the institutions are running into a loss.

Another way to put the matter is in terms of the balance sheet. The difference between lending and borrowing rates will cause the lending institution to become technically insolvent, in the sense that the market value of its assets will be insufficient to cover its liabilities. The reason for this is that its liabilities are related to the *face* value of its mortgage assets, but the *market* value of these assets—the present value of the cash flow stream due from the debtor, discounted at the current high rate—will be below the face value by a factor not too far from the ratio of the contractual rate to the current market rate. Both losses and technical insolvencies have occurred on a large scale among lending institutions since the late 1960s, and especially in the 1970s and 1980s, because of this fact.

But, one might ask, why have there not been *more* bankruptcies? The basic reason is that a losing bank does not have to close as long as it can pay depositors interest and principal, using reserves, liquidation of assets, and most important, the so-called "Ponzi" technique of attracting more deposits.[2] Similarly, technical insolvency need not lead to bankruptcy as long as the depositors do not step forward to be repaid. And on the whole they do not. Federal deposit insurance has seen to that. Those depositors who were concerned with potential bankruptcy did not see the dangers—if they looked at anything at all, it was at the book value of assets. This value was inflated through some "creative financing," which was tolerated by the regulatory agencies that were anxious to keep things going and hide the disaster.

---

[1]Fisher's Law says that the nominal rate of interest consists of two components: the real rate of interest plus the anticipated rate of inflation over the investment period.
[2]This is a technique of acquiring funds fraudulently by using the funds of new investors to pay existing investors.

Of course, some institutions went under or were taken over by other institutions with subsidies provided by the Federal Saving and Loan Insurance Corporation (FSLIC).[3] This did not help much, however. Both old and new institutions became engaged in highly speculative undertakings on the ground that if the speculation was successful the management would reap part of the profits, and if the speculation was unsuccessful, there would be no cost to depositors since they were covered by the deposit insurance, recently raised to $100,000.

The gangrene within the S&L industry progressed until finally, in 1989, President Bush launched his $150 billion rescue plan. It is interesting that although this plan involves a complete overhaul of the regulatory system, there is so far no indication of any new regulation requiring the kind of investment policy that would have prevented the tragedy of the last 20 years, namely matching maturities!

How can this requirement be achieved? One obvious way is for institutions that primarily finance fixed-rate mortgages to lengthen their liabilities through term deposits or analogous instruments. That is, they would match every 30-year fixed-rate mortgage issued with an equal dollar amount of long-term deposits. This was actually done in recent years, but only to a modest extent. In fact, it is doubtful that this approach could go very far in solving the problem, for what has made S&Ls so popular is unquestionably the highly liquid, riskless nature of their deposits. If they were allowed to finance mortgages only by long-term deposits, one might expect a substantial decline in the volume of funds available to them for mortgage financing; few depositors are interested in tying up funds for long periods.

A second approach consists of redesigning the traditional mortgage to produce an asset with a return that would match the short-term market rates, thus better matching the cost of liabilities. One instrument which satisfies these requirements, and which has won considerable popularity, is the so-called adjustable-rate mortgage (ARM).

[3]Prior to the passage of FIRREA, federal deposit insurance for S&Ls was provided by the Federal Saving and Loan Insurance Corporation. The Savings Association Insurance Fund (SAIF) has replaced FSLIC. SAIF is administered by the Federal Deposit Insurance Corporation.

ARMs have been popular with lenders because they shift interest rate risk from the lender to the borrower. To be sure, the risk resulting from falling rates tends to be shifted from the borrower to the lender, but then this risk is borne by the lenders anyway, at least in part, because of the repayment option given to the borrower. Thrifts, accordingly, prefer to hold ARMs in their portfolio rather than fixed-rate mortgages, because ARMs provide a better matching with their liabilities.

CHARACTERISTICS OF AN ARM

In an ARM, the contract rate is reset periodically in accordance with some appropriately chosen benchmark index (or reference base), typically one based on a short-term interest rate. This approach already has been applied to many other market instruments such as floating-rate notes, adjustable-rate preferred stock, and floating-rate certificates of deposit.

When a short-term interest rate is used as the benchmark index, depository institutions such as S&Ls are able to improve the matching of their returns to their cost of funds. Equivalently, an instrument earning the market rate can be expected to remain close to par whether interest rates rise or fall,[4] thus avoiding the problems of technical insolvency that plagued the S&Ls relying on the traditional mortgage. Note also that, with high and variable inflation, an adjustable-rate, in principle, reduces risk for the borrower as well—a reduction of inflation will generally be accompanied by a fall in the benchmark index, which will benefit borrowers with an adjustable-rate contract. Adjustable-rate contracts outstanding in the United States call for resetting the interest rate either every month, six months, one year, two years, three years, or five years. In recent years, ARMs typically have had reset periods of six months, one year, or five years. The interest rate at the reset date is equal to a benchmark index plus a spread. The spread is typically between 100 and 200 basis points, reflecting market conditions, the features of the ARM, and the

---

[4]The extent to which it will deviate from par will depend on the degree to which the spread on the instrument deviates from the market-required spread.

increased cost of servicing an ARM compared to a fixed-rate mortgage.[5]

While the early 1980s saw the first major production of ARMs, there were attempts in the early 1970s by the Federal Home Loan Bank Board (FHLBB) to obtain congressional approval to authorize thrifts to use this instrument for residential lending. Facing opposition from interest groups that perceived such a mortgage design as a dangerous financing vehicle during a period of rising interest rates, Congress denied approval. In California, however, state chartered S&Ls were permitted to originate ARMs. The thrift problem heated up in the late 1970s, and Congress shifted its position in 1978, granting approval to the FHLBB to authorize ARMs. In December 1978, the FHLBB experimented with this mortgage design, restricting its use to federally chartered S&Ls in the state of California, where state chartered S&Ls had already gained experience with this mortgage instrument. There the popularity of the ARM was immediately apparent. A Federal Home Loan Bank of San Francisco survey found that in 1979 more than 40% of mortgages originated were ARMs.

When the ARM market began, there was a proliferation of ARM designs. In early 1984, for example, Professor Jack Guttentag estimated that there were between 400 and 500 different types of ARM products.[6] As he noted, the desire for product differentiation by competing lending institutions was the reason for the lack of standardization of ARM products. The negative side effect, however, was lack of liquidity because of the unique features of each product. As the market developed and ARM passthroughs were issued, standardization of ARM products increased.

The dramatic growth in the ARM market for conventional single-family mortgages as measured by mortgage originations for the years 1984 to 1990 and its share of all originations is shown in Table 6-1. While this indicates that the share of ARMs twice exceeded 50% in the years 1984 to 1989, it

[5]While there are no data available, one estimate is that it costs 10 to 15 basis points more to service an ARM. See Michael J. Lea, "The Margin of Success," *Secondary Mortgage Markets* (Spring 1986), p. 24.
[6]Jack M. Guttentag, "Recent Changes in the Primary Mortgage Market," *Housing Finance Review* (July 1984), pp. 221–255.

Table 6-1

Origination of Conventional Single-Family, Fixed-Rate, and Adjustable-Rate Mortgages, 1984–1990

Year	Amount ($ millions)			Share of Total (%)	
	Fixed	Adjustable	Total	Fixed	Adjustable
1984	$ 81,379	$ 93,703	$175,082	46%	54%
1985	108,958	90,100	199,058	55	45
1986	279,326	82,800	362,126	77	23
1987	249,776	126,400	376,176	66	34
1988	159,559	178,200	337,759	47	53
1989	195,586	111,600	307,186	64	36
1990	268,478	104,000	372,478	72	38

Source: Adapted from *Secondary Mortgage Markets* (Summer 1991) by permission of Freddie Mac. All rights reserved.

masks the fact that there were months when ARM origination exceeded 60% of total monthly origination and that in 1987 it reached a peak of almost 70%. This can be seen in Figure 6-1. The same figure also shows the relationship between the share of ARMs and the fixed-rate mortgages available in the market for mortgage loans. As can be seen, when mortgage rates were relatively high, such as in 1984 and 1989 (as well as in 1983 which is not shown in the figure), homeowners preferred adjustable-rate mortgages rather than fixed-rate mortgages. As interest rates declined in 1985 and 1986, homeowners preferred locking in the relatively low rate via fixed-rate mortgages.

The problem with the ARMs originated by thrifts and held in their portfolio was that they were designed in a way that violated the matching principle. They were not "pure" ARMs—that is, an ARM that contained no feature restricting the contract rate the borrower would pay nor any subsidy to the borrower that would reduce the thrift's spread income. Too many borrowers were reluctant to accept ARMs because they feared that a rise in interest rates would cause a sudden jump in mortgage payments, and some additional features had to be included to overcome this reluctance. We will discuss these features later. Some observers feel that in an attempt to

Figure 6-1

Effect of Interest Rates on ARM Originations

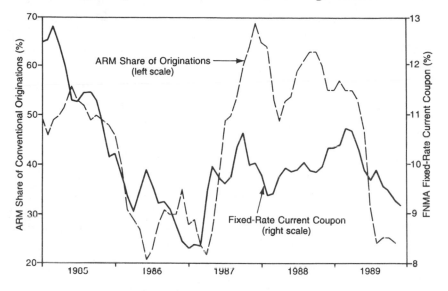

Source: Robert Gerber, "Adjustable Rate Mortgages," in Frank J. Fabozzi, ed., *The Handbook of Mortgage-Backed Securities,* 3d ed. (Chicago: Probus Publishing, 1992).

increase mortgage origination production, thrifts have been too aggressive, resulting in features that have reduced the profitability of ARMs.[7]

Benchmark Indexes

Two categories of benchmark indexes have been used in ARMs: (1) indexes based on market-determined rates, and (2) indexes based on the cost of funds for thrift. Market-determined rates have been limited to Treasury-based indexes, unlike the more popular benchmark index used in

[7]Michael J. Lea, "An Empirical Examination of Loan Features," *Housing Finance Review* (January 1985), pp. 467–481; Paul A. Willax, "ARMs: A Case of Product Overdevelopment," *American Banker,* February 11, 1988, pp. 4, 10–11. Studies that dispute this are Jan K. Brueckner and James R. Follain, "The Rise and Fall of the ARM: An Econometric Analysis of Mortgage Choice," *Review of Economics and Statistics* (February 1988), pp. 93–102; J. Gordon Douglas, Jan E. Luytjes, and John J. Feid, "Economic Analysis of Thrifts' Pricing of Adjustable-Rate Mortgages," memo. (Washington, D.C.: Office of Thrift Supervision, November 1989).

the Eurodollar floating-rate market, the London Interbank Offered Rate (LIBOR). The various indexes within each category are summarized below. The benchmark index will have an important impact on the performance of ARMs and on how they are priced. Moreover, since the benchmark index is not perfectly correlated with the investor's cost of funds, this risk must be reflected in the spread.

Treasury-based indexes. Three Treasury-based indexes that have been used as benchmarks, the one-year constant maturity Treasury (CMT) rate, the five-year CMT, and the six-month Treasury bill rate. The CMT rates are based on the CMT yield curve constructed for each trading day by the Federal Reserve Bank of New York and published weekly in the Federal Reserve's *Statistical Release H15*. The CMT yield curve has yields for the most actively traded Treasuries with maturities of one, two, three, five, seven, ten, and thirty years, based on closing bid-yields submitted by five major dealer firms. The one-year CMT and five-year CMT are taken from the CMT yield curve. The six-month Treasury bill index is based on the weekly auction of six-month Treasury bills. Since the auction is done on a competitive basis, there is a range of rates realized by winning bidders. The six-month Treasury bill index, reported weekly in the *Statistical Release H15,* is the weighted average of the winning yield bids, where the weight is the amount sold at each bid rate.

Since there are at least four rates published for each of the Treasury-based indexes each month, the mortgage agreement must specify which weekly rate will be used. Typically, the weekly index rate used to set the new mortgage rate is the one issued just before the fifteenth of the month in which the rate will be reset. Some lenders use an average of weekly rates over a specified time period. For example, the index for First Nationwide's Certainly Affordable Mortgage Loans is based on the six-month average of the weekly six-month Treasury bill index.

ARMs that rely on Treasury-based indexes are preferred by nonthrift investors. Of the three indexes, the most popular is the one-year CMT.

Cost of funds for thrifts indexes. These indexes are calculated based on the monthly weighted average interest cost for liabilities of thrifts. The two more popular are the 11th Federal Home Loan Bank Board District Cost of Funds and the National Cost of Funds Index, the former being the most popular. Another index that has been used is the Federal Home Loan Bank Contract Rate.

The 11th District includes the states of California, Arizona, and Nevada. The cost of funds is calculated by first computing the monthly interest expenses for all thrifts included in the 11th District. The interest expenses are summed and then divided by the average of the beginning and ending monthly balances. The index value is reported with a one-month lag. For example, June's 11th District Cost of Funds is reported in July. The contract rate for an index based on the 11th District Cost of Funds is usually reset according to the previous month's reported index rate. For example, if the reset date is August, the index rate reported in July will be used to set the contract rate. Consequently, there is a two-month lag before the average cost of funds is reflected in the contract rate. This is obviously an advantage to the borrower when interest rates are rising and a disadvantage to the investor. The opposite is true when interest rates are falling.

While most thrifts will argue that the 11th District Cost of Funds is an appropriate index because it fairly represents their cost of funds, this is not quite accurate. In fact, the 11th District Cost of Funds is generally higher than the cost of funds of most regions in the country, reflecting the dominance of California thrifts, which have typically accounted for more than 85% of the thrifts in the 11th District.

The National Cost of Funds Index is calculated based on all federally insured S&Ls. A median cost of funds is calculated rather than an average. This index is reported with a delay of about six weeks. The contract rate is typically reset based on the most recently reported index value.

Since liabilities are closely tied to the calculated cost of funds index, thrifts prefer ARMs benchmarked to cost of funds indexes.

The index will have an important impact on the performance of an ARM. This can be seen from Figure 6-2, which compares the movement of the one-year CMT rate, the 11th District Cost of Funds Index, and three-month LIBOR for the

Figure 6-2

ARM Index Levels

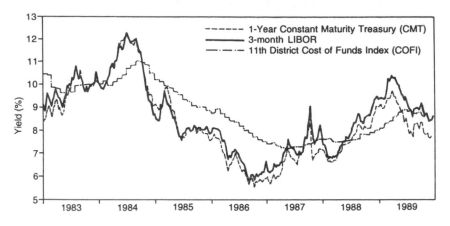

Source: Robert Gerber, "Adjustable Rate Mortgages," in Fabozzi, ed., *The Handbook of Mortgage-Backed Securities,* 3d ed.

period January 1983 to December 1989. Notice that the 11th District Cost of Funds (1) exhibits less volatility than the one-year CMT rate and (2) has a tendency to lag behind movements of the one-year Treasury rate. We observe these two characteristics for the 11th District Cost of Funds because of the manner in which it is calculated. The index is a composite cost of funds that includes both historical and current costs. When interest rates are rising, the composite interest cost will include the lower historical cost and the higher current cost. The average will therefore be lower than the current cost. The opposite is true when interest rates are falling. The implication is that when interest rates are falling (rising), an ARM indexed off the 11th District Cost of Funds will pay a higher (lower) rate than an ARM indexed off the one-year Treasury rate.

The frequency with which the contract rate resets varies with the index used. For ARMs indexed to the one-year Treasury rate, the mortgage rate is generally reset once a year. The monthly mortgage payments for the year are then based on the new indexed mortgage rate. For ARMs indexed to the 11th District Cost of Funds, the mortgage rate typically adjusts monthly. However, the monthly mortgage payments are adjusted once a year.

Features of Adjustable-Rate Mortgages

To encourage borrowers to use ARMs rather than fixed-rate mortgages, mortgage originators generally offer an initial contract rate that is less than the prevailing market mortgage rate. This below-market initial contract rate, set by the mortgage originator based on competitive market conditions, is commonly referred to as a *teaser rate*. At the reset date, the benchmark index plus the spread determines the new contract rate. For example, suppose that one-year ARMs are typically offering a 100 basis point spread over the one-year CMT rate. Suppose also that the current one-year CMT rate is 6.5%, so that the initial contract rate should be 7.5%. The mortgage originator might set an initial contract rate of 6.75%, a rate 75 basis points below the current index rate plus the spread.

A pure ARM is one that resets periodically and has no other terms that affect the monthly mortgage payment. However, the monthly mortgage payment, and hence the investor's cash flow, are affected by other terms. These terms are linked to (1) periodic caps and (2) lifetime rate caps and floors.

Periodic caps. There are two types of periodic caps: rate caps and payment caps. Rate caps limit the amount that the contract rate may increase or decrease at the reset date. The rate cap is expressed in percentage points. The most common rate cap on annual reset loans is 2%.

From an option's perspective, what is a periodic cap on the interest rate? Effectively the lender or investor has given the homeowner the right to borrow money at a below-market interest rate. Thus, the lender or investor has sold an option on an interest rate to the homeowner. In fact, since the cap goes into effect each year, the lender or investor has not sold one option but a package of options to the homeowner. The lender must be compensated for selling these options.

ARMs with payment caps are not as common as those with rate caps. Payment caps limit the change in the monthly mortgage *payment* rather than in the interest rate at the reset date. Note that while there is no restriction on how much the contract rate may change, there is a restriction on the amount that the monthly mortgage payment may change. There is no corresponding restriction on what the debtor is debited for. Accordingly, with a payment cap there can be negative amortization—a situation in which the periodic payment is insufficient to cover accrued interest and thus the mortgage balance increases. This is because the cap on the monthly mortgage payment results in a payment that is insufficient to cover the higher mortgage interest used for debiting. The shortfall is added to the principal. With a rate cap there is no negative amortization.[8]

The impact of the two types of periodic caps on the cash flow and mortgage balance is illustrated in Table 6-2. The first ARM in the table is based on a 2% rate cap structure while the second ARM is based on a 7.5% payment cap structure. The underlying mortgage for both ARMs is a 30-year, $100,000 mortgage with a spread of 200 basis points over the index rate. The initial index rate is 8.5%, which means that the initial contract rate should be 10.5%. In the illustration it is assumed that the initial contract rate for both mortgages is a teaser rate of 8.5% and that the contract rate and monthly mortgage payment reset annually. The second column in the table shows the assumed index rate for each year. In the first year, the monthly mortgage payment and the end-of-year mortgage balance are identical for both mortgages. In the second year, the index rate is assumed to increase to 9.5%.

In the absence of any rate cap, the contract rate would be reset at 11.5%. Because of the 2% rate cap, the contract rate for the first ARM in the second year is restricted to 10.5%, an increase of only 200 basis points over the initial contract rate. For the second instrument, the contract rate increases to 9.5% plus 2%, or 11.5%. To amortize the mortgage balance at the end of the first year at an 11.5% contract rate, the monthly mortgage payment would have to increase from $768.91 (the first year's monthly mortgage payment at an 8.5% contract rate) to $986.80. However, the 7.5% payment cap restricts the monthly mortgage payment to $826.58 (1.075 times $768.91).

---

[8]An alternative approach is to extend the maturity of the loan.

Table 6-2

Rate Cap Structure vs. Payment Cap Structure

Year	Index Rate	Index Plus Margin	Rate Cap Structure			Payment Cap Structure		
			Mortgage Rate	Beginning Balance	P&I Payment	Mortgage Rate	Beginning Balance	P&I Payment
1	8.50%	10.50%	8.50%	$100,000	$ 768.91	8.50%	$100,000	$ 768.91
2	9.50	11.50	10.50	99,244	912.39	11.50	99,244	826.58
3	10.50	12.50	12.50	98,690	1,060.63	12.50	100,819	888.57
4	12.50	14.50	13.50	98,275	1,135.87	13.50	102,874	955.21
5	11.50	13.50	13.50	97,888	1,135.87	13.50	105,455	1,026.86
6	9.00	11.00	11.50	97,446	990.51	11.50	107,492	1,053.54
7	7.00	9.00	9.50	96,729	853.90	9.00	106,631	974.53
8	4.00	6.00	7.50	95,624	728.07	6.00	104,445	901.44
9	5.00	7.00	7.00	94,004	398.85	7.00	99,767	833.83
10	6.00	8.00	8.00	92,153	755.93	8.00	96,646	792.91

*$100,000 original principal balance. 30-year original term.

Source: Bella S. Borg and Andrew S. Carron, "The Valuation of Adjustable Rate Mortgages," in Frank J. Fabozzi, ed., *The Handbook of Mortgage-Backed Securities*, rev. ed. (Chicago: Probus Publishing, 1988), p. 800.

Monthly interest alone for the first month of the second year on the mortgage balance at the beginning of the second year is $951.09 ($99,244 times 0.115/12). The difference of $124.51 between the interest for that month of $951.09 and the new monthly mortgage payment of $826.58 is added to the mortgage balance. That is, the 7.5% payment cap has resulted in negative amortization for this ARM. In the second month of the second year, the interest is greater than $951.09 because the mortgage balance has increased. Thus, more than $124.51 would be added to the mortgage balance. At the end of the second year, the mortgage balance is $100,819.

From the lender's perspective, payment caps have two opposite effects on default risk. On the one hand, in the absence of payment caps, it is possible for the monthly mortgage payment to rise to a level such that the borrower will be incapable of making loan payments and therefore default on the loan. Capping the monthly mortgage payment reduces this possibility. On the other hand, negative amortization may raise the mortgage balance to an amount in excess of the market value of the property, encouraging the borrower to default. Current regulations make default more likely because they specify that if negative amortization brings the mortgage balance to 125% of the appraised value at the time the loan was originated, the contract rate will be revised to the rate specified by the benchmark index plus the spread. The monthly mortgage payment will then be revised based on the new contract rate to fully amortize the new mortgage balance over the loan's remaining life. Consequently, the spread over the benchmark index on a payment-capped ARM must reflect the perceived net effect on default risk.

Lifetime caps and floors. Prior to 1987, most ARMs had an upper limit on the contract rate that could be charged over the life of the loan. The Competitive Equality Banking Act of 1987 requires that all single-family mortgages originated have such a limit on the contract rate. This lifetime loan cap is expressed in terms of the initial rate, the most common lifetime cap being 5% to 6%. For example, if the initial mortgage rate is 7% and the lifetime cap is 5%, the maximum interest rate that the lender can charge over the life of the loan is 12%. Many ARMs also have a lower limit on the interest rate that can be charged over the life of the loan.

Once again, looking at the lifetime cap in terms of an option, the lender or investor has effectively sold an option on an interest rate to the homeowner. What about a lifetime floor? In this case, the homeowner is compensating the lender or investor should the interest rate fall below the floor. Therefore, the homeowner has sold the lender or investor an option. From the lender or investor's perspective, an ARM with a lifetime cap and floor is equivalent to a "collar"—a maximum and minimum interest rate. This, then, is equivalent to selling an option (the cap) at one interest rate and buying an option (the floor) at a lower interest rate.

HYBRID MORTGAGES

There are mortgage designs that share features of fixed-rate and adjustable-rate mortgages. These are described below.

Convertible Mortgages

There are ARMs that can be converted into fixed-rate mortgages. These are called *convertible ARMs*. Approximately three-quarters of ARMs originated in recent years have been convertible ARMs. There are also fixed-rate mortgages that can have their mortgage rate lowered if rates fall by some predetermined level. These are called *reducible fixed-rate mortgages* (FRMs) or convertible FRMs. Unlike convertible ARMs, reducible FRMs have not been a popular financing vehicle among borrowers. Convertible ARMs and reducible FRMs are hybrid mortgages with built-in refinancing options. The motivation for the development of these mortgages has been the high rates of refinancing since 1983, particularly in late 1986 and early 1987. These hybrid mortgage instruments reduce the cost of refinancing.[9]

With a convertible ARM, the borrower has the choice of converting to a fixed-rate mortgage. The new contract may be either (1) a rate determined by the lender or (2) a market-

---

[9]For a more detailed discussion of these instruments, see Arnold Kling, "Refinancing Express," *Secondary Mortgage Markets* (Spring 1988), pp. 2–6.

determined rate. As an example of the latter, the rate may be set at some spread over the mortgage commitment rates established by one of the agencies that purchases mortgages. The trend is toward a market-determined rate. A borrower is typically able to convert at any time between the first and fifth dates at which the mortgage rate is reset. The lender charges a nominal fee for conversion.

With a fixed-rate mortgage that may be adjusted downward, the borrower can only exercise the option to have the contract rate adjusted if the benchmark index rate falls below a certain level, called the *trigger rate*. The new contract rate will be equal to the trigger rate. Usually the conversion option is not granted for the entire life of the mortgage, but only for the first five or six years.

Convertible mortgage instruments reduce the cost of refinancing substantially. However, investors in convertible ARMs and reducible FRMs must be compensated for holding them, since they have effectively sold an option to borrowers. Investors must therefore determine whether they are receiving fair compensation for selling these options. In the case of reducible FRMs, the borrower effectively has also sold the investor a floor on an interest rate, since the contract rate cannot decline below the trigger rate; thus the lender must compensate the borrower for this option in the form of a lower cost. The advantage to the servicer of the mortgage is that the servicing fee is continued. Convertible ARMs have been securitized by Freddie Mac and Fannie Mae.

Arnold Kling, senior economist of Freddie Mac's financial research department, believes that if reducible FRMs are eventually as successful as convertible ARMs, there will be a trend toward more "hybrid" mortgage instruments in the future.[10] He poses the possibility of an ARM with a zero life cap, for which the interest rate never increases above the initial rate. For example, consider an ARM given that (1) it has an initial rate of 11%, (2) the mortgage rate is set at a 200 basis point spread over the one-year Treasury index, and (3) the mortgage rate adjusts every year. If in the next year, the one-year Treasury index is 8%, the rate on the mortgage will

---

[10] Ibid., p. 6.

reset at 10%. If in the following year the one-year Treasury rate is 8.6%, the mortgage rate will reset at 10.6%. However, if in the third year the one-year Treasury index is 12%, the mortgage rate will reset at 11%, the initial mortgage rate. To make such a mortgage instrument attractive to investors, the initial mortgage rate must be set at a rate above existing rates on fixed-rate mortgages and/or borrowers must be charged additional fees.

Balloon/Reset Mortgages

A mortgage design long used in Canada is the rollover mortgage. In this mortgage design the borrower is given long-term financing by the lender, but at specified future dates the contract rate is renegotiated. Thus, the lender is providing long-term funds for what is in effect a short-term borrowing, how short depending on the frequency of the renegotiation period. Effectively it is a short-term balloon loan in which the lender agrees to provide financing for the remainder of the term of the mortgage. The balloon payment is the original amount borrowed less the amount amortized.

The FHLBB attempted to introduce this mortgage design in January 1980 when it proposed a prototype rollover mortgage design. The prototype called for the contract rate to be renegotiated every three to five years (with the specific time period being determined at the time the mortgage is originated), with a maximum contract rate change of 50 basis points for each year in the renegotiation period (i.e., 150 basis points if renegotiated every three years and 250 if every five years), and with the lender guaranteeing to provide new financing. There were several proposals as to how the new contract rate should be determined.

Although rollover mortgages were hailed as an important step in alleviating the mismatch problem faced by thrifts, they did not catch on until 1990. They are now called *balloon/reset mortgages,* or simply *balloon mortgages*; Fannie Mae and Freddie Mac purchase these mortgages for pooling. Freddie Mac's 30-year balloon/resets, for example, can have either a renegotiation period of five years ("30-due-in-5" FRMs) or seven years ("30-due-in-7" FRMs). If certain conditions are met, Freddie Mac guarantees the extension of the loan. The contract rate set by Freddie Mac is based on its 30-year, single-family, fixed rate, 60-day delivery mortgage rate. If the borrower elects to extend the mortgage, a $250 processing fee is charged. Moreover, the servicer of the mortgage retains the servicing fee.

ASSESSMENT OF VARIABLE-RATE MORTGAGES

On the whole, the variable-rate mortgage and its variants have the merit of providing a manageable solution to the problem of mismatch of maturities. To borrowers, such mortgages also reduce the risk associated with uncertain inflation. Unfortunately, the merits of the ARM have been significantly impaired by the arbitrary and misguided constraints imposed by the regulatory authority, particularly through interest caps. These caps, meant to protect the borrower, might make sense if rates were unilaterally set by the lender, but they do not make sense when they are tied to an objective market rate, or to the cost of funds for the lending institution. Furthermore, we know that an increase in nominal rates tends to occur when there is an appreciable rise in inflation, in which case the borrower, in general, can afford to pay the higher interest rate while it lasts. The main effect of caps is to increase the risk of inflation to intermediary lenders that have no way of putting a cap on the rate they have to pay. Nor is a lower cap an adequate compensation, since borrowers have the right to repay. Of course, some of the expected loss will tend to be recouped by a higher spread, and thus finally unloaded on some borrowers; but even so it would be best to leave the matter to private bargaining.

Unfortunately, regulators have still not grasped these simple principles. Nor have they understood that the so-called protection of consumers is generally paid for by the consumer in the form of higher rates or other less favorable terms. Finally, the variable-rate mortgage is not a satisfactory answer to inflation-swollen interest rates because it does not address the tilt problem. In Chapter 7 this problem is explained, along with mortgage designs that have been proposed to resolve it.

7

The Tilt Problem and the Creation of Other Mortgage Instruments

Inflation since the 1970s has produced devastating effects on the housing industry all over the world. The rise in mortgage rates that has accompanied, and roughly matched, the rise in inflation has placed home ownership out of the reach of major portions of the population, notably the young and the first-time buyers. In this chapter we will look at mortgage designs—both currently used and proposed—that have attempted to cope with the problem created by inflation. This problem is called the tilt problem.

THE TILT PROBLEM

The fixed-rate, level-payment, fully amortized mortgage was designed so that the borrower would repay the debt in constant nominal installments. This form of repayment would be considered highly desirable from the debtor's point of view as long as inflation was zero or small, because a level nominal repayment rate in that case implies a level *real* rate of repayment. But when there is significant inflation, the traditional mortgage turns into a malfunctioning, very undesirable vehicle for home financing. The reason is not, as is frequently supposed, that inflation increases interest rates. To be sure, with a 10% rate of inflation we would expect nominal interest rates to rise by roughly 10 percentage points—say, from 5% to 15%. But this rise does not, per se, make the lender any better off or the borrower any worse off, since the increase is offset by inflation losses and gains, leaving the real rate largely unchanged. The higher interest rate is generally compensated for by the erosion of the principal in terms of purchasing power. (In nominal terms, the higher rate is offset by the rise in the value of the property.)

Rather, the reason for the unsatisfactory performance of the traditional mortgage lies in the "tilt" effect: with 10% steady inflation, if the nominal payment is level, the real payment will decrease at 10% per year. By the twentieth year, it will be down to some 15% of the initial installment payment. If the creditor is to receive the same real amount in the absence of inflation, the gradual erosion of the repayments in terms of purchasing power will have to be made up by sufficiently high initial real (and hence nominal) payments. Indeed, with the interest rate rising from 5% to 15%, the first payment on a long-term mortgage will rise roughly threefold.

The nature of the distortion or tilt in the real payment path is illustrated in Figure 7-1 for different rates of inflation. Notice that for an 8% rate of inflation, the path starts at more than twice the no-inflation level, to terminate at well below half. The high initial payment caused by inflation has the effect of foreclosing home ownership to large segments of the population or forcing buyers to scale down their demands. Indeed, not many people would be able to pay a multiple of what they were paying in the preinflation period for the same facilities. This is especially true in the case of young people who have little asset accumulation.

The first thing to note about this problem is that it is not addressed by the adjustable-rate mortgage. That mortgage uses throughout a nominal interest rate comparable to the fixed-rate mortgage. In particular, the critical early payment will be roughly as high as it is with a traditional mortgage. Actually, one can show that the ARM is, in some ways, even worse for borrowers than the traditional mortgage. It starts with a rate as high as the traditional mortgage independently of inflation, and will make a substantial jump every time the

Figure 7-1

Nature of the Tilt Problem: Real Value of Monthly Payments

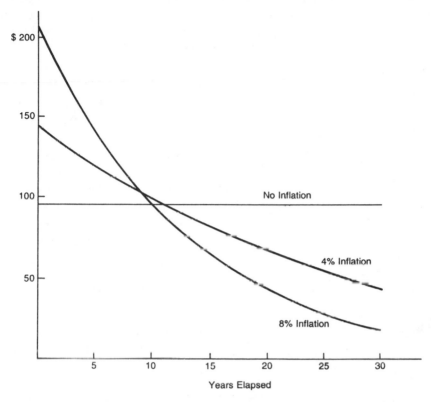

Years Elapsed

Source: D. Tucker, "The Variable-Rate Graduated-Payment Mortgage," *Real Estate Review* (Spring 1975), p. 72.

interest rate is adjusted and the payment shifts from one nominal level to another—even though the rate of payment is level as long as the interest rate does not change.

Can the tilt problem be remedied? It is clear that in principle a solution must involve reducing the interest rate used in the early payments and recouping later. Several approaches (with many variants) have been offered: graduated-payment mortgages, growing equity mortgages, tiered-payment mortgages, shared-appreciation mortgages, price-level-adjusted mortgages, and dual-rate mortgages.

GRADUATED-PAYMENT MORTGAGE (GPM)

The original graduated-payment mortgage exploited an interesting property of the traditional mortgage payment formula. If in that formula the fixed interest rate R is replaced with a lower rate, say R minus x, and at the same time the level stream is replaced with one that grows at the rate of $x\%$ per year, then the new stream has the same present value, when discounted at R, as the level stream. If the rate of inflation over the life of the contract were roughly, say, $p\%$ per year, and known with certainty, then the GPM could provide a very satisfactory answer to the inflation tilt problem. By choosing x equal to p, one could offer a mortgage for which the first payment was at the real rate R minus p, and for which subsequent payments grew in nominal terms at the rate of inflation p while staying level in real terms.

Note that if x is large enough (larger than beginning amortization as a percent of principal), in the early years the nominal payments might be insufficient to cover interest at $R\%$ plus amortization. In this case nominal principal would initially rise. That is, there would be *negative amortization.* However, if payments keep growing at x per year, amortization must eventually turn positive, and will necessarily (by construction) be completed by the end of the contract. The initial negative amortization, if any, will be larger, the longer the contract (because the share of amortization in the payment declines with maturity), and the larger is x (and hence p).

Unfortunately, the rate of inflation is most unlikely to be constant over a couple of decades, and in any event it is unforeseeable with any degree of accuracy. Under these conditions the GPM is not likely to succeed in ensuring the debtor anything approaching a level real repayment stream. In particular, if p is chosen below realized inflation, the real payments will decline in time, and thus start too high and end too low; if p is overestimated, the payments will start too low.

The original GPM described above is no longer in use. What is popular instead are modified versions introduced by the FHA in 1976, under which the nominal payment grows at a constant rate during a portion of the life of the contract, and thereafter leveling off. The main reason why these modified plans are the ones most in use is that they are the ones that the FHA has declared eligible for their insurance—presumably because the mortgages are deemed less risky in nominal terms—and insurance is highly desirable for the borrower as well as for the lender.

GPM Plans

The terms of a GPM plan include (1) the mortgage rate, (2) the term of the mortgage, (3) the number of years over which the monthly mortgage payment will increase (and when the level payments will begin), and (4) the annual percentage increase in the mortgage payments. The most popular 30-year GPM plan calls for monthly payments that increase by 7.5% for five years, then at the beginning of the sixth year remain constant for the remaining 25 years. The monthly mortgage payments under this GPM program for a $100,000, 30-year, 10% mortgage would be: (1) $667.04 per month in the first year, (2) $717.00 per month in the second year, (3) $770.84 in the third year, (4) $828.66 in the fourth year, (5) $890.80 in the fifth year, and (6) $957.62 for the remaining term of the mortgage, beginning with the sixth year. For a level-payment, fixed-rate, 30-year mortgage, the monthly mortgage payment would be $877.57.

Table 7-1 compares the amount of the outstanding mortgage balance at the end of each year for this particular GPM and a level-payment, fixed-rate mortgage. Notice that there is negative amortization of the GPM for the first four years. It is not until year 10 that the outstanding mortgage balance is below the original mortgage balance.

Five 30-year GPM plans currently available are summarized below:

	Plan				
	I	II	III	IV	V
Annual increase in monthly payment	2.5%	5.0%	7.5%	2.0%	3%
Years of increase	5	5	5	10	10

Table 7-1

Comparison of Outstanding Mortgage Balance for a Level-Payment, Fixed-Rate Mortgage and a Popular GPM

Term of mortgage: 30 years
Original balance: $100,000
Mortgage rate: 10%

GPM: Monthly mortgage payment increases by 7.5% per year for 5 years

Year	Outstanding mortgage balance at end of year	
	Level-payment fixed rate	GPM
1	$99,444	$102,090
2	98,830	103,769
3	98,152	104,949
4	97,402	105,526
5	96,574	105,383
6	95,660	104,385
7	94,649	103,282
8	93,533	102,064
9	92,300	100,719
10	90,938	99,233
11	89,433	97,591
12	87,771	95,777
13	85,934	93,773
14	83,906	91,559
15	81,665	89,113
16	79,189	86,412
17	76,454	83,427
18	73,432	80,130
19	70,094	76,488
20	66,407	72,464
21	62,333	68,019
22	57,833	63,108
23	52,862	57,684
24	47,370	51,691
25	41,303	45,071
26	34,601	37,757
27	27,197	29,678
28	19,018	20,752
29	9,982	10,892
30	0	0

The level payment for a $100,000, 30-year, 10% fixed-rate mortgage would be $877.57. For the five GPM plans, the initial and final monthly mortgage payments for a $100,000, 30-year, 10% mortgage are:

	I	II	III	IV	V
Initial payment	$800.58	$730.58	$667.04	$780.04	$734.58
Final payment	$905.76	$932.44	$957.62	$950.86	$987.20

The first three GPM plans qualify for inclusion in certain types of mortgage passthroughs discussed in Chapter 8. The majority of the GPMs underlying certain types of passthroughs are Plan III graduated-payment mortgages because, as can be seen from the table above, they have the lowest initial monthly mortgage payment. While all three types of GPMs may be found within the pool of mortgages that makes up the collateral for a passthrough, analysts typically assume all GPMs are of the Plan III type.

It should be apparent from our description of the GPM's terms that it cannot solve the mismatch problem or provide a satisfactory answer to the tilt problem, at least as long as inflation is high and unpredictably variable. This shortcoming has probably contributed to the decreasing popularity of GPMs in recent years. In fact, the only two basic mortgage designs that can provide a more or less foolproof solution to both problems are the price-level-adjusted mortgage and the dual-rate mortgage that we describe later in this chapter.

GROWING EQUITY MORTGAGE (GEM)

A growing equity mortgage is a fixed-rate mortgage with monthly mortgage payments that increase over time. The initial monthly mortgage payment is the same as for a traditional mortgage. By increasing the monthly mortgage payments, the principal of the GEM is repaid faster. For example, a 30-year $100,000 GEM loan with a contract rate of 9.5% might call for an initial monthly payment of $840.85 (the same as a traditional 9.5%, 30-year mortgage loan). However, the

GEM payment would gradually increase, and the GEM might be fully paid in only 15 years. GEMs have been securitized.

The fixed rate, increasing mortgage payment characteristic of this mortgage design seems similar to the graduated-payment mortgage. There is a major difference. The initial monthly mortgage payment for a GEM is the same as for a traditional mortgage; for a GPM it is less. Consequently, unlike a GPM, a GEM has no negative amortization.

TIERED-PAYMENT MORTGAGE (TPM)

The tiered-payment mortgage is designed to allow an initial monthly mortgage payment less than that of a traditional mortgage. The mortgage rate is fixed over the life of the loan. However, the initial mortgage payments are based on an interest rate of 300 to 500 basis points below the prevailing market rate. Monthly mortgage payments subsequently increase to an amount that would be paid on a traditional mortgage. Unlike a GPM, a TPM has no negative amortization. But how can the borrower pay an initial below-market rate and still pay a higher mortgage rate over the life of the loan without negative amortization?

The structural design that permits this is the establishment of an interest-earning account from which the interest shortfall can be made up each month. This investment account is established at the beginning of the loan by either the borrower, the seller of the property, the home builder, the borrower's employer, or a relative. A TPM therefore resembles a GPM (without negative amortization) from the borrower's perspective but a traditional mortgage from the lender's perspective.

This mortgage design is not new. It was introduced in the early 1980s and was referred to as a pledged-account mortgage (PAM) or FLIP (for flexible loan-insurance program). The latter was in recognition of the FLIP Mortgage Corporation, which pioneered this mortgage design. It was not until the late 1980s, however, that TPMs became popular. By 1989, origination of this mortgage design was estimated to be between \$200 and \$300 million, primarily in 15-year mortgages.[1] TPMs were by then being used to back collateralized mortgage obligation structures. In the second half of 1989, 15-year TPMs were used as collateral for three collateralized mortgage obligation structures issued by Freddie Mac.

SHARED-APPRECIATION MORTGAGE (SAM)

With a shared-appreciation mortgage, the borrower repays the loan in two parts: (1) by a traditional mortgage at a below-market rate, and (2) by yielding to the lender a share of the house appreciation at the sale of the house or at some other stated time. The extent to which the lender can share in the price appreciation determines by how much the mortgage rate will be reduced below the prevailing rate. For example, in early 1981 when mortgage rates reached 15%, lenders commonly offered a one-third participation program. This means that the mortgage rate would be cut by one third and the lender would share in one-third of the price appreciation.

The only good feature of this mortgage design is that, as with the GPM, in the presence of significant inflation the monthly payments start below the level corresponding to the traditional mortgage. But this positive result is acquired at the cost of many serious shortcomings. First, the lender must take an equity position, shared with the owner, which seriously limits the class of possible lenders. Second, this mortgage design involves a high risk for the lender, since the level nominal payment on the mortgage component means that, after a while, the portion of his real debt repaid by the borrower falls below what it would be in a traditional mortgage with no inflation, and hence, a fortiori, below what it would be with the dual-rate mortgage discussed later. The third shortcoming is the complexity of defining price appreciation. For example, suppose the homeowner makes improvements in the property

---

[1]Lynn M. Edens, "New Mortgage Designs: Tiered Payment, Balloon, Two-Step, and Fixed/Adjustable Rate Hybrid Mortgages," in Frank J. Fabozzi, ed., *The Handbook of Mortgage-Backed Securities,* 3d ed. (Chicago: Probus Publishing, 1992).

that enhance its economic value. Does the lender have the right to share in the price appreciation attributable to the improvement? If not, how is the economic value of the improvement measured? Finally, it is difficult to securitize this type of mortgage design, which means that investor demand for SAMs is reduced.

All told, this mortgage design is one of the least rational variants of the traditional mortgage, and this explains its very limited acceptance.

THE PRICE-LEVEL-ADJUSTED MORTGAGE (PLAM)

The price-level-adjusted mortgage is similar to the traditional mortgage except that monthly payments are designed to be level in purchasing power terms rather than in nominal terms, and that the fixed rate is in the real rather than the nominal rate.

The real rate is the interest rate that one could expect to prevail if there were no inflation in the economy. It can be estimated by taking the market nominal rate and subtracting the expected inflation rate, which might in turn be approximated by the recent inflation experience. The evidence suggests that in the United States, the real rate, in contrast to the nominal one, tends to remain fairly stable in time around a value of 3% to 4%.

To compute the monthly payment under a PLAM, we must first establish the terms of the contract, namely: (1) the real interest rate, (2) the term of the loan, and (3) the index to be used to measure the price level, usually the Consumer Price Index (CPI). We can then compute, from an ordinary mortgage table, the annual payment and the unpaid balance at the end of each year, corresponding to the stipulated real interest and maturity. These figures represent payments and balances in real terms. To compute the payments actually due in each year, we simply multiply the real payment by an inflation correction factor equal to the ratio of the stipulated index in the last year to the value of the index in the initial year. Similarly, to compute the actual debt, we multiply the real debt by the inflation correction factor.

Table 7-2 illustrates the required computations for a PLAM that has a 4% real rate and a 30-year maturity and that relies on the CPI. Columns 2 and 3 report the real payments and the real ending balance, which correspond to those for a traditional mortgage with the same specifications. Column 4 shows the inflation correction factor based on actual experience for the years 1977 through 1987, and fictitious figures thereafter. Note that the figures in this column are the ratio of the price index in the current year to that in the *initial* year; it is not the rate of inflation but its accumulated rate plus one. We see that for year 1 the correction is 1.076, implying an inflation rate of 7.6%. This figure is used to correct the ending balance for year 1, which is reported in column 6. It cannot be used to correct the year 1 payment because the information is available only after it is too late. Thus in column 5, which shows the corrected payments, the figures for the first two years are the same as the uncorrected ones in column 2, but the payment for year 2 is corrected by using the correction factor for year 1, that is, (477.4)(1.076) = 513.7. Similarly, for every subsequent row, the figure in column 5 is the product of column 1 and column 4 lagged one year. By the end of the contract, in the thirtieth year, the debt has been fully amortized—a necessary consequence of the fact that the underlying contract in real terms is fully amortized by then (see, for example, the last row in columns 3 and 6).

Calculation of the periodic payment can be accomplished in an alternative way that may be instructive in terms of our discussion of the dual-rate mortgage. In this alternative procedure, the ending balance for each year is computed as above, but the payment for each year is the level payment corresponding to a 4% mortgage rate, a maturity equal to the remaining life of the PLAM, and a debt equal to the balance for the previous year as given in column 6. To illustrate, consider the calculation of the payment for year 10. At this point the mortgage has 20 years of remaining life. Using this maturity and an interest rate of 4%, the level annuity factor per month is .005873. (This can be found from a mortgage table or can be inferred from Table 7-2 as the ratio of the monthly payment rate in column 2 to the balance at the end of the year before, in column 3.) Multiplying this factor by the balance at

Table 7-2

Hypothetical 30-year $100,000 PLAM

(1) Year	Zero Inflation		Based on 1977–1987 Incomes, House Prices, and Inflation						
	(2) Monthly Payment	(3) Ending Balance	(4) CPI Ratio	(5) Monthly Payment	(6) Ending Balance	(7) Monthly Income	(8) Current PTI* Ratio	(9) House Value	(10) Current LTV
0	$477.42	$100,000	1.000	$ 477.42	$100,000	$ 2,388	20.0	$125,000	80.0
1	477.42	98,239	1.076	477.42	105,705	2,657	18.0	140,750	75.1
2	477.42	96,406	1.198	513.70	115,455	2,928	17.5	160,455	72.0
3	477.42	94,499	1.359	571.75	128,449	3,210	17.8	175,698	73.1
4	477.42	92,514	1.499	648.93	138,702	3,524	18.4	191,160	72.6
5	477.42	90,448	1.591	715.77	143,877	3,707	19.3	195,556	73.6
6	477.42	88,297	1.642	759.43	144,951	3,941	19.3	199,467	72.7
7	477.42	86,059	1.712	783.74	147,352	4,292	18.3	205,451	71.7
8	477.42	83,730	1.772	817.44	148,382	4,528	18.1	209,150	70.9
9	477.42	81,307	1.806	846.05	146,824	4,772	17.7	212,705	69.0
10	477.42	78,784	1.873	862.12	147,533	4,977	17.3	217,597	67.8
11	477.42	76,159	2.015	894.02	153,455	5,540	16.1	245,015	62.6
12	477.42	73,426	2.243	961.97	164,668	6,105	15.8	279,317	59.0

13	477.42	70,532	2.545	1,070.67	179,660	6,691	16.0	305,852	58.7
14	477.42	67,623	2.808	1,215.21	189,856	7,347	16.5	332,767	57.1
15	477.42	64,543	2.979	1,340.38	192,262	7,729	17.3	340,420	56.5
16	477.42	61,357	3.074	1,422.14	188,560	8,216	17.3	347,229	54.3
17	477.42	58,001	3.206	1,467.65	185,971	8,947	16.4	357,646	52.0
18	477.42	54,529	3.319	1,550.76	180,957	9,439	16.2	364,083	49.7
19	477.42	50,915	3.382	1,584.33	172,176	9,949	15.9	370,273	46.5
20	477.42	47,154	3.507	1,614.45	165,358	10,376	15.6	378,789	43.7
21	477.42	43,240	3.773	1,674.17	165,157	11,549	14.5	426,516	38.3
22	477.42	39,167	4.200	1,801.41	164,486	12,727	14.2	486,229	33.8
23	477.42	34,927	4.767	2,004.96	166,484	13,949	14.4	532,420	31.3
24	477.42	30,515	5.258	2,275.64	160,434	15,316	14.9	579,273	27.7
25	477.42	25,923	5.578	2,510.03	144,606	16,112	15.6	592,597	24.4
26	477.42	21,144	5.757	2,663.14	121,722	17,127	15.5	604,449	20.1
27	477.42	16,170	6.004	2,748.36	97,092	18,651	14.7	622,582	15.6
28	477.42	10,994	6.214	2,866.54	68,322	19,677	14.6	633,789	10.8
29	477.42	5,607	6.355	2,966.87	55,505	20,740	14.3	644,563	5.5
30	477.42	0	6.567	3,025.24	0	21,632	14.0	659,388	0.0

Table assumes a 4% real interest rate, 80% initial LTV, 20% PTI ratio, and 1% annual house depreciation relative to a new house.

*Payment-to-income.

Source: Susan E. Woodward and David A. Crowe, ''A Power-Packed Mortgage,'' Secondary Mortgage Markets (Fall 1988), p. 6, by permission of Freddie Mac.

the end of the year before in column 6, $146,824, we arrive at a payment for the year of $862, which coincides with the figure in column 5.

The behavior of the monthly payment and of the ending balance in columns 5 and 6 may raise questions about the desirability of this type of instrument, considering that by the end of the contract the payment is over six times as large as at the start—an increase of 500%. Similarly, because of negative amortization, the ending balance keeps growing through the first half of the mortgage life; by the fifteenth year the debt has just about doubled. In other words, the debtor, instead of repaying, has kept getting deeper and deeper in debt. In reality, these results are simply the consequence of the prevailingly high and persistent inflation assumed in the illustration, which causes the price level to rise by some six and a half times.

We know from columns 2 and 3 that in fact the real payment stays perfectly flat, and this is the only feature of the contract that should be relevant. The data on the behavior of average nominal income from 1977 to 1987, columns 7 and 8, show that it rose even faster than inflation, and that, accordingly, the ratio of the monthly nominal payment to monthly income would actually have decreased if such a mortgage had been outstanding in this period. Similarly, column 9, relying on estimates of the average value of a house, implies that the house's market value was rising substantially faster than the debt; by the fifteenth year, when the debt was at its peak, the debt-to-value ratio had declined from 0.80 to 0.57.

It may be objected that "average experience" is of no help to an individual borrower; for many people, income may not keep up with inflation and hence with the payment. Though this risk exists, and may affect the probability of default, exactly the same risk exists with the traditional mortgage in the absence of significant inflation; in both cases the payment is level in real terms, and while most people may be expected to enjoy rising (or at least nondecreasing) real income, many fall short. But let's remember that insufficient real income is, generally, not a cause of default costly to the lender; as long as the market value of the property exceeds the debt balance, it will pay the owner who cannot afford it any longer to sell the house and settle the debt, rather than default. Thus what matters most is the loan-to-value ratio: here again, the risk is no more than for a traditional mortgage with a stable price level. It may in fact be less, as it is not uncommon in times of inflation for house prices to rise faster than the general price level.

It is, of course, true that a PLAM provides less protection to the lender than does a traditional mortgage in the presence of significant inflation, because a traditional mortgage amortizes the debt faster. But that is because inflation, through the unintended tilt or front-loading effect, affords extra protection to the lender that was not intended by the designers of the traditional mortgage, or required by the lender, in the absence of inflation. It would seem that rational investors, if they are prepared to invest in a traditional mortgage with stable prices, should be equally willing to invest in a PLAM. In fact, the PLAM has distinct advantages for any investor interested in the real rather than in the nominal outcome of the investment, for it protects the investor as well as the borrower against purchasing power uncertainty.

Some difficulty might arise if thrift institutions wanted to offer a PLAM, since they would be earning the real rate while having to pay their depositors the market nominal rate. Actually, there need be no problem—what the institution would earn is the real rate plus the annual revaluation of the subject property, and the sum of the two might be expected to be close to the nominal market rate (Fisher's Law). In addition, the intermediaries, if the contract real rate had been correctly chosen, could undertake to offer a new type of indexed deposit earning a real fixed rate on an indexed principal, although this might require appropriate changes in regulation.

The PLAM is not a new concept; it has been used for decades in many countries with high inflation, where the housing industries could not possibly have survived with the traditional mortgage. These include Finland right after World War II, many South American countries, and Israel. Somewhat surprisingly, it has not been used to any significant extent in the United States. This is largely because no innovation in home financing has been possible without some sanction from government regulators, and regulators have been unimaginative and have shown themselves rather disinclined toward real indexation of any type. Critical in this respect has been HUD's lack of approval for FHA insurance. Quite recently, however, HUD has seemed about ready to change this attitude and to issue regulations to standardize these mortgages. PLAM may soon be making its debut in the United States.

THE DUAL-RATE MORTGAGE (DRM)

The dual-rate mortgage, which has also been referred to as the inflation-proof mortgage (IPM), is similar in spirit and its objective to the PLAM: payments start low—at current mortgage rates of around 10%, payments would start at approximately 30% to 40% below those required by the traditional mortgage or by the ARM. They then rise smoothly at the rate of inflation, if any, achieving, like the PLAM, annual payments approximately level in terms of purchasing power. Finally, by construction, the debt is fully amortized by the end of the contract.

The DRM differs from the PLAM in that the amount owed by the borrower is computed on the basis of a floating short-term rate. This has several important consequences. First, just as in the case of other instruments where a fluctuating rate is indexed to short-term market rates, the market value of the instrument is not subject to interest rate risk but should instead remain close to par, except of course for credit risk. Second, there is little prepayment risk, i.e., little danger of the borrower taking the option to repay when rates fall, for the DRM rate would automatically fall. And finally, it can be financed through the existing institution of short-term nominal deposits.

A DRM requires specification of three parameters:

1. The "payment" rate, which is a real rate of interest fixed for the life of the loan, much as with a PLAM. The purpose of this rate is not to establish *how much* the debtor will pay but rather *how* the amount will be paid, i.e., to make possible a desir-

able and affordable distribution of payments over the life of the instrument.

2. The "effective" or "debiting" rate, a short-term rate that, as in the ARM, determines how much the borrower effectively pays (or is debited for) and how much the creditor earns. It changes periodically—say, once a year—on the basis of an agreed-upon reference short-term rate such as the one-year Treasury bill.

3. The life of the mortgage, just as for any other fully amortized mortgage contract.

Given these three parameters, the calculation of the periodic payment is straightforward, as illustrated in Table 7-3. In any year the payment, shown in column 3, is obtained exactly as for the PLAM, i.e., by multiplying the balance outstanding at the beginning of the year, reported in column 1, by the annuity factor appropriate to a mortgage contracted at the *payment* rate and with maturity equal to the number of years remaining until the end of the contract. The calculations in the table are based on a payment rate of 7% and a 20-year life, so the annuity factor reported in column 2 turns out to be 0.0943. Multiplying by the initial balance of column 1, we obtain the first-year annual payment of $9,439 in column 3, implying a monthly payment of $787. To compute the balance at the beginning of the second year (1973), we take the first-year balance and subtract amortization in the first year.

Now recall that the amortization of the debt is equal to the annual payment less the amount of interest for which one is liable (whether paid in cash or added to the debt). The essential feature of the DRM is that the interest for which the debtor is liable in a given year is calculated by multiplying the initial balance by the *effective* rate, and not the payment rate. In Table 7-3, the chosen debiting rate is the one-year Treasury bill rate for the first week of each year, plus 2%. Its value for year t is reported in column 4—for the first year it is 6.28%. Thus the amount of interest we arrive at for the first year is $6,280 (column 5), and the amortization in column 6 is the difference between the first-year payment (column 3) and the

Table 7-3

Performance of a 20-year DRM Beginning in 1972 with a Payment Rate of 7%

	(1) Outstanding Principal	(2) Payment Factor	(3) Total Annual Payment	(4) Effective Interest Rate	(5) Interest Charged	(6) Amortization (3)−(5)	(7) Principal Year End (1)−(6)	(8) Deflator	(9) Inflation Rate	(10) Payment over Deflator (3)/(8)×100	(11) Payment over Per Capita Disposable Income 1972 = 100	(12) Principal over Deflator (7)/(8)	(15) Payment over Residential Rent Index 1972 = 100
Year													
1972	100,000.00	0.09439	9,439.00	0.0628	6,280.00	3,159.00	96,841.00	100.00	—	9,459.00	100	96,841.00	100
1973	96,841.00	0.09675	9,369.57	0.0789	7,640.75	1,728.61	95,112.39	105.70	0.06	8,864.11	89	89,985.34	95
1974	95,112.39	0.09941	9,455.12	0.0942	8,959.59	495.54	94,616.85	116.40	0.10	8,123.20	81	81,288.40	91
1975	94,616.85	0.10243	9,691.60	0.0883	8,354.67	1,356.94	93,279.92	125.30	0.08	7,734.68	78	74,444.87	89
1976	93,279.92	0.10586	9,874.61	0.0781	7,285.16	2,589.45	90,690.47	131.70	0.05	7,497.67	74	68,860.15	86
1977	90,690.47	0.10979	9,956.91	0.0729	6,611.33	3,345.57	87,344.89	139.30	0.06	7,147.85	68	62,703.03	82
1978	87,344.89	0.11434	9,987.02	0.0928	8,105.61	1,881.41	85,463.49	149.10	0.07	6,698.21	62	57,319.62	77
1979	85,463.49	0.11965	10,225.71	0.1241	10,606.02	−380.31	85,843.80	162.50	0.09	6,292.71	57	52,826.65	73
1980	85,843.80	0.12590	10,807.73	0.1406	12,069.64	−1,261.90	87,105.70	179.00	0.10	6,057.84	55	48,662.40	71
1981	87,105.70	0.13536	11,616.42	0.1608	14,006.60	−2,390.18	89,495.88	194.10	0.08	5,984.76	55	46,108.13	70
1982	89,495.88	0.14238	12,742.42	0.1632	14,605.73	−1,863.30	91,359.19	205.30	0.06	6,206.73	56	44,500.33	72
1983	91,359.19	0.15349	14,022.72	0.1078	9,848.52	4,174.20	87,184.99	214.00	0.04	6,552.67	56	40,740.65	77
1984	87,184.99	0.16747	14,600.87	0.1000	8,718.50	5,882.37	81,302.61	226.84	0.06	6,436.64	54	35,841.39	75
1985	81,302.61	0.18555	15,085.70	0.1000	8,130.26	6,955.44	74,347.18	240.45	0.06	6,273.95	52	30,919.96	74
1986	74,347.18	0.20980	15,598.04	0.1000	7,434.72	8,163.52	66,183.86	243.88	0.06	6,119.82	50	25,966.94	73
1987	66,183.86	0.24389	16,141.58	0.1000	6,618.39	9,523.20	56,660.66	270.17	0.06	5,974.60	49	20,972.22	72
1988	56,660.66	0.29523	16,727.95	0.1000	5,666.07	11,061.86	45,598.80	286.38	0.06	5,841.16	47	15,922.47	71
1989	45,598.80	0.38105	17,375.42	0.1000	4,559.88	12,815.54	32,783.26	303.56	0.06	5,723.85	46	10,799.49	70
1990	32,783.26	0.55509	18,132.09	0.1000	3,278.33	14,855.77	17,929.49	321.78	0.06	5,634.99	45	5,572.03	70
1991	17,929.49	1.10000	19,722.44	0.1000	1,792.95	17,929.49	0.00	341.08	0.06	5,782.29	46	0.00	72
Totals			260,572.70		160,572.70	100,000.00							

interest due (column 5). Subtracting the amortization from the initial balance, one arrives at the initial balance for the second year (column 1, second row), which is used in turn to compute the second-year payment, and so on. To summarize:

1. The annual payment (column 3) equals the initial balance (column 1) times the annuity factor (column 2).
2. Initial balance equals the previous year's balance less the previous year's amortization (column 6).
3. Amortization (column 6) equals the annual payment (column 3) less interest due (column 5).
4. Interest due equals the previous balance (column 1) times the debiting or effective rate (column 4).

A few observations are appropriate here. First, as the table reveals, negative amortization is possible with this instrument because the debiting rate can exceed the annuity factor if inflation is high enough. Second, in principle, the DRM resembles the PLAM in several ways:

1. For both instruments the current payment is the previous balance times the same annuity factor.
2. In the PLAM the balance in year t is the balance at $t-1$ times (1 − an amortization factor corresponding to the real rate and remaining life + rate of inflation). For the DRM the balance at t is the balance at $(t-1)$ times (1 − an amortization factor as above + debiting rate − real rate). If we choose a real rate for a PLAM that is the same as the payment rate for a DRM, the only difference between the two instruments is that the PLAM's balance tends to be driven up through inflation, while the DRM balance grows through the difference between the nominal and the real rate. Thus, if Fisher's Law held precisely, the two instruments would be identical. Deviations will arise because Fisher's Law may fail to hold, especially in the short run. In this case we can show that the PLAM debtor will end up paying precisely the real rate

set in the contract, while the DRM borrower will end up paying the average effective real rate over the period. In the period covered by the example, the borrower would have fared somewhat better with a DRM.

If the DRM and the PLAM are so similar, why does the annual payment in Table 7-3 decline so steadily in real terms? The reason is that the real rate used in Table 7-2 is much higher than the 4% used in Table 7-3. There are two justifications for our choice of the higher rate. This first is that, once we allow for the intermediation spread, we believe that the 4% is too low. The second is that we have allowed the lender some extra protection by assuming a payment rate higher than the best guess of the real rate. Notice that raising the payment rate will result in faster amortization, tilting the payment schedule down, as in the table.

Despite their overall similarity, the DRM appears to have several advantages over the PLAM. One is the opportunity to reduce the lender's credit risk without increasing total interest costs, by raising the payment rate above the estimated real rate, thus accelerating the amortization in real terms. A second advantage is that it reduces the price risk for lenders. The PLAM is, after all, a fixed-rate contract, and although the real rate has turned out to be relatively stable, significant movements cannot be ruled out over a 20- to 30-year span. The DRM, by contrast, as a variable rate instrument should tend to remain always close to par (aside from credit risk). A further important advantage is that because the lender always earns the short-term market rate, the mortgage can be financed through short-term deposits without violating the principle of matching maturities.

So far the DRM has had rather limited application in the United States, in large measure because it has not yet received FHA approval for insurance. It has had some application abroad and should also have a future in the United States after the PLAM has been introduced. There are a number of variants of the DRM that improve the working of the instrument in some direction at the cost of deterioration in other directions.

The French and Mexican Mortgage

It is worthwhile to mention two more "inflation-proof" mortgage designs, which are at present unknown in the United States but have had successful applications abroad. We will label them the "French" mortgage and the "Mexican" mortgage, respectively, after the countries in which they were first applied.[2] Both are dual-rate mortgages and combine elements of the PLAM and the DRM; they offer advantages over the traditional instruments for both lenders and borrowers under many, though not all, circumstances.

The French mortgage is designed to achieve affordability and at the same time eliminate the interest rate or price risk inherent in any long-term contract using a fixed long-term rate, like the fixed-rate mortgage or the PLAM (although the risk is smaller for a PLAM because the real rate is less volatile). The way the price risk is eliminated is the same as for the DRM, namely by charging the borrowers a variable short-term rate—the debiting rate—in principle the same rate that is applicable to the ARM, or DRM. However, what really distinguishes the French mortgage is its novel approach to the determination of the repayment schedule: it is entirely different from that applicable to the ARM and, instead, is basically the same as that which applies to the PLAM. That is, the first payment is computed from the traditional mortgage formula and the desired term, say n, but uses as the interest rate a "payment" rate equal to the long-term real rate, as in the PLAM and DRM (or possibly a modestly different one—see below); all subsequent payments are indexed to inflation p, just as in the PLAM. The difference between the payment and the amount debited in any given period represents the amortization of the remaining principal.

The effective maturity—the time when the debit is fully amortized—depends in a predictable way on the payment rate, the desired term embodied in computing the first payment, and the average ex-post real market rate $(R\text{-}p)$. But it cannot be accurately foreseen because the real rate is not

[2]For a more detailed description of these mortgages and their properties see Denise DiPasquale and Franco Modigliani, *Mortgage Design and Affordable Home Ownership*, Massachusetts Institute of Technology, December 1991 (in publication).

known until it is realized. This is clearly a drawback of this type of mortgage. Still, the instrument has an "expected" term to maturity in the sense that, if the payment rate equals the average real rate, then the term will coincide with the desired term, n. If the payment rate exceeds the real rate, the loan amortizes faster than the PLAM, and conversely. This property of the French mortgage implies that the risk of exceeding the intended maturity can be controlled by choosing a larger payment rate.

One concern that may arise with respect to the French mortgage as well as the PLAM (and the DRM) is that, in the course of inflation, incomes of some borrowers may fail to keep pace with rising prices. Since the payment escalates as fast as inflation, the nominal payment might rise faster than the debtor's income, making it hard for him to meet his obligations and increasing the probability of nonperformance. This problem is unlikely to arise with a traditional mortgage since the constant nominal payment, while causing the front loading, also implies a gradually decreasing real payment.

This problem is dealt with by the Mexican mortgage by indexing payments not to overall inflation, as in the French mortgage, but to a wage index. Clearly with this instrument there should be no danger of payments outgrowing income on the average. As long as the wage index is appropriately chosen to reflect average wage experience, income will keep pace, on the average, with the increases in payments. The Mexican mortgage, in principle, could be indexed to wage indices in specific sectors of the economy or to an overall wage index. The idea behind the Mexican mortgage is to permit the borrower to amortize his debt by paying a constant number of monthly labor hours, and thus a constant fraction of his labor income, over the term of the loan. However, it shares with the French mortgage the drawback that maturity is uncertain; it shortens if real wages rise.

Summary of Advantages and Disadvantages
of Alternative Instruments

All the dual-rate mortgages share several desirable properties:

1. Because the first payment is based on a long-term *real* rate, and further payments are indexed on prices, these instruments eliminate (or control) the problem of the inflation-induced front loading and tilt that is characteristic of mortgages currently in use. This not only reduces the initial burden of home ownership but also, for any given ceiling in the payment-to-income ratio, permits the borrower to qualify for a larger loan, the same as he could obtain without inflation. Thus, the inflation-proof instruments offer a solution to the most severe problems facing a first-home buyer under sustained inflation.

2. All three mortgages possess an important measure of flexibility with respect to the real payment stream, which neither the traditional mortgage nor the PLAM possess. It is achieved by contracting for a payment rate somewhat different from the long-run real rate. In the case of the French mortgage, raising the payment rate raises the level of real payment above the PLAM, accelerates the amortization, and shortens the maturity; the same type of change occurs with the Mexican mortgage. In the case of the DRM, the maturity is not affected, but raising the payment rate has the effect of front loading, thus producing a downward tilt of the real payment and faster amortization, to any desired extent.

3. All inflation-proof mortgages offer the borrower and the lender the opportunity to contract for a stream of monthly payments and receipts which is fully predictable in real terms (or nearly so for the DRM). This is a property that neither of the currently used mortgages possess in the presence of significantly variable inflation.

4. Because the French and Mexican mortgages, like the DRM and ARM, guarantee the lender a floating, short-term nominal rate, their market value can be expected to remain, at all times, close to par. This feature eliminates the lender's price risk associated with any fixed long-term rate, be it nominal

as in the traditional mortgage, or real as in the PLAM.

5. For the same reason, lenders no longer face a pre-payment risk, as debtors cannot take advantage of declines in long-term rates.

Against these advantages, the dual-rate mortgages do have some possible drawbacks.

1. For the French and Mexican mortgages, the most serious drawback probably is their uncertain maturity. From the investor's point of view, an unpaid balance at the end of the expected term is an investment which should have market value equal to face value. Hence it should not involve a serious loss. From the borrower's point of view, it means that because the real rate turned out higher than assumed in establishing the payment rate, payment has been spread out over a longer period in lieu of being higher throughout. In the case of the DRM, the only consequence of underestimating the real rate will be some unintended upward tilt. This possible consequence should not prove too serious, especially since real income tends to rise with age and productivity, and because the positive tilt can be controlled through the payment rate.

2. Under any of the three contracts as well as the PLAM, the initial payment is lower than that of the traditional mortgage or the ARM—the more so the greater inflation. It follows that the initial amortization will also be slower, depending on inflation. In fact, if inflation is sufficiently rapid, the amortization may even be negative for awhile;[3] that is, the nominal debt may keep rising instead of falling (see the PLAM example illustrated in Table 7-2).

This possibility is illustrated by a set of simulations of all the different contracts carried out by DiPasquale and

---

[3]This will tend to occur whenever inflation exceeds the amortization rate, which can easily happen at the beginning of the contract when the scheduled rate of amortization is low.

Modigliani for mortgages with a 20-year maturity initiated in 1975, using the debiting rates and the inflation actually observed over the period.[4] It is found that, though inflation never exceeded 10%, still for all the inflation-proof mortgages the unamortized debt tends initially to rise to a peak about eight years after the contract starts. In the PLAM and DRM, one does not get back to the starting level of debt until past the middle of the contract; only the old mortgages exhibit positive amortization throughout.

These results might suggest that the new mortgages should prove unacceptable to lenders. But in reality the simulation results reported above are rather uninformative. To be meaningful, the unamortized principal must be adjusted for inflation, i.e., deflated by the price index in order to provide a measure of the real remaining debt. It is shown in DiPasquale and Modigliani that for the three dual-rate mortgages, the path of the real unamortized debt depends on the choice of the payment rate relative to the average ex-post real rate. For the French mortgage and the DRM, if their payment rate is equal to the average ex-post real rate, the path of the remaining real principal will be the same as that of a PLAM with the same real rate. On the average, the same proposition holds for the Mexican mortgage if the real wage is constant. Now the path of the real remaining principal for a PLAM is, by construction, precisely the same as that of a traditional mortgage with the same maturity and rate when prices are stable.

It follows that, provided the payment rate does approximate the ex-post average real rate, from the point of view of real amortization, the four instruments are no riskier than a traditional mortgage with stable prices since they amortize as fast in real terms. If the payment rate is prudently chosen at an appropriate margin over the expected average real rate (which one should realize does not affect the actual interest paid by the borrower), amortization will be faster, and the three dual-rate instruments actually will be safer than a traditional mortgage under price stability.

The same conclusions can be reached through simulation, looking not at the behavioral, real remaining principal

[4]DiPasquale and Modigliani, *Mortgage Design and Affordable Home Ownership.*

but at another risk measure, the loan-to-value ratio. If the payment rate is chosen prudently, the three instruments generate a loan-to-value ratio decreasing faster than a PLAM or traditional mortgage with no inflation. Of course the result does not necessarily hold when we compare the amortization path of the new instrument with that of a traditional mortgage, in the presence of inflation and interest rates swollen by the inflation premium. In that case, the real amortization speeds up, providing more safety to the lender than the PLAM and the other inflation-proof mortgages. This is because inflation, through the unintended tilt or front-loading effect, offers the lender extra protection that was not intended by the designers of the traditional mortgage or required by the lender in the absence of inflation—an extra protection acquired at the expense of affordability. Furthermore with variable inflation, a traditional mortgage is much riskier than with price stability. A rational, risk-averse investor, preparing to invest in a traditional mortgage during the period of relative price stability up to the mid-1950s, should have been ready to invest in any of the new inflation-proof instruments from the point of view of safety of principal.

Problems and Opportunities in Implementation

The implementation of these new instruments presents new opportunities, but also may require some changes. These will be surveyed only briefly here but a more extensive treatment is provided by DiPasquale and Modigliani.[5]

First, with respect to underwriting standards, many, like those having to do with credit worthiness and property appraisal, would remain largely unchanged. Among the standards that may need revisions are the loan-to-value (LTV) ratio and payment-to-income (PTI) ratio. In view of the negative nominal amortization, a somewhat lower LTV might be justified—although in real terms amortization should not be slower and might even be faster, depending on the payment rate. There may then be an opportunity, especially in the case of a DRM, to negotiate the LTV with the payment rate and

[5] Ibid.

resulting tilt simultaneously. Similarly, the rising stream of nominal repayment, characterizing all the inflation-proof instruments, may suggest the opportunity to tighten the PTI ratio standards—though, again, one should not expect the stream to rise in real terms. As for the DRM, the real tilt can again be controlled through the payment rate and some negative tilt may be desirable even for the borrower as his payments will become easier to meet over the life of the mortgage. But there is a trade-off between the tilt and the size of the initial payments and, therefore, also the size of the mortgage he can qualify for. It is precisely the possibility of controlling the tilt and relevant variables through the payment rate that makes the DRM such a flexible and active instrument.

Another problem of implementation concerns taxation of both borrowers and lenders. A problem arises for all four inflation-proof mortgages because the interest actually paid and received on the initial balance for the period is the payment rate which is different from the interest rate accrued in the period, namely the sum of the payment rate and the rate of inflation. The tax treatment of the instrument will clearly differ from country to country. In the case of the United States, the Internal Revenue Service has just issued regulations for the PLAM only (though one can infer the treatment of the other instruments). As shown by DiPasquale and Modigliani, the treatment of lenders is the same as for a traditional mortgage, but that of borrowers is somewhat more favorable.[6]

Another interesting aspect of implementation relates to the question as to who should be interested in acquiring and holding these newer instruments. The DRM, French, and Mexican mortgages, which earn the current short-term rates, should prove suitable for all the investors that now invest in ARMs, including those holding certain classes of collateralized mortgage obligations. The only difference is that the stream of cash income from the investment would take a different shape. It would be roughly constant in purchasing power terms instead of front-loaded ones. Thrift institutions wishing to finance them with ordinary deposits would need to reinvest in the existing loan to the extent that the nominal amortization

[6]See also *Federal Reporter*, January 9, 1990.

was negative; this should happen only with substantial inflation and should not be difficult to finance since, with inflation, deposits typically rise in tune with inflation. In the case of the PLAM, the investment does not return the short-term market rate; however it does return the long-term real rate, plus the annual revaluation of the debt at the rate of inflation. The sum of these two components of return should be approximately equal to the nominal rate, though, admittedly, with some risk of slippage.

A more interesting possibility is for thrift institutions to offer an indexed deposit, earning the real rate plus the rate of inflation. Such contracts have had limited offering, in part because of the difficulty of hedging them. The new instruments would be ideal for that purpose. Finally, insurance companies may find the new instruments attractive in order to hedge indexed contracts such as annuities or life insurance.

CONCLUSIONS

In this chapter and the previous two, we have described and analyzed the properties of several major instruments and a host of minor ones designed to finance the acquisition of houses. The availability of such a variety of instruments greatly enhances the realm of choices available to finance home ownership. Because households have varying combinations of income and wealth, some are blocked from home ownership by the high initial payments and/or by the size of the down payment required, and yet others cannot meet the income standards required. Furthermore the severity of these constraints varies with the rate of inflation.

The analysis of the various mortgages presented in this chapter points to the relative advantages and disadvantages of these instruments for dealing with these problems.

As DiPasquale and Modigliani have pointed out, these alternative instruments should not be viewed as a replacement for the traditional mortgage or ARM, but rather as an urgently needed potential addition to the menu of mortgage options available. Increasing the number of mortgage options will significantly expand affordability.

8

Features of Passthrough Securities

A mortgage passthrough security is the basic mortgage-backed security and is the subject of this chapter and Chapter 9. As explained in Chapter 1, a passthrough is created when one or more mortgage holders form a collection (pool) of mortgages and sell shares or participation certificates in the pool. A pool may consist of several thousand mortgages or only a few mortgages. From the passthrough, two derivative mortgage-backed securities are created: collateralized mortgage obligations and stripped mortgage-backed securities. These securities are the subject of Chapter 11.

INVESTOR PREFERENCE FOR PASSTHROUGHS

Risk-averse investors prefer to invest in a fractional pool rather than a single mortgage loan, for many of the same reasons that investors prefer to hold a diversified portfolio of stocks rather than an individual stock. Individual mortgage loans expose the investor to unique (or unsystematic) risk and systematic risk. The risks in this case are: (1) the risk that the homeowner will prepay the mortgage at any unfavorable time, and (2) that the borrower may default on the loan. The former risk is called prepayment risk. In Chapter 9 we will see that changes in mortgage rates are one reason that prepayments occur.

Prepayment risk can be divided into systematic and unsystematic prepayment risk. Systematic prepayment risk with respect to prepayments is the unfavorable change in prepayments caused by changes in mortgage rates. Systematic risk with respect to default rates represents widespread default rates caused by a severe economic recession. Unsystematic prepayment risk is the risk of an adverse change in the speed of prepayments that are not affected by changes in mortgage rates. Holding a diversified portfolio of mortgage loans in the form of a passthrough reduces most unsystematic risk, leaving only systematic risk. In addition, the liquidity of a passthrough is considerably better than that of an individual mortgage loan.

CASH FLOW CHARACTERISTICS

The cash flow of a passthrough depends on the cash flow of the underlying mortgages. It consists of monthly mortgage payments representing interest, the scheduled repayment of principal, and any prepayments.

Payments are made to security holders each month. Neither the amount nor the timing, however, of the cash flow from the pool of mortgages is identical to that of the cash flow passed through to investors. The monthly cash flow for a passthrough security is less than the monthly cash flow of the underlying mortgages by an amount equal to servicing and other fees. The other fees are those charged by the issuer or guarantor of the passthrough for guaranteeing the issue.[1] The coupon rate on a passthrough security is less than the contract rate on the underlying pool of mortgage loans by an amount equal to the servicing and guaranteeing fees.

The timing of the cash flow is also different. The monthly mortgage payment is due from each mortgagor on the first day of each month. There is a delay in passing through the corresponding monthly cash flow to the security holders, which varies by the type of passthrough. Because of prepayments, the cash flow of a passthrough is not known with

---

[1] Actually, the servicer pays the guarantee fee to the issuer or guarantor.

certainty. The various conventions for constructing cash flows are the subject of the next chapter.

AGENCY PASSTHROUGHS

As we explained in Chapter 2, there are three major types of passthroughs, guaranteed by the following organizations: Government National Mortgage Association, Federal Home Loan Mortgage Corporation, and Federal National Mortgage Association. These are called agency passthroughs. Tables 2-1 and 2-2 in Chapter 2 show outstanding passthroughs and their origination, respectively. Agency passthroughs are sold with minimum par value denominations of $25,000.

Features of Agency Passthroughs

Features of passthroughs vary not only by agency but also by program offered. The features of a passthrough will have an impact on its investment characteristics (particularly its prepayment characteristics). These general features, summarized below and discussed further when we review the various agency programs, can be classified into six groups: (1) the type of guarantee, (2) the number of lenders with mortgage loans that are permitted in the pool, (3) the mortgage design of the loans, (4) the characteristics of the mortgage loans in the pool, (5) the payment procedure, and (6) the minimum pool size.

Type of guarantee. An agency can provide two types of guarantees. One type of guarantee is the timely payment of both interest and principal, meaning the interest and principal will be paid when due, even if any of the mortgagors fail to make the monthly mortgage payments. Passthroughs with this type of guarantee are referred to as *fully modified passthroughs.* The second type guarantees both interest and principal payments; however, it only guarantees the timely payment of interest. The scheduled principal is passed through as it is collected with a guarantee that the scheduled payment will be made no later than a specified date. Passthroughs with this type of guarantee are called *modified passthroughs*.

Number of lenders permitted in the pool. A pool may consist of mortgages originated by a single lender or multiple lenders. A single-lender pool has mortgage loans concentrated in one geographical area or in a few states. In multiple-lender pools, the underlying mortgage loans have greater geographical diversification of borrowers.

Mortgage design of the loans. In the previous three chapters, we described a variety of mortgage designs. Agency passthroughs have pools of loans with various mortgage designs.

Characteristics of the mortgage loans in the pool. Not all mortgage loans are permitted in a pool that collateralizes a passthrough. The underwriting standards established by the agency define the permissible loans. These key underwriting standards are summarized below:

- *mortgage loans permitted in the pool:* Mortgage loans can be classified as government-insured or -guaranteed loans and conventional loans.
- *maximum size of a loan:* For agency securities, the loan limits are reset annually.
- *amount of seasoning permitted:* The seasoning of a mortgage loan refers to the time that has passed since the loan was originated.
- *assumability of mortgages:* If a mortgage loan may be taken over by another borrower, the loan is said to be assumable.
- *maturity:* Programs are available with mortgage loans of different maturities. For example, a pool can have a stated maturity of 30 years, even though not all of the mortgage loans in the pool have a maturity of 30 years, since seasoned loans may be included.
- *net interest spread permitted:* The contract rate on a mortgage loan is also called the coupon rate or gross coupon rate. The net coupon rate is the difference between the coupon rate and fees for servicing

and agency guaranteeing. The maximum net interest spread that permits a mortgage loan to qualify for inclusion in a pool varies.

Payment procedure. Differences in payment procedure involve payment delays and the method of payment.

- *payment delays:* Payment delays for passthroughs occur for two reasons. First, monthly payments by homeowners are made in arrears. That is, the payments for the funds borrowed in, say, March are due on the first of the month of April, the normal delay when investing in whole loans. When the payments are received, they must be processed and the checks mailed to passthrough investors. The actual delay for passthrough investors—that is, the number of days that payment is delayed beyond the normal delay—varies with the agency and agency program. The "stated delay" of a passthrough is the normal delay plus the actual delay. If the payment is made on the fifteenth of the month, then the actual delay is 14 days, since the monthly payment would have been due on the first of the month. If the stated delay for a passthrough is 44 days, then the actual delay is 14 days.
- *method of payment:* By method of payment, we mean how many monthly checks will be sent to an investor that owns several pools of an agency. There can be either one check for all pools or multiple checks.

Minimum pool size. In creating passthroughs, an agency will establish a minimum pool size.

Government National Mortgage Association MBSs

Ginnie Mae passthroughs are guaranteed by the full faith and credit of the U.S. government. For this reason, Ginnie

Mae passthroughs are viewed as risk-free in terms of default risk, just like Treasury securities. The security guaranteed by Ginnie Mae is a mortgage-backed security.

Ginnie Mae MBSs are issued under one of two programs: GNMA I (established in 1970) and GNMA II (established in 1983). Because the latter program is more attractive, as we explain below, Ginnie Mae permits qualified passthroughs issued under the GNMA I program to be converted into the GNMA II program.

Type of guarantee. All Ginnie Mae MBSs are fully modified passthroughs.

Number of lenders permitted in the pool. Only single-lender pools are permitted under the GNMA I program; both single-lender and multiple-lender pools are allowed in the GNMA II program. Single-lender pools issued under the GNMA II program are called *custom pools;* multiple-lender pools are called *jumbo pools.*

Mortgage design of the loans. Under the two programs, passthroughs with different types of collateral are issued. Both programs issue passthroughs that are backed by single-family (SF) mortgages, graduated-payment mortgages, growing equity mortgages, and mobile or manufactured home loans. The large majority of GNMA MBSs are backed by single-family mortgages, where a single-family mortgage is a loan for a 1-to-4 family primary residence with a level-payment fixed-rate mortgage. A Ginnie Mae MBS of this type is referred to as a "GNMA SF MBS."

Mortgage-backed securities backed by adjustable-payment mortgages (APMs) are issued under the GNMA II program. For an APM the monthly mortgage payment changes periodically, based on some index. An example of an adjustable-payment mortgage is the adjustable-rate mortgage described in Chapter 6. Not all ARMs qualify for inclusion in the pools that collateralize Ginnie Mae APM mortgage-backed securities. To qualify, the ARM must (1) adjust annually and (2) be indexed off the weekly average yield of the one-year constant maturity Treasury.

Characteristics of the mortgage loans in the pool. The key underwriting standards for the mortgage loans are summarized below:

- *mortgage loans permitted in the pool:* Only mortgage loans insured or guaranteed by either the Federal Housing Administration, the Veterans Administration, or the Farmers Home Administration can be included in a mortgage pool guaranteed by Ginnie Mae.
- *maximum size of a loan:* The maximum loan size is set by Congress, based on the maximum amount that the FHA or VA may guarantee. The maximum for a given loan varies with the region of the country and type of residential property. At the time of this writing, the maximum FHA loan is $124,187 for regions of the country designated as high-cost regions; for a VA loan it is $184,000.
- *amount of seasoning permitted:* In both programs, only newly originated mortgage loans may be included in a pool. These are defined as mortgage loans that have been seasoned less than 24 months.
- *assumability of mortgages:* Assumable mortgages are permitted in the pool.
- *maturity:* Within the single-family MBS, there are pools in which the security is collateralized by 30-year and 15-year mortgages. The 15-year pools are commonly referred to as "midgets."
- *net interest spread permitted:* In the GNMA I program, only net interest spreads of 50 basis points are permitted; for the GNMA II program, the net interest spread may vary from 50 to 150 basis points.

Payment procedure. The stated delays for GNMA I and II programs are 45 and 50 days, respectively. Thus, corresponding actual delays are 14 and 19 days.

There is also a difference between the two programs in the method of payment. In the GNMA I program, payments are made by the individual servicers. In the GNMA II program, payments from all pools owned by an investor are consolidated and paid in one check by the central paying agent, Chemical Bank.

Minimum pool size. The minimum pool size varies by program and the type of mortgage design. For the more popular program, the GNMA SF MBS, the minimum pool size is $1 million for the GNMA I program and for custom pools issued under the GNMA II program. For the jumbo pool, it is $500,000.

Table 8-1 lists the outstanding remaining mortgage balance of GNMA 30-year MBSs backed by single-family mortgages by coupon. Also shown is the number of pools outstanding by coupon and the remaining term of the pools.

Federal Home Loan Mortgage Corporation PC

The second largest type of agency passthrough is the participation certificate issued by Freddie Mac. Although a guarantee of Freddie Mac is not a guarantee by the U.S. government, most market participants view Freddie Mac PCs as similar, although not identical, in creditworthiness to Ginnie Mae passthroughs.

Freddie Mac has a variety of programs from which it creates PCs. The most important programs are the Cash Program and Guarantor/Swap Program, which we discussed in Chapter 2. The PCs created under the first program are called *Cash PCs* or *Regular PCs*, while those created under the second program are called *Swap PCs*. In the fall of 1990, Freddie Mac introduced its *Gold PC*, which as we shall explain below has stronger guarantees and shorter stated payment delays. Gold PCs are issued in both programs, and will be the only type of PC issued in the future.

Type of guarantee. Freddie Mac offers both modified passthroughs and fully modified passthroughs. All non-Gold PCs that have been issued as part of its Cash Program and almost all that have been issued as part of its Guarantor/Swap Program are modified passthroughs. There are a very small number of non-Gold PCs in the latter program that are fully modified passthroughs. All Gold PCs issued are fully modified passthroughs.

Table 8-1

30-Year Ginnie Mae Single-Family MBSs Outstanding by Coupon as of October 1991

| Coupon | Projected Rem Term | All Pools | | |
		# of Pools	Rem Bal ($ millions)	Rem Term
6 1/2		1,270	1,111.6	135
7		556	648.7	278
7 1/2	315	5,783	6,624.7	236
8	330	16,865	26,264.0	266
8 1/2	352	12,738	30,526.3	317
9	340	33,391	99,751.9	313
9 1/2	330	28,278	83,622.9	320
10	310	21,804	56,444.0	321
10 1/2	310	7,359	11,649.1	316
11	310	11,561	12,051.0	274
11 1/2	295	9,591	6,676.1	263
12	290	8,115	4,254.6	273
12 1/2	293	6,455	2,330.1	258
13	277	4,077	1,248.0	256
13 1/2	274	2,297	577.6	254

Source: Goldman, Sachs & Co.

For modified PCs issued by Freddie Mac, the scheduled principal is passed through as it is collected, with Freddie Mac guaranteeing only that the scheduled payment will be made no later than one year after it is due.

Number of lenders permitted in the pool. The Cash Program includes only multiple-lender pools. (Recall that in this program Freddie Mac purchases mortgage loans from various lenders and then creates a pool to collateralize the PCs.) In the Guarantor/Swap Program, there are both single-lender and multiple-lender pools.

Mortgage design of the loans. There are pools with fixed-rate, level-payment mortgage loans, adjustable-rate mortgage loans, and balloon/reset mortgage loans. A wide variety of ARM PCs are issued under both the Cash and Guarantor/Swap programs. There are Treasury-indexed ARM pools and cost-of-funds-indexed ARM pools. The latter includes the 11th District Cost of Funds, the National Cost of Funds, and the Federal Home Loan Bank Contract Rate, which we discussed in Chapter 6.

For an ARM to be included in a PC, its annual cap must be restricted. There are both Cash ARM PCs and Swap ARM PCs with a 1% annual cap and with a 2% annual cap. There are also pools with convertible ARMs, which we discussed in Chapter 6.

Characteristics of the mortgage loans in the pool. The key underwriting standards for the mortgage loans are summarized below:

- *mortgage loans permitted in the pool:* The majority of PCs are backed by conventional mortgage loans. There are a small portion of PCs that are backed by FHA- and VA-guaranteed mortgage loans.
- *maximum size of a loan:* For both Freddie Mac and Fannie Mae, the maximum loan size is set each year based on the annual percentage change in the average price of conventionally financed homes as determined by the Federal Home Loan Bank Board. The maximum loan for a 1-to-4 family residence depends on the number of units. For example, at the time of this writing, the maximum loan for one unit is $202,300.[2]
- *amount of seasoning permitted:* There are no limits on seasoning for either program.
- *assumability of mortgages:* No assumable mortgages are permitted in a pool.
- *maturity:* There are 30-year and 15-year Freddie Mac Regular and Swap PCs. The 15-year Regular PCs are called "gnomes" and Swap PCs are called "non-gnomes."
- *net interest spread permitted:* In general, the net interest spread can be 50 to 250 basis points for both programs.

Payment procedure. The stated delay for non-Gold PCs issued as part of either program is 75 days, and the actual delay is 44 days. The Gold PCs have a shorter payment delay;

---

[2] For property in the states of Alaska and Hawaii, loan limits are 50% higher.

the stated delay is 45 days, the actual delay 14 days. One monthly check is received in both programs for all pools an investor owns.

Minimum pool size. The minimum pool size for the Cash Program and Guarantor/Swap Program is $50 million and $1 million, respectively.

Tables 8-2, 8-3, and 8-4 provide information about outstanding remaining mortgage balances of 30-year FHLM PCs by coupon issued under the Regular, Guarantor, and Gold programs, respectively. The number of pools, the remaining term, and the weighted average coupon of the underlying mortgage loans are also shown.

Federal National Mortgage Association MBS

The passthroughs issued by Fannie Mae are mortgage-backed securities (MBSs). Like a Freddie Mac PC, a Fannie Mae MBS is not the obligation of the U.S. government.

Table 8-2

30-Year Freddie Mac Regular PCs Outstanding by Coupon as of October 1991

Coupon	Projected Rem Term	All Pools			
		# of Pools	Rem Bal ($ millions)	WAC	Rem Term
6 1/2					
7					
7 1/2	324	4	119.2	8.55	153
8	350	21	2,002.7	9.29	245
8 1/2	350	21	1,893.8	9.69	255
9	353	44	9,161.6	10.05	281
9 1/2	354	75	16,694.3	10.27	305
10	350	61	9,603.2	10.65	299
10 1/2	345	20	1,372.6	11.23	296
11	335	12	684.3	11.91	238
11 1/2	300	8	165.9	12.21	229
12	253	29	497.6	12.74	227
12 1/2	241	27	504.1	12.87	219
13	224	9	103.5	13.55	223
13 1/2		7	70.2	12.78	209

Source: Goldman, Sachs & Co.

Table 8-3

30-Year Freddie Mac Guarantor PCs Outstanding by Coupon as of October 1991

Coupon	Projected Rem Term	All Pools # of Pools	Rem Bal ($ millions)	WAC	Rem Term
6 1/2		396	797.5	7.41	106
7	310	1,017	2,486.8	8.23	163
7 1/2	290	1,297	3,849.2	8.96	230
8	300	5,962	15,870.1	9.00	230
8 1/2	340	9,156	18,963.1	9.30	265
9	345	13,492	30,492.6	9.77	292
9 1/2	340	17,008	35,188.8	10.12	302
10	310	12,086	21,385.8	10.60	299
10 1/2	310	4,215	5,747.0	11.11	291
11	341	2,451	2,233.4	11.72	262
11 1/2	341	1,641	981.4	12.18	230
12	280	1,640	764.1	12.72	213
12 1/2	260	999	370.4	13.17	213
13	224	587	161.6	13.68	207
13 1/2		209	47.5	14.10	201

Source: Goldman, Sachs & Co.

Table 8-4

30-Year Freddie Mac Gold PCs Outstanding by Coupon as of October 1991

Coupon	Projected Rem Term	All Pools # of Pools	Rem Bal ($ millions)	WAC	Rem Term
6 1/2		18	87.0	7.15	111
7	327	25	166.8	7.94	134
7 1/2	290	37	767.5	9.13	268
8	350	172	1,494.2	8.99	277
8 1/2	350	1,476	7,792.1	9.28	337
9	354	4,724	29,753.8	9.67	342
9 1/2	348	2,819	16,924.2	10.13	333
10	310	919	6,238.9	10.58	325
10 1/2	310	148	1,060.2	11.10	321
11	335	30	79.0	11.67	287
11 1/2	300	6	25.6	12.19	203
12	253	8	13.8	13.07	214
12 1/2	241	3	8.0	13.42	220
13	224				

Source: Goldman, Sachs & Co.

Fannie Mae also has a swap program similar to that of Freddie Mac, through which it issues most of its MBSs.

There are four standard MBS programs established by Fannie Mae, which we discuss below. In addition to its regular programs, Fannie Mae issues securities known as "boutique" securities. These are securities that are issued through negotiated transactions and not backed by one of the mortgage loan types in its regular program.

Type of guarantee. All Fannie Mae MBSs are fully modified passthroughs.

Number of lenders permitted in the pool. The Cash Program includes only multiple-lender pools. (Recall that in this program Fannie Mae purchases mortgage loans from various lenders and then creates a pool to collateralize the PCs.) In the Guarantor/Swap program there are both single-lender and multiple-lender pools.

Mortgage design of the loans. Three of the four standard programs have pools backed by mortgage loans that are level-payment fixed-rate mortgages. The fourth standard program is an MBS collateralized by adjustable-rate mortgage loans. These ARMs are adjusted to the one-year Treasury index; they have a 2% annual adjustment cap and a lifetime cap of 6%.

In its boutique program, the passthroughs can be backed by either fixed-rate or adjustable-rate conventional mortgage loans. In the former case, there are boutique securities in which the underlying mortgage loans are GPMs, GEMs, and balloons. The boutique securities backed by adjustable-rate mortgage loans can have, as their underlying mortgages, conventional ARMs indexed off the Federal Home Loan Bank's 11th District Cost of Funds.

Characteristics of the mortgage loans in the pool. The key underwriting standards for the mortgage loans are summarized below:

- *mortgage loans permitted in the pool:* Two of the four standard programs are backed by conventional mortgages. One is backed by FHA-insured or VA-guaranteed mortgages. The two programs backed by conventional mortgages are called *Conventional*

MBSs. The MBSs that are backed by FHA-insured or VA-guaranteed mortgages are called *Government MBSs.*

- *maximum size of a loan:* The maximum loan size is the same as for Freddie Mac PCs.
- *amount of seasoning permitted:* There are no limits on seasoning.
- *assumability of mortgages:* No assumable mortgages are permitted in a pool.
- *maturity:* The two programs backed by conventional mortgages are 30-year and 15-year MBSs, commonly referred to as the *Conventional Long-Term* and *Conventional Intermediate-Term MBSs,* respectively. The 15-year MBSs are also known as "dwarfs." The MBSs that are backed by 30-year FHA-insured or VA-guaranteed mortgages are called *Government Long-Term MBSs.*
- *net interest spread permitted:* In general, the net interest spread can be 50 to 250 basis points for both programs.

Payment procedure. The stated delay is 55 days and the actual delay 24 days.

Minimum pool size. The minimum pool size is $1 million.

Information about the outstanding remaining mortgage balance, number of pools, and weighted average coupon of 30-year FHLMC MBSs by coupon is reported in Table 8-5.

CONVENTIONAL PASSTHROUGHS

Conventional passthroughs, also called *private label passthrough securities* and *AA passthroughs,* are issued by thrifts, commercial banks, and private conduits.[3] As we explained in Chapter 2, private conduits purchase nonconforming mortgages, pool them, and then sell passthroughs in which the collateral is the underlying pool of nonconforming mort-

---

[3]At one time these passthroughs were referred as "Connie Macs."

Table 8-5

30-Year Fannie Mae MBSs Outstanding by Coupon as of October 1991

Coupon	Projected Rem Term	All Pools			
		# of Pools	Rem Bal ($ millions)	WAC	Rem Term
6 1/2		276	667.5	7.40	111
7		445	1,199.6	7.96	154
7 1/2	300	691	2,144.0	8.72	209
8	345	3,249	10,050.8	8.83	259
8 1/2	350	7,355	25,455.3	9.26	300
9	354	16,809	71,567.4	9.68	326
9 1/2	348	18,621	69,655.0	10.11	323
10	310	11,172	33,240.9	10.60	316
10 1/2	310	3,269	6,691.7	11.13	303
11	340	2,329	2,372.1	11.73	274
11 1/2	340	1,545	947.2	12.27	245
12	280	2,151	943.1	12.77	237
12 1/2	236	1,497	480.6	13.30	234
13	257	1,079	264.0	13.77	233
13 1/2		319	56.3	14.27	222

Source: Goldman, Sachs & Co.

gages. The private conduits that issue passthroughs are doing what the government created the agency conduits to do, without any guarantees (implicit or explicit) from the U.S. government.

Although the amount of conventional passthroughs is small compared to agency passthroughs, this market can be expected to grow significantly for the reasons explained in Chapter 2. Table 2-2 shows origination of private passthroughs. As of September 1991, the outstanding amount of private-label passthroughs was $92 billion.

Unlike agency passthroughs, conventional mortgage passthroughs must be registered with the Securities and Exchange Commission. As noted in Chapter 2, registration requirements have been modified by the SEC to accommodate the nuances of passthrough underwriting.

Conventional mortgage passthroughs are rated by commercial rating agencies such as Moody's and Standard &

Poor's. To obtain a high investment quality rating of double A or better, so that they can qualify under the Secondary Market Enhancement Act of 1984, they are supported by credit enhancements. The importance of this private credit enhancement should not be underestimated. The development of private credit enhancement is the key to the success of this market and, indeed, the key to the development of all asset securitization.

Credit Enhancement

Credit enhancement may take any one of several forms: (1) corporate guarantees, (2) letters of credit, (3) bond insurance, or (4) senior/subordinated interests.

With a corporate guarantee, the issuer of a conventional passthrough uses its own credit rating to back the security. Citicorp and Travelers, two issuers of conventional passthroughs, enhance their issues in this way. The cost of a letter of credit is relatively high because of the limited number of financial institutions willing to issue such guarantees, and therefore this form of credit enhancement is not common. With the third form of credit enhancement, an insurance bond is obtained to cover timely payment of interest and principal. The rating of the insurance company that writes the policy must be equal to or higher than the rating that the issuer seeks for the passthrough. For example, if an issuer seeks a double-A rating for the passthrough, it cannot obtain insurance from an insurance company with a single-A rating. Financial Guarantee Insurance Corporation (FGIC), Financial Security Assurance (FSA), and Capital Markets Assurance Corporation (CAPMAC) are insurance companies that underwrite policies for conventional passthroughs.

Senior/subordinated structure. The fourth form of credit enhancement is the senior/subordinated structure, also known as the *A/B passthrough*. In this structure a mortgage pool is partitioned into senior certificates and subordinated certificates. The senior certificate holder has priority on the cash flow from the underlying collateral. It is the senior certificates that are rated and sold to investors as conventional passthroughs. The subordinated certificates absorb the default risk. They can be either retained or sold to investors willing to accept the greater default risk.

The amount of subordinated certificates relative to senior certificates within a mortgage pool will determine its credit rating. The greater the portion of subordinated certificates relative to senior certificates, the higher the credit rating that can be obtained. In rating conventional passthroughs, Moody's and Standard & Poor's have established credit support guidelines for a benchmark pool of high-quality loans needed to determine a specific rating. The specific pool of mortgage loans to be rated is then compared to the benchmark pool, adjusted for any deviations of the pool under consideration and the benchmark pool.[4] Consideration is given to the distribution of loan-to-value ratios in the pool to be rated, the expected severity of loss, the size of the pool, the geographic concentration of the loans, the quality of the servicing agent, and hazard coverage.

In addition to credit support, protection is required in a senior/subordinated structure to ensure against a temporary shortfall in the cash flow from the subordinated class needed to satisfy payments to the senior class. The safeguards against such shortfalls can take one of two forms: a reserve fund or a shifting interest mechanism. With the former, a reserve fund is created by diverting principal payments from the subordinated class; this fund then serves to protect against cash flow shortfalls in the payments to the senior class. No reserve fund is created in a shifting mechanism structure. Protection against shortfalls is accomplished by diverting prepayments that would otherwise be payable to the subordinated class and directing them to the senior class. This distribution mechanism effectively increases the amount of subordination of the subordinated class.

Since 1988, the senior/subordinated (or A/B passthrough) structure has been the most common structure. As

---

[4] A description of the rating methodology used by Moody's is given in *Moody's Approach to Rating Whole Loan Mortgage-Backed Securities* (Moody's Investor Services, January 1987). For Standard & Poor's, the methodology is described in *Credit Review* (Standard & Poor's, October 19, 1987). For a numerical illustration of the methodology, see the appendix to Anand Bhattacharya and Peter J. Cannon, "Senior-Subordinated Mortgage Pass-Throughs," in Frank J. Fabozzi, ed., *Advances and Innovations in Bond and Mortgage Markets* (Chicago: Probus Publishing, 1989).

explained in Chapter 2, the increased use of this structure was not an accident. Certain Internal Revenue regulations concerning the tax treatment of multiclass passthroughs made this structure feasible. However, the recent capital guidelines for banks require that those issuing conventional passthroughs—such as Citicorp—hold capital against these pools. Consequently, the use of this structure by banks may decline in the future.

Mortgage Design of the Loans

The underlying pool of conventional mortgage loans may be fixed-rate or adjustable-rate. Prior to 1987, most conventional passthroughs were backed by fixed-rate mortgage loans; after 1987, the majority of conventional passthroughs issued were collateralized by adjustable-rate mortgage loans.

SECONDARY MARKET TRADING MECHANICS

In Chapter 2, we discussed the secondary market for mortgage-backed securities. Table 2-4 of that chapter shows trading activity of all agency MBSs. Here we will confine our discussion to the trading mechanics unique to passthroughs.

Passthroughs are quoted in the same manner as U.S. Treasury coupon securities. A quote of 94-05 means 94 and 5/32nds of par value, or 94.15625% of par value. As explained in Chapter 9, the yield corresponding to a price must be qualified by an assumption concerning prepayments.

Passthroughs are identified by a pool prefix and pool number. This information is provided by the agency. The prefix indicates the type of passthrough. For example, a pool prefix of 20 for a Freddie Mac PC means that the underlying pool consists of conventional mortgages with an original maturity of 15 years. A pool prefix of AR for a Ginnie Mae MBS means that the underlying pool consists of adjustable-rate mortgages. The pool number indicates the specific mortgages underlying the passthrough and the issuer of the passthrough.

Many trades occur while a pool is still unspecified and therefore no pool information is known at the time of the trade. As we noted earlier, this kind of trade is known as a "TBA" (to be announced) trade. What does an investor that purchases, say, $1 million GNMA 8's on a TBA basis receive? The investor can receive up to three pools, the pool numbers being announced shortly before the settlement date. Why three possible pools? Because the Public Securities Association (PSA) has established guidelines for standards of delivery and settlement of mortgage-backed securities,[5] under which our hypothetical TBA trade would permit three possible pools to be delivered. The option of what pools to deliver is left with the seller, as long as they satisfy the PSA guidelines. In contrast to TBA trades, a pool number may be specified. In this case the transaction will involve the delivery of the pool specifically designated.[6]

There are many seasoned issues of the same agency with the same coupon rate outstanding at a given point in time. Each issue is backed by a different pool of mortgage loans. For example, there are many seasoned pools of GNMA 8's. One issue may be backed by a pool of mortgage loans in which all the properties are located in California, while another may be backed by a pool of mortgage loans in which all the properties are in New Jersey. Yet another may be backed by a pool of mortgage loans in which the properties are from several regions of the country. Which pool are dealers referring to when they talk about GNMA 8's? They are not referring to any specific pool. Instead they mean a generic security. However, the prepayment characteristics of passthroughs with underlying pools from different parts of the country are different. Thus, the projected prepayment rates for passthroughs reported by dealer firms are for generic passthroughs. A particular pool purchased may have a materially different pre-

[5]Public Securities Association, *Uniform Practices for the Clearance and Settlement of Mortgage-Backed Securities*. More specifically, the requirement for good delivery permits a maximum of three pools per $1 million traded, or a maximum of four pools per $1 million for coupons of 12% or more.

[6]For a further discussion of specified pools, see Chuck Ramsey and J. Michael Henderson, "Specified Pools," in Frank J. Fabozzi, ed., *The Handbook of Mortgage-Backed Securities*, rev. ed. (Chicago: Probus Publishing, 1988), pp. 115–130.

payment speed from the generic. Moreover, when an investor purchases a passthrough without specifying a pool number, the seller can deliver the worst-paying pools from its portfolio as long as they satisfy good delivery requirements.

In addition, in TBA trades there is another advantage granted to the seller. PSA delivery standards permit an under- or overdelivery tolerance of 2.5% per million traded. This means that if $1 million of par value is sold at par, the seller may deliver to the buyer passthroughs with a par value anywhere between $975,000 and $1,025,000. This delivery option is valuable. To understand why, suppose that interest rates decline between the trade date and the settlement date. The value of passthroughs will rise and therefore it will be beneficial for the seller to deliver less than $1 million. The opposite is true if interest rates rise between the trade date and the settlement date: the seller will deliver $1,025,000.

Investors must recognize the valuable delivery options that are granted to the seller in a TBA trade. These options can be taken away from the seller by engaging in a specified trade. However, the cost of such a trade, as measured by the bid-ask spread, is larger than for a TBA trade, with the difference being dependent on the specific pool sought by the buyer.[7]

Dollar Rolls

In the government securities market, dealers can finance their inventory position by using an instrument known as a *repurchase agreement,* or simply, a *repo.* In a repo, a dealer uses government securities purchased as collateral for borrowing funds. The counterparty to the transaction is a client of the dealer. The counterparty lends funds. The customer willing to be a counterparty to a repo would be one that is interested in making a short-term investment. At the end of

[7]Readers familiar with Treasury bond and note futures contracts recognize that the seller of the contract has several delivery options. There have been numerous published studies that have attempted to estimate the economic value of the various delivery options. To our knowledge, no such studies have been undertaken to assess the economic value of the delivery option in a TBA trade. This information would be useful for buyers considering a TBA trade or paying a higher price for a specified pool trade.

the repo term, the dealer pays the customer the amount borrowed plus accrued interest, and the government security is returned to the dealer.

The dealer can also use a repo to cover a short position in a government security.[8] In this case the dealer seeks a customer that may need funds and that possesses the specific government security that the dealer is short. The dealer agrees to loan funds to the customer with the sought-after government security used as collateral. At the end of the repo term, the dealer receives the funds lent plus interest and returns an identical government security to the customer.

Thus, a repo is used by a dealer to either finance a long position in a government security or cover a short position. The key is that at the end of the repo term, the same security is returned to the counterparty.

This vehicle for covering a short position is less practical in the passthrough market. Dealers would like to borrow passthroughs to cover a short position but would find it difficult to return a passthrough backed by the same pool borrowed from the customer.

A vehicle created for the passthrough market to overcome this drawback is the dollar roll transaction. It is similar to a repo in that it is a collateralized borrowing. However, at the end of the term of the agreement, the dealer firm agrees to return a "substantially identical" passthrough, not necessarily the identical one borrowed.[9]

This arrangement has made the secondary market operate more smoothly, since it enables dealers to cover short positions more easily. The yield offered on dollar roll transactions is lower[10] than in the repo market, reflecting the risk that the lender of the securities faces—namely, the risk that the dealer firm may return passthroughs less attractive than those it borrowed.

---

[8]This is often referred to as a reverse repo.

[9]The obvious question is: What is a "substantially identical" passthrough? The conditions that must be met for a passthrough to satisfy the substantially identical standard are described in "Definition of the Term *Substantially the Same* for Holders of Debt Instruments as Used in Certain Audit Guides and a Statement of Position," The American Institute of Certified Public Accountants, Statement of Position 90-3, February 13, 1990.

[10]A lower yield is beneficial to the lender of the securities (which is effectively borrowing funds) because it means a lower financing rate.

FORWARD, FUTURES, AND OPTIONS ON PASSTHROUGH SECURITIES

In Chapter 3 we explained the various instruments that originators can use to hedge the interest rate risk associated with originating mortgages. Investors and dealers are also concerned with the adverse effects of interest rate movements on their portfolio or position. In the remainder of this chapter we briefly describe several contracts that are available. The reader is referred to Chapter 3 for a general description of forward, futures, and options (including futures options).

Forward and Futures Contracts

A forward contract is a contract negotiated between two parties, and the agreement is not traded on an organized exchange. There is an active forward market for passthroughs. The forward contract requires that the seller deliver to the buyer a specified amount of passthroughs at a predetermined date in the future at the forward price. The specific pools that must be delivered are not indicated; that is, the forward contract involves a TBA pool, where the seller has the right to deliver any pools that satisfy the PSA standards for good delivery. Forward contracts in this market settle on a specific date each month depending on the type of passthrough (Ginnie Mae, Fannie Mae, or Freddie Mac) and the coupon. Typically, the maximum maturity is three months.

A futures contract is an exchange-traded product. The Chicago Board of Trade began trading a futures contract on a GNMA passthrough in June 1989.[11] It is a cash-settlement contract. Each month a new GNMA futures contract begins trading with settlement in four months. The underlying GNMA

---

[11]In October 1975, the CBOT introduced the GNMA Collateralized Deposit Receipt futures contract. This contract was the first interest-rate futures contract traded in the United States. The contract was based on a GNMA passthrough with a coupon rate of 8%. Delivery of any other coupon was permissible with appropriate adjustments to the invoice price, a delivery practice followed in the Treasury bond futures contract. The contract was unsuccessful and was discontinued a few years later. In September 1978, the CBOT introduced the Certificate Delivery GNMA futures contract. About three years later, this contract was discontinued.

is one with a specific coupon, the coupon being established by the CBOT based on the current coupon GNMA for the month that the contract begins trading.

Options

There is a futures option traded on the CBOT in which the underlying futures contract is the GNMA futures contract just described. This contract is basically used to hedge current coupon GNMAs. Using it to hedge other coupons introduces basis risk, which was described in Chapter 3.

There is also an active over-the-counter market developing for passthrough securities. These contracts are customized by dealer firms for their clients. Because of the customization, the underlying passthrough can be for any coupon, any strike price, and any expiration date sought by the customer. The disadvantage of all over-the-counter options is the exposure to counterparty risk and the lack of liquidity. The latter feature is typically unimportant to a customer.

9

Price and Yield Conventions for Passthroughs

A basic tenet of finance is that the price of a financial asset is equal to the present value of its expected cash flow. Consequently, to determine the price of a financial asset it is necessary to (1) estimate the expected cash flow and (2) discount that cash flow at an appropriate interest rate (or set of interest rates). Neither (1) nor (2) is easy to do for a passthrough, since its cash flow depends on the cash flow of the underlying pool of mortgage loans. As explained in Chapter 5, the cash flow of a mortgage loan consists of monthly mortgage payments representing interest, the scheduled repayment of principal, and any prepayments. Because prepayments are difficult to predict accurately, the cash flow of a passthrough cannot be known with certainty. Determining the appropriate interest rate (or rates) at which to discount the cash flow is not a simple matter either. It is complicated not just by default risk, but more important, by the complexity of the prepayment option given to all the borrowers whose mortgage loans are in the pool.

In this chapter we discuss the various conventions for calculating the price and yield of a passthrough. We refer to these measures as conventions because they are based on prepayment benchmarks established in the industry. Moreover, yield measures have well-known deficiencies that make them inappropriate for assessing the value of any asset except a zero-coupon instrument. In Chapter 13 we present several methodologies to evaluate passthroughs.

We begin this chapter with an explanation of the various prepayment benchmark conventions. Our aim here is simply to illustrate the mechanics involved. At the end of this chapter, we describe the genesis of the convention currently in use and critically evaluate it. In Chapter 10, we discuss factors that affect prepayments. Given the estimated prepayment rate, we then show how the cash flow, yield, and price of a passthrough are calculated. While we walk the reader through all of the calculations, most practitioners will use software available from vendors that provide standard fixed-income calculations.

PREPAYMENT BENCHMARK CONVENTIONS

Estimating the cash flow from a passthrough requires forecasting prepayments. Several conventions have been used as a benchmark for prepayment rates: (1) Federal Housing Administration experience, (2) the constant prepayment rate, and (3) the Public Securities Association prepayment benchmark.[1] Although the first is no longer used, we discuss it because of its historical significance.

FHA Experience

At one time, the most commonly used benchmark for prepayment rates was the prepayment experience for 30-year mortgages derived from an FHA probability table on mortgage survivals. Using FHA experience, the cash flow is projected for a mortgage pool, assuming that the prepayment rate is the same as the FHA experience ("100% FHA") or some multiple of FHA experience (faster than FHA experience or slower than FHA experience).

[1] In the early stages of the development of the passthrough market, cash flows were calculated assuming no prepayments for 12 years. In the twelfth year, all the mortgages in the pool were assumed to prepay. This approach was naive and was replaced by the "FHA prepayment experience" approach.

Despite their popularity in the past, prepayment projections based on FHA experience were not necessarily indicative of the prepayment rate for a particular pool. The explanation for their unreliability is that FHA experience represents an estimate of prepayments on all FHA-insured mortgages originated over various interest rate periods. Since prepayment rates are tied to interest rate cycles, an average prepayment rate over various cycles does not have much value for estimating prepayments. In addition, a new FHA table is published periodically, leading to confusion as to which FHA table prepayments should be based on. Consequently, the estimated prepayments using FHA experience may be misleading, and the resulting cash flow stream is not meaningful for valuing passthroughs.

Constant Prepayment Rate

Another benchmark for projecting prepayments and the cash flow of a passthrough is to assume that some fraction of the remaining principal in the pool is prepaid *each* month for the remaining term of the mortgages. The prepayment rate assumed for a pool, called the *constant prepayment rate* (CPR),[2] is based on the characteristics of the pool (including its historical prepayment experience) and the current and expected future economic environment. The advantage of this approach is its simplicity. What's more, it allows for quick analysis of changes in economic conditions that influence prepayment rates and changes in the historical prepayment pattern of a pool.

The CPR is an annual prepayment rate. To estimate monthly prepayments, the CPR must be converted into a monthly prepayment rate, commonly referred to as the *single monthly mortality rate* (SMM). The following formula can be used to determine the SMM for a given CPR:

$$\text{SMM} = 1 - (1 - \text{CPR})^{1/12} \qquad (1)$$

[2] One dealer firm, Bear Stearns, refers to this convention as the constant prepayment percentage (CPP).

For example, suppose that the CPR used to estimate prepayments is 6%. The corresponding SMM is:

$$\begin{aligned} SMM &= 1 - (1 - .06)^{1/12} \\ &= 1 - (.94)^{.083333} = .005143 \end{aligned}$$

An SMM of w% means that approximately w% of the remaining mortgage balance at the beginning of the month after subtracting the scheduled principal payment will prepay that month. That is,

prepayment for month t = SMM × (beginning mortgage balance for month t − scheduled principal for month t)

For example, suppose that an investor owns a pass-through in which the remaining mortgage balance at the beginning of some month is $50,525. Assuming that the SMM is 0.5143% and the scheduled principal payment is $67, then the estimated prepayment for the month is:

$$.005143 \times (\$50,525 - \$67) = \$260$$

PSA Standard Prepayment Benchmark

Although initially developed for collateralized mortgage obligations, the Public Securities Association standard prepayment benchmark[3] has been applied to project cash flows for all mortgage-related securities. The PSA standard prepayment benchmark is expressed as a monthly series of annual constant prepayment rates. The basic PSA model assumes that prepayment rates will be low for newly originated mortgages and then will speed up as the mortgages become seasoned.

---

[3]This benchmark is commonly referred to as a prepayment model, suggesting that it can be used to estimate prepayments. As we explain in Chapter 10, characterization of this benchmark as a prepayment model is inappropriate.

The PSA standard benchmark assumes the following prepayment rates for 30-year mortgages:

(1) a CPR of 0.2% for the first month, increased by 0.2% per month for the next 30 months until it reaches 6% per year, and

(2) a 6% CPR for the remaining years.

This benchmark is referred to as "100% PSA" and can be expressed as follows:

$$\text{if } t \leq 30 \text{ then CPR} = \frac{6\% \, t}{30}$$
$$\text{if } t > 30 \text{ then CPR} = 6\%$$

where t is the number of months since the mortgage originated.

Slower or faster speeds are then referred to as some percentage of PSA. For example, 50% PSA means one-half the CPR of the PSA prepayment rate; 150% PSA means one and a half the CPR of the PSA prepayment rate.

The CPR is converted to an SMM using equation 1. For example, the SMMs for month 5, month 20, and months 31 through 360 assuming 100% PSA are calculated as follows:

$$\text{for month 5: CPR} = \frac{6\% \, (5)}{30} = 1\% = .01$$

$$\text{SMM} = 1 - (1 - .01)^{1/12}$$
$$= 1 - (.99)^{.083333} = .000837$$

$$\text{for month 20: CPR} = \frac{6\% \, (20)}{30} = 4\% = .04$$

$$\text{SMM} = 1 - (1 - .04)^{1/12}$$
$$= 1 - (.96)^{.083333} = .003396$$

$$\text{for months 31–360: CPR} = 6\%$$

$$\text{SMM} = 1 - (1 - .06)^{1/12}$$
$$= 1 - (.94)^{.083333} = .005143$$

The SMMs for month 5, month 20, and months 31 through 360 assuming 150% PSA are computed as follows:

$$\text{for month 5: CPR} = \frac{6\% \ (5)}{30} = 1\% = .01$$
$$150\% \ \text{PSA} = 1.5 \ (.01) = .015$$

$$\text{SMM} = 1 - (1 - .015)^{1/12}$$
$$= 1 - (.985)^{.083333} = .001259$$

$$\text{for month 20: CPR} = \frac{6\% \ (20)}{30} = 4\% = .04$$
$$150\% \ \text{PSA} = 1.5 \ (.04) = .06$$

$$\text{SMM} = 1 - (1 - .06)^{1/12}$$
$$= 1 - (.94)^{.083333} = .005143$$

$$\text{for months 31--360: CPR} = 6\% = .06$$
$$150\% \ \text{PSA} = 1.5 \ (.06) = .09$$

$$\text{SMM} = 1 - (1 - .09)^{1/12}$$
$$= 1 - (.91)^{.083333} = .007828$$

Notice that the SMM assuming 150% PSA is not just 1.5 times the SMM assuming 100% PSA. It is the CPR that is a multiple of the CPR assuming 100% PSA.

The SMMs for month 5, month 20, and months 31 through 360 assuming 50% PSA are as follows:

$$\text{for month 5: CPR} = \frac{6\% \ (5)}{30} = 1\% = .01$$
$$50\% \ \text{PSA} = 0.5 \ (.01) = .005$$

$$\text{SMM} = 1 - (1 - .005)^{1/12}$$
$$= 1 - (.995)^{.083333} = .000418$$

$$\text{for month 20: CPR} = \frac{6\% \ (20)}{30} = 4\% = .04$$
$$50\% \ \text{PSA} = 0.5 \ (.04) = .02$$

$$\text{SMM} = 1 - (1 - .02)^{1/12}$$
$$= 1 - (.98)^{.083333} = .001682$$

for months 31–360: CPR = 6% = .06

$$50\% \text{ PSA} = 0.5\,(.06) = .03$$

$$\text{SMM} = 1 - (1 - .03)^{1/12}$$
$$= 1 - (.97)^{.083333} = .002535$$

Once again, notice that the SMM assuming 50% PSA is not just one-half the SMM assuming 100% PSA. It is the CPR that is a multiple of the CPR assuming 100% PSA.

CONSTRUCTING THE PROJECTED CASH FLOW

To construct a cash flow schedule for a passthrough based on some assumed prepayment rate (or prepayment rates), the formulas presented in this section are used.

Projected Monthly Mortgage Payment

The formula to obtain the projected monthly mortgage payment for any month is:

$$\overline{MP}_t = \overline{MB}_{t-1}\left[\frac{[i\,(1 + i)^{n-t+1}]}{[(1 + i)^{n-t+1} - 1]}\right]$$

where

$\overline{MP}_t$ = projected monthly mortgage payment for month t

$\overline{MB}_{t-1}$ = projected mortgage balance at the end of month $t-1$ given prepayments have occurred in the past (which is the projected mortgage balance at the beginning of month t)

n = original number of months of mortgage

i = simple monthly interest rate (annual interest rate/12)

Projected Monthly Mortgage Interest and Servicing

To compute the portion of the projected monthly mortgage payment that is interest, the following formula can be used:

$$\bar{I}_t = \overline{MB}_{t-1}\, i \tag{3}$$

where

$\bar{I}_t$ = projected monthly interest for month t.

Equation 3 states that the projected monthly interest is found by multiplying the mortgage balance at the end of the previous month by the monthly interest rate. The projected monthly interest rate can be divided into two parts: (1) the projected net monthly interest rate after the servicing fee and (2) the servicing fee.[4] The formulas are as follows:

$$\overline{NI}_t = \overline{MB}_{t-1}\, (i - s) \tag{4}$$

$$\bar{S}_t = \overline{MB}_{t-1}\, s \tag{5}$$

where

$\overline{NI}_t$ = projected interest net of servicing fee for month t

$\bar{S}_t$ = projected servicing fee for month t

s = servicing fee rate

Projected Monthly Scheduled Principal and Prepayment

The projected monthly scheduled principal payment is found by subtracting the projected monthly interest from the projected monthly mortgage payment. In terms of our notation:

$$\overline{SP}_t = \overline{MP}_t - \bar{I}_t$$

[4]Extension to the guaranteeing fee is straightforward.

where

$$\overline{SP}_t = \text{projected monthly scheduled principal payment for month t}$$

As explained earlier, the projected monthly principal prepayment is found by multiplying the SMM by the difference between the outstanding balance at the beginning of the month (the ending balance in the previous month), and the projected scheduled principal payment for the month. That is,

$$\overline{PR}_t = SMM_t\,(\overline{MB}_{t-1} - \overline{SP}_t)$$

where

$$\overline{PR}_t = \text{projected monthly principal prepayment for month t}$$
$$SMM_t = \text{assumed single monthly mortality rate for month t}$$

Investor's Cash Flow

The cash flow to the investor is then the sum of (1) the projected monthly interest net of the servicing fee, (2) the projected monthly scheduled principal payment, and (3) the projected monthly principal prepayment. That is,

$$\overline{CF}_t = \overline{NI}_t + \overline{SP}_t + \overline{PR}_t$$

where

$$\overline{CF}_t = \text{projected cash flow for month t}$$

Alternatively, this can be expressed as:

$$\overline{CF}_t = \bar{I}_t + \overline{SP}_t + \overline{PR}_t - \bar{S}_t$$

Illustrations

The following illustrations show how to apply the formulas presented above.

Suppose that an investor owns a passthrough with an original mortgage balance of $100,000, a mortgage rate of 9.5%, a 0.5% servicing fee, and 360 months to maturity. Suppose also that the investor believes a CPR of 6% is appropriate.

Using our notation:

$$MB_0 = \$100,000$$
$$n = 360$$
$$i = 0.0079167 \; (.095/12)$$
$$s = 0.0004167 \; (0.005/12)$$
$$CPR = 6\%$$

Earlier we showed that a CPR of 6% is equal to an SMM of 0.5143%. Thus,

$$SMM_t = 0.005143 \quad \text{for all } t \; (t = 1, \ldots, 360)$$

Table 9-1 shows the projected cash flow for this passthrough for selected months. We will explain the meaning of the fourth column in Table 9-1 shortly.

Suppose that for the passthrough in the previous illustration the assumed CPR is 8.5% instead of 6%. The SMM would be .007375. Table 9-2 shows the projected cash flow for selected months.

Suppose that the PSA prepayment model is used to project prepayments for the passthrough. In particular, assume that the investor believes the mortgages will prepay at 100% PSA. Table 9-3 shows the cash flow for the passthrough for selected months. The SMMs shown in the third column agree with those computed earlier in this chapter. If instead of 100% PSA, 150% PSA is assumed, the cash flow for the passthrough for selected months is shown in Table 9-4. The SMMs shown in the third column are the same as those we computed earlier. Finally, suppose the prepayment rate is assumed to be 50% PSA. For selected months, Table 9-5 shows the cash flow.

Short Cut Approach

In the formulas given above, the process begins with a determination of the monthly mortgage balance at the beginning of the month given prepayments that have occurred in the past. While this can be determined using the procedure shown in Tables 9-1 through 9-5, there are formulas that can be used to compute the projected cash flow without knowing the mortgage balance at the beginning of the month. First, it is necessary to introduce the following concept:[5]

Let

$$\overline{b}_t = (1 - SMM_t)(1 - SMM_{t-1}) \ldots (1 - SMM_2)$$
$$(1 - SMM_1)$$

where

$\overline{b}_t$ = the projected mortgage balance in month t per $1 of the original principal given prepayments through month t

Then, the projected monthly mortgage payment in month t is:

$$\overline{MP}_t = \overline{b}_{t-1} MP$$

where

MP = monthly mortgage payment on the original principal assuming no prepayments

---

[5]See the appendix to Lakhbir S. Hayre and Cyrus Mohebbi, "Mortgage Pass-Through Securities," in Frank J. Fabozzi, ed., *Advances and Innovations in the Bond and Mortgage Markets* (Chicago: Probus Publishing, 1990).

Table 9-1

Projected Cash Flow Assuming a 6% CPR

Original balance $100,000
Mortgage rate 9.5%
Servicing fee 0.5%
Term 360 months
CPR 6%

t (1)	$\overline{MB}_{t-1}$ (2)	SMM_t (3)	$\overline{b}_{t-1}$ (4)	$\overline{MP}_t$ (5)	$\overline{SP}_t$ (6)	$\overline{I}_t$ (7)	$\overline{PR}_t$ (8)	$\overline{S}_t$ (9)	$\overline{CF}_t$ (10)	$\overline{MB}_t$ (11)
1	100,000	0.005143	1.00000	841	49	792	514	41	1,313	99,437
2	99,437	0.005143	0.99486	837	49	787	511	41	1,306	98,876
3	98,876	0.005143	0.98974	832	49	783	508	40	1,300	98,319
4	98,319	0.005143	0.98465	828	50	778	505	40	1,293	97,764
5	97,764	0.005143	0.97959	824	50	774	503	39	1,286	97,211
6	97,211	0.005143	0.97455	819	50	770	500	39	1,280	96,662
7	96,662	0.005143	0.96954	815	50	765	497	39	1,273	96,115
8	96,115	0.005143	0.96455	811	50	761	494	38	1,266	95,571
9	95,571	0.005143	0.95959	807	50	757	491	38	1,260	95,029
10	95,029	0.005143	0.95465	803	50	752	488	37	1,253	94,490
11	94,490	0.005143	0.94974	799	51	748	486	37	1,247	93,954
12	93,954	0.005143	0.94486	794	51	744	483	36	1,240	93,420
13	93,420	0.005143	0.94000	790	51	740	480	36	1,234	92,889
14	92,889	0.005143	0.93517	786	51	735	477	36	1,228	92,361
15	92,361	0.005143	0.93036	782	51	731	475	35	1,221	91,835
16	91,835	0.005143	0.92557	778	51	727	472	35	1,215	91,312
17	91,312	0.005143	0.92081	774	51	723	469	35	1,209	90,791
18	90,791	0.005143	0.91608	770	52	719	467	34	1,202	90,273
19	90,273	0.005143	0.91136	766	52	715	464	34	1,196	89,757
20	89,757	0.005143	0.90668	762	52	711	461	33	1,190	89,244
21	89,244	0.005143	0.90201	758	52	707	459	33	1,184	88,733
...	...	...	...	...	...	...	...	...	...	...

t	$\overline{MB}_{t-1}$	SMM_t	$\overline{b}_{t-1}$	$\overline{MP}_t$	$\overline{SP}_t$	$\overline{I}_t$	$\overline{S}_t$	$\overline{PR}_t$	$\overline{CF}_t$	$\overline{MB}_t$
:	:	:	:	:	:	:	:	:	:	:
31	84,248	0.005143	0.85668	720	53	667	433	30	1,123	83,761
32	83,761	0.005143	0.85228	717	54	663	431	29	1,117	83,277
33	83,277	0.005143	0.84789	713	54	659	428	29	1,112	82,795
34	82,795	0.005143	0.84353	709	54	655	426	29	1,106	82,316
35	82,316	0.005143	0.83919	706	54	652	423	28	1,100	81,839
36	81,839	0.005143	0.83488	702	54	648	421	28	1,094	81,364
:	:	:	:	:	:	:	:	:	:	:
98	56,315	0.005143	0.60643	510	64	446	289	14	785	55,962
99	55,962	0.005143	0.60332	507	64	443	287	14	781	55,610
100	55,610	0.005143	0.60021	505	64	440	286	15	776	55,260
:	:	:	:	:	:	:	:	:	:	:
209	25,380	0.005143	0.34215	288	87	201	130	3	414	25,163
210	25,163	0.005143	0.34039	286	87	199	129	3	412	24,947
211	24,947	0.005143	0.33864	285	87	197	128	3	409	24,732
:	:	:	:	:	:	:	:	:	:	:
357	526	0.005143	0.15951	134	130	4	2	0	136	394
358	394	0.005143	0.15869	133	130	3	1	0	135	262
359	262	0.005143	0.15788	133	131	2	1	0	133	131
360	131	0.005143	0.15706	132	131	1	0	0	132	0

Key:

$\overline{MB}_{t-1}$ = projected mortgage balance at the end of month $t-1$

SMM_t = single monthly mortality

$\overline{b}_{t-1}$ = $(1 - SMM_{t-1})(1 - SMM_{t-2}) \ldots (1 - SMM_1)$

$\overline{MP}_t$ = projected monthly mortgage payment for month t

$\overline{SP}_t$ = projected monthly scheduled principal payment for month t

$\overline{I}_t$ = projected monthly interest for month t

$\overline{PR}_t$ = projected monthly principal prepayment for month t

$\overline{S}_t$ = projected servicing fee for month t

$\overline{CF}_t$ = projected cash flow for month t

Table 9-2

Projected Cash Flow Assuming an 8.5% CPR

Original balance $100,000
Mortgage rate 9.5%
Servicing fee 0.5%
Term 360 months
CPR 8.5%

t (1)	$\overline{MB}_{t-1}$ (2)	SMM_t (3)	$\overline{b}_{t-1}$ (4)	$\overline{MP}_t$ (5)	$\overline{SP}_t$ (6)	$\overline{I}_t$ (7)	$\overline{PR}_t$ (8)	$\overline{S}_t$ (9)	$\overline{CF}_t$ (10)	$\overline{MB}_t$ (11)
1	100,000	0.007375	1.00000	841	49	792	737	41	1,536	99,214
2	99,214	0.007375	0.99262	835	49	785	731	41	1,525	98,433
3	98,433	0.007375	0.98530	828	49	779	726	40	1,514	97,658
4	97,658	0.007375	0.97804	822	49	773	720	39	1,502	96,889
5	96,889	0.007375	0.97082	816	49	767	714	39	1,491	96,126
6	96,126	0.007375	0.96366	810	49	761	709	38	1,480	95,368
7	95,368	0.007375	0.95656	804	49	755	703	38	1,469	94,615
8	94,615	0.007375	0.94950	798	49	749	697	37	1,458	93,869
9	93,869	0.007375	0.94250	793	49	743	692	36	1,448	93,127
10	93,127	0.007375	0.93555	787	49	737	686	36	1,437	92,391
11	92,391	0.007375	0.92865	781	49	731	681	35	1,426	91,661
12	91,661	0.007375	0.92180	775	49	726	676	35	1,416	90,936
13	90,936	0.007375	0.91500	769	49	720	670	34	1,405	90,216
14	90,216	0.007375	0.90825	764	49	714	665	34	1,395	89,501
15	89,501	0.007375	0.90155	758	50	709	660	33	1,384	88,792
16	88,792	0.007375	0.89490	752	50	703	655	33	1,374	88,088
17	88,088	0.007375	0.88830	747	50	697	649	32	1,364	87,389
18	87,389	0.007375	0.88175	741	50	692	644	32	1,353	86,696
19	86,696	0.007375	0.87525	736	50	686	639	31	1,343	86,007

20	86,007	0.007375	0.86879	731	50	681	634	31	1,333	85,323
21	85,323	0.007375	0.86239	725	50	675	629	30	1,323	84,645
:	:	:	:	:	:	:	:	:	:	:
:	:	:	:	:	:	:	:	:	:	:
31	78,757	0.007375	0.80085	673	50	623	580	26	1,228	78,127
32	78,127	0.007375	0.79495	668	50	619	576	25	1,218	77,501
33	77,501	0.007375	0.78908	664	50	614	571	25	1,209	76,880
34	76,880	0.007375	0.78326	659	50	609	567	25	1,200	76,263
35	76,263	0.007375	0.77749	654	50	604	562	24	1,191	75,651
36	75,651	0.007375	0.77175	649	50	599	558	24	1,182	75,044
:	:	:	:	:	:	:	:	:	:	:
:	:	:	:	:	:	:	:	:	:	:
98	45,289	0.007375	0.48770	410	52	359	334	9	735	44,904
99	44,904	0.007375	0.48410	407	52	355	331	9	729	44,522
100	44,522	0.007375	0.48053	404	52	352	328	9	723	44,142
:	:	:	:	:	:	:	:	:	:	:
:	:	:	:	:	:	:	:	:	:	:
209	15,906	0.007375	0.21444	180	54	126	117	1	296	15,735
210	15,735	0.007375	0.21286	179	54	125	116	1	293	15,565
211	15,565	0.007375	0.21129	178	54	123	114	1	291	15,396
:	:	:	:	:	:	:	:	:	:	:
:	:	:	:	:	:	:	:	:	:	:
357	236	0.007375	0.07170	60	58	2	1	0	62	177
358	177	0.007375	0.07117	60	58	1	1	0	61	117
359	117	0.007375	0.07064	59	58	1	0	0	60	58
360	58	0.007375	0.07012	59	58	0	0	0	59	0

*See the key in Table 9-1.

Table 9-3

Projected Cash Flow Assuming 100% PSA

Original balance $100,000
Mortgage rate 9.5%
Servicing fee 0.5%
Term 360 months
PSA 100%

t (1)	$\overline{MB}_{t-1}$ (2)	SMM_t (3)	$\bar{b}_{t-1}$ (4)	$\overline{MP}_t$ (5)	$\overline{SP}_t$ (6)	$\bar{I}_t$ (7)	$\overline{PR}_t$ (8)	$\bar{S}_t$ (9)	$\overline{CF}_t$ (10)	$\overline{MB}_t$ (11)
1	100,000	0.000166	1.00000	841	49	792	17	42	816	99,934
2	99,934	0.000333	0.99983	841	50	791	33	42	832	99,851
3	99,851	0.000501	0.99950	840	50	790	50	42	849	99,751
4	99,751	0.000669	0.99900	840	50	790	67	42	865	99,634
5	99,634	0.000837	0.99853	839	51	789	83	42	881	99,500
6	99,500	0.001005	0.99749	839	51	788	100	41	897	99,349
7	99,349	0.001174	0.99649	838	51	787	117	41	913	99,181
8	99,181	0.001343	0.99552	837	52	785	133	41	929	98,996
9	98,996	0.001512	0.99398	836	52	784	150	41	944	98,795
10	98,795	0.001682	0.99248	835	52	782	166	41	959	98,576
11	98,576	0.001852	0.99081	833	53	780	182	41	975	98,341
12	98,341	0.002022	0.98898	832	53	779	199	41	989	98,089
13	98,089	0.002192	0.98698	830	53	777	215	41	1,004	97,821
14	97,821	0.002363	0.98481	828	54	774	231	41	1,018	97,536
15	97,536	0.002535	0.98248	826	54	772	247	41	1,033	97,235
16	97,235	0.002706	0.97999	824	54	770	263	41	1,047	96,917
17	96,917	0.002878	0.97734	822	55	767	279	40	1,060	96,584
18	96,584	0.003050	0.97453	819	55	765	294	40	1,074	96,235
19	96,235	0.003223	0.97155	817	55	762	310	40	1,087	95,870

20	95,870	0.005396	0.96842	814	55	759	325	40	1,100	95,489
21	95,489	0.005569	0.96515	812	56	756	341	40	1,113	95,093
:	:	:	:	:	:	:	:	:	:	:
:	:	:	:	:	:	:	:	:	:	:
31	90,860	0.005143	0.92392	777	58	719	467	38	1,206	90,336
32	90,336	0.005143	0.91917	773	58	715	464	38	1,200	89,814
33	89,814	0.005143	0.91444	769	58	711	462	37	1,193	89,294
34	89,294	0.005143	0.90974	765	58	707	459	37	1,187	88,777
35	88,777	0.005143	0.90506	761	58	703	456	37	1,180	88,263
36	88,263	0.005143	0.90041	757	58	699	454	37	1,174	87,751
:	:	:	:	:	:	:	:	:	:	:
:	:	:	:	:	:	:	:	:	:	:
98	60,735	0.005143	0.65403	550	69	481	312	25	837	60,354
99	60,354	0.005143	0.65067	547	69	478	310	25	832	59,975
100	59,975	0.005143	0.64732	544	70	475	308	25	827	59,597
:	:	:	:	:	:	:	:	:	:	:
:	:	:	:	:	:	:	:	:	:	:
209	27,372	0.005143	0.36901	310	94	217	140	11	459	27,138
210	27,138	0.005143	0.36711	309	94	215	139	11	436	26,905
211	26,905	0.005143	0.36522	307	94	213	138	11	434	26,673
:	:	:	:	:	:	:	:	:	:	:
:	:	:	:	:	:	:	:	:	:	:
357	567	0.005143	0.17205	145	140	4	1	0	147	425
358	425	0.005143	0.17115	144	141	3	1	0	145	283
359	283	0.005143	0.17027	143	141	2	1	0	144	141
360	141	0.005143	0.16939	142	141	1	0	0	142	0

*See the key in Table 9-1.

Table 9-4

Projected Cash Flow Assuming 150% PSA

Original balance $100,000
Mortgage rate 9.5%
Servicing fee 0.5%
Term 360 months
PSA 150%

t (1)	$\overline{MB}_{t-1}$ (2)	SMM_t (3)	$\bar{b}_{t-1}$ (4)	$\overline{MP}_t$ (5)	$\overline{SP}_t$ (6)	$\bar{I}_t$ (7)	$\overline{PR}_t$ (8)	$\bar{S}_t$ (9)	$\overline{CF}_t$ (10)	$\overline{MB}_t$ (11)
1	100,000	0.000250	1.00000	841	49	792	25	42	824	99,926
2	99,926	0.000501	0.99975	841	50	791	50	42	849	99,826
3	99,826	0.000753	0.99925	840	50	790	75	42	874	99,701
4	99,701	0.001005	0.99850	840	50	789	100	42	898	99,551
5	99,551	0.001258	0.99749	839	51	788	125	41	923	99,375
6	99,375	0.001512	0.99624	838	51	787	150	41	947	99,174
7	99,174	0.001767	0.99473	836	51	785	175	41	970	98,947
8	98,947	0.002022	0.99297	835	52	783	200	41	994	98,695
9	98,695	0.002278	0.99096	833	52	781	225	41	1,017	98,419
10	98,419	0.002535	0.98871	831	52	779	249	41	1,040	98,117
11	98,117	0.002792	0.98620	829	52	777	274	41	1,062	97,791
12	97,791	0.003050	0.98345	827	53	774	298	41	1,084	97,440
13	97,440	0.003309	0.98045	824	53	771	322	41	1,106	97,065
14	97,065	0.003569	0.97720	822	53	768	346	40	1,127	96,665
15	96,665	0.003829	0.97371	819	53	765	370	40	1,148	96,242
16	96,242	0.004090	0.96998	816	54	762	393	40	1,169	95,794
17	95,794	0.004352	0.96602	812	54	758	417	40	1,189	95,324
18	95,324	0.004615	0.96181	809	54	755	440	40	1,209	94,830
19	94,830	0.004878	0.95737	805	54	751	462	40	1,228	94,313

20	94,315	0.005143	0.95270	801	54	747	485	39	1,247	93,774
21	93,774	0.005407	0.94780	737	55	742	507	39	1,266	93,213
:	:	:	:	:	:	:	:	:	:	:
:	:	:	:	:	:	:	:	:	:	:
51	87,224	0.007828	0.88695	746	55	691	682	36	1,392	86,487
52	86,487	0.007828	0.88001	740	55	685	677	36	1,381	85,755
53	85,755	0.007828	0.87312	734	55	679	671	36	1,369	85,028
54	85,028	0.007828	0.86628	728	55	673	665	35	1,358	84,308
55	84,308	0.007828	0.85950	723	55	667	660	35	1,347	83,593
56	83,593	0.007828	0.85277	717	55	662	654	35	1,335	82,884
:	:	:	:	:	:	:	:	:	:	:
:	:	:	:	:	:	:	:	:	:	:
98	48,647	0.007828	0.52386	440	55	385	380	20	801	48,211
99	48,211	0.007828	0.51976	457	55	382	377	20	794	47,779
100	47,779	0.007828	0.51569	454	55	378	374	20	787	47,350
:	:	:	:	:	:	:	:	:	:	:
:	:	:	:	:	:	:	:	:	:	:
209	16,241	0.007828	0.21895	134	56	129	127	7	304	16,059
210	16,059	0.007828	0.21724	135	56	127	125	7	301	15,878
211	15,878	0.007828	0.21554	131	56	126	124	7	299	15,699
:	:	:	:	:	:	:	:	:	:	:
:	:	:	:	:	:	:	:	:	:	:
357	226	0.007828	0.06842	58	56	1	1	0	58	169
358	169	0.007828	0.06789	57	56	1	1	0	58	112
359	112	0.007828	0.06735	57	56	1	0	0	57	56
360	56	0.007828	0.06683	56	56	0	0	0	56	0

*See the key in Table 9-1.

Table 9-5

Projected Cash Flow Assuming 50% PSA

Original balance $100,000
Mortgage rate 9.5%
Servicing fee 0.5%
Term 360 months
PSA 50%

t (1)	$\overline{MB}_{t-1}$ (2)	SMM_t (3)	$\overline{b}_{t-1}$ (4)	$\overline{MP}_t$ (5)	$\overline{SP}_t$ (6)	$\overline{I}_t$ (7)	$\overline{PR}_t$ (8)	$\overline{S}_t$ (9)	$\overline{CF}_t$ (10)	$\overline{MB}_t$ (11)
1	100,000	0.000083	1.00000	841	49	792	8	42	808	99,942
2	99,942	0.000166	0.99992	841	50	791	17	42	816	99,876
3	99,876	0.000250	0.99975	841	50	791	25	42	824	99,801
4	99,801	0.000333	0.99950	840	50	790	33	42	832	99,718
5	99,718	0.000417	0.99917	840	51	789	42	42	840	99,625
6	99,625	0.000501	0.99875	840	51	789	50	42	848	99,524
7	99,524	0.000585	0.99825	839	51	788	58	41	856	99,415
8	99,415	0.000669	0.99766	839	52	787	66	41	864	99,296
9	99,296	0.000753	0.99700	838	52	786	75	41	872	99,169
10	99,169	0.000837	0.99625	838	53	785	83	41	879	99,054
11	99,054	0.000921	0.99541	837	53	784	91	41	887	98,890
12	98,890	0.001005	0.99449	836	53	783	99	41	894	98,757
13	98,757	0.001089	0.99349	835	54	782	108	41	902	98,576
14	98,576	0.001174	0.99241	834	54	780	116	41	909	98,406
15	98,406	0.001258	0.99125	833	54	779	124	41	916	98,227
16	98,227	0.001343	0.99000	832	55	778	132	41	923	98,041
17	98,041	0.001427	0.98867	831	55	776	140	41	930	97,846
18	97,846	0.001512	0.98726	830	56	775	148	41	937	97,642
19	97,642	0.001597	0.98576	829	56	773	156	41	944	97,431

Age										
20	97,431	0.001682	0.98419	328	56	771	164	41	951	97,211
21	97,211	0.001765	0.98253	326	57	770	172	41	957	96,982
:	:	:	:	:	:	:	:	:	:	:
:	:	:	:	:	:	:	:	:	:	:
31	94,566	0.002535	0.96161	309	60	749	240	39	1,009	94,267
32	94,267	0.002535	0.95917	307	60	746	239	39	1,006	93,968
33	93,968	0.002535	0.95674	304	61	744	238	39	1,003	93,669
34	93,669	0.002535	0.95431	302	61	742	237	39	1,001	93,371
35	93,371	0.002535	0.95189	300	61	739	237	39	998	93,073
36	93,073	0.002535	0.94948	798	62	737	236	39	995	92,776
:	:	:	:	:	:	:	:	:	:	:
:	:	:	:	:	:	:	:	:	:	:
98	75,332	0.002555	0.81122	882	36	596	191	31	841	75,056
99	75,056	0.002555	0.80917	880	36	594	190	31	839	74,779
100	74,779	0.002555	0.80711	879	37	592	189	31	837	74,503
:	:	:	:	:	:	:	:	:	:	:
:	:	:	:	:	:	:	:	:	:	:
209	45,399	0.002555	0.61204	515	155	359	115	19	610	45,129
210	45,129	0.002555	0.61049	513	156	357	114	19	609	44,859
211	44,859	0.002555	0.60894	512	157	355	113	19	607	44,589
:	:	:	:	:	:	:	:	:	:	:
:	:	:	:	:	:	:	:	:	:	:
357	1,386	0.002555	0.42037	553	342	11	3	1	356	1,041
358	1,041	0.002555	0.41930	553	344	8	2	0	354	695
359	695	0.002555	0.41824	552	346	6	1	0	352	348
360	348	0.002555	0.41718	551	348	3	0	0	351	0

*See the key in Table 9-1.

The projected scheduled principal payment is found as follows:

$$\overline{SP}_t = \overline{b}_{t-1} P_t$$

where

P_t = scheduled principal payment on the original balance assuming no prepayments.

Once MP and P_t are computed, the other values necessary to compute the projected cash flow can be easily determined. The formulas for MP and P_t were given in Chapter 5.

To illustrate the above formulas, consider the passthrough we have been using in the previous illustrations. Assuming a CPR of 6%, for month 210, the projected monthly mortgage payment is:

$$\overline{MP}_{210} = \overline{b}_{209} MP$$

It can be shown that the monthly mortgage payment assuming no principal prepayments is $840.85. Since the SMM is 0.005143 for each month, then:

$$\overline{b}_{209} = (1 - .005143)(1 - .005413)\ldots(1 - .005143)$$

The above product is multiplied 209 times, or equivalently:

$$\overline{b}_{209} = (1 - .005143)^{209} = .34039$$

So,

$$\overline{MP}_{209} = (.34039)\,\$840.85 = \$286$$

The projected scheduled principal payment is:

$$\overline{SP}_{210} = \overline{b}_{209} P_{210}$$

We showed that scheduled principal payment in month 210 assuming no prepayments is $255.62. The projected scheduled principal is then:

$$\overline{SP}_{210} = (.34039)\ \$255.62 = \$87$$

Notice that both of the values we computed agree with the values for month 210 shown in Table 9-1.

CASH FLOW YIELD

Given the projected cash flow and the price of a passthrough, its yield can be calculated. The yield is the interest rate that will make the present value of the expected cash flow equal to the price.[6] A yield computed in this manner is known as a *cash flow yield*.

Bond Equivalent Yield

For a passthrough, the yield that makes the present value of the cash flow equal to the price is a monthly interest rate. The next step is to annualize the monthly yield. According to market convention, to compare the yield for a passthrough to that of a Treasury or corporate bond, the monthly yield should not be annualized by just multiplying the monthly yield by 12. The reason is that a Treasury bond and a corporate bond pay interest semiannually, while a passthrough has a monthly cash flow. By reinvesting monthly cash flows, the passthrough holder has the opportunity to generate greater interest than can be earned by a bond holder who has only semiannual coupon payments to reinvest. Therefore, the yield on a passthrough must be calculated so as to make it comparable to the yield to maturity for a bond. This is accomplished by computing the *bond equivalent yield*, which is a market

---

[6]Letting CF_t denote the cash flow in month t, T the number of months remaining to maturity, P the price of the passthrough, and y_M the monthly mortgage cash flow yield, then y_M is found by solving the following equation using a trial-and-error process:

$$P = \sum_{t=1}^{T} \frac{CF_t}{(1 + y_M)^t}$$

convention for annualizing any fixed-income instrument that pays interest more than one time per year. The bond equivalent yield is found by doubling a semiannual yield. For a passthrough security, the semiannual yield is:

$$\text{semiannual cash flow yield} = (1 + y_M)^6 - 1$$

where

$\qquad y_M$ = monthly interest rate that will equate the present value of the projected monthly cash flow to the price of the passthrough

The bond equivalent yield is found by doubling the semiannual cash flow yield; that is

$$\text{bond equivalent yield} = 2\,[(1 + y_M)^6 - 1]$$

Illustrations

Suppose that a passthrough with a gross coupon rate of 9.5%, a servicing fee of 0.5%, 360 months remaining to maturity (a newly originated passthrough), and original principal of $100,000 can be purchased for $94,521. To compute the cash flow yield, a prepayment assumption must be made. Assuming that the prepayment rate is 100% PSA, the cash flow would be as shown in Table 9-3. Assuming that the first monthly cash flow is 30 days from now, the interest rate that will make the present value of the cash flow assuming 100% PSA equal to the price of $94,521 is 0.8333% (0.008333). The bond equivalent yield is then 10.21%, as shown below:

$$y_M = 0.008333$$

$$\text{bond equivalent yield} = 2\,[(1.008333)^6 - 1] = .1021$$

Suppose that the passthrough security in the previous illustration can be purchased for $105,985. Assuming a prepayment rate of 200% PSA, the interest rate that will make the present value of the cash flow equal to $105,985 is 0.006667

(0.6667%). The bond equivalent yield is

$$y_M = 0.006667$$

$$\text{bond equivalent yield} = 2\,[(1.006667)^6 - 1] = .0813 = 8.13\%$$

PRICE

Given the required yield for a passthrough, its price is simply the present value of the projected cash flow. However, care must be taken in determining the monthly interest rate that should be used to compute the present value of each monthly cash flow.

To convert a bond equivalent yield to a monthly interest rate, the following equation can be used:

$$y_M = [1 + (0.5)\ \text{bond equivalent yield}]^{1/6} - 1$$

Illustrations

Once again, consider the passthrough used in our previous illustration. Suppose that (1) the investor requires an 8.13% yield on a bond equivalent basis, and (2) the prepayment rate assumed by the investor is 150% PSA. The corresponding monthly interest rate for a bond equivalent yield of 8.13% is 0.6667% (0.006667) as shown below:

$$y_M = [1 + (0.5)\,.0813]^{1/6} - 1$$
$$= [1.04065]^{.16667} - 1 = 0.006667$$

The projected cash flow based on 150% PSA would be the same as in Table 9-4. Discounting the projected cash flow at 0.6667% gives a price of $106,710.

Suppose that instead of 8.13%, the investor wants a yield of 12.30%. Also assume that the investor believes that a 25% PSA rate is appropriate to project the cash flow. The monthly interest rate is determined as follows:

$$y_M = [1 + (0.5) .1230]^{1/6} - 1$$
$$= [1.0615]^{.16667} - 1 = 0.01$$

Discounting the projected cash flow based on 25% PSA would give a price of $79,976.

BEWARE OF CONVENTIONS

Everyone knows that there are 365 days in a non–leap year, but not all fixed-income instruments assume a 365-day year. Some pay interest assuming a year that consists of 360 days. This is simply a market convention. Doubling of a semi-annual yield to annualize a yield (the bond equivalent yield) is another example of a market convention.

The PSA prepayment benchmark is also simply a market convention. It is the product of a study by the PSA based on FHA prepayment data. Data that the PSA committee examined seemed to suggest that mortgages became seasoned (i.e., prepayment rates tended to level off) after 30 months and the CPR tended to be 6%. How did the PSA come up with the CPRs used for months 1 through 29? They were not based on empirical evidence. Instead, a linear increase from month 1 to month 30 such that at month 30 the CPR is 6% was selected. Moreover, the same benchmark or seasoning process is used in quoting passthroughs regardless of the collateral—30- and 15-year loans, fixed- and adjustable-rate loans, and conventional and VA/FHA-insured loans.

Astute money managers recognize that the CPR is a convenient convention enabling market participants to quote yield and/or price but that it has many limitations in determining the value of a passthrough. Studies that we discuss more fully in the next chapter have demonstrated that the seasoning process assumed by the PSA benchmark does not fit recent prepayment experience. One study of fixed-rate passthroughs found that the seasoning process takes considerably longer than 30 months.[7] How much longer depends on the type of collateral. Freddie Mac and Fannie Mae passthroughs (which are backed by conventional mortgage loans) were found to take longer to season than Ginnie Mae passthroughs (which are backed by FHA/VA-insured mortgage loans). In a study of the prepayment behavior of one-year constant maturity Treasury ARMs, it was found that prepayments exhibited the following pattern: they tended to season in about 26 months at a CPR of 15.6% until about month 46, then gradually declined for the next 30 months, finally reaching a second seasoning pattern in month 77 at a 12.3% CPR.[8] Cost-of-funds-indexed ARMs exhibited a similar seasoning behavior pattern. This two-plateau seasoning pattern is far different from the PSA's single-plateau seasoning pattern.

Consequently, care must be exercised in using any measure that is based on the PSA prepayment benchmark. In Chapter 10, factors that affect prepayments are discussed.

[7] David Jacob et al., "The Seasoning of Prepayment Speeds and Its Effect on the Average Lives and Values of MBS," in Frank J. Fabozzi, ed., *The Handbook of Mortgage-Backed Securities*, 3d ed. (Chicago: Probus Publishing, 1992).

[8] Scott F. Richard and Lynn M. Edens, "Prepayment and Valuation Modeling for Adjustable Rate Mortgage-Backed Securities," in Fabozzi, ed., *The Handbook of Mortgage-Backed Securities*, 3d ed.

10

Factors Affecting Prepayment Behavior

In Chapter 9 we explained the conventions used to construct cash flows based on some prepayment benchmark. In this chapter we discuss the factors that have been observed to affect prepayments. Prepayments occur for one of the following three reasons. First, for a variety of reasons a homeowner may sell the property, resulting in the outstanding balance being paid off (if the mortgage loan is not assumable). Second, the homeowner may obtain a lower cost of financing when mortgage rates in the market decline below the contract rate. This is referred to as refinancing and results in the outstanding balance being paid off. Finally, for a variety of reasons a homeowner may elect to repay a portion of the outstanding balance. Motivation for such prepayments is also related to the current interest rate on bonds relative to the contract rate. As interest rates decline, homeowners who are able to accumulate savings may find that the partial repayment of their mortgage balance offers a better investment opportunity than investing in long-term bonds.

Below we describe four factors that affect prepayment behavior: (1) prevailing mortgage rate, (2) characteristics of the underlying mortgage pool, (3) seasonal factors, and (4) general economic activity.

PREVAILING MORTGAGE RATE

The current mortgage rate affects prepayments in three ways. First, the spread between the prevailing mortgage rate and the contract rate affects the incentive to refinance. Second, the path of mortgage rates since the loan was originated affects prepayments through a phenomenon referred to as *refinancing burnout*. Both the spread and path of mortgage rates affect prepayments that are the product of refinancing. The third way in which the prevailing mortgage rate affects prepayments is through its effect on the affordability of housing and housing turnover. We discuss each below.

Spread Between Contract Rate and Prevailing Mortgage Rate

The single most important factor affecting prepayments because of refinancing is the current level of mortgage rates relative to the contract rate. The greater the difference between the two, the greater the incentive to refinance the mortgage loan. For refinancing to make sense, the interest savings must be greater than the total costs associated with the process. These costs include legal expenses, origination fees, title insurance, and the value of the time associated with obtaining another mortgage loan. Some of these costs—such as title insurance and origination points—will vary proportionately with the amount to be financed. Other costs such as the application fee and legal expenses are typically fixed.

Historically, it has been observed that when mortgage rates fall to more than 200 basis points below the contract rate, prepayment rates increase. This can be seen in Figure 10-1, which shows the prepayment rate (as measured in terms of CPR) for the period January 1984 to November 1987 for GNMA 13s, as well as the spread between the mortgage coupon (which is a 13.5% contract rate, since the servicing fee is 50 basis points) and the mortgage rate three months earlier.[1] The

---

[1]Lakhbir S. Hayre, Kenneth Lauterbach, and Cyrus Mohebbi, "Prepayment Models and Methodologies," in Frank J. Fabozzi, ed., *Advances and Innovations in Bond and Mortgage Markets* (Chicago: Probus Publishing, 1989), p. 331.

Figure 10-1

Prepayment Rates and Coupon Spreads for GNMA 13s

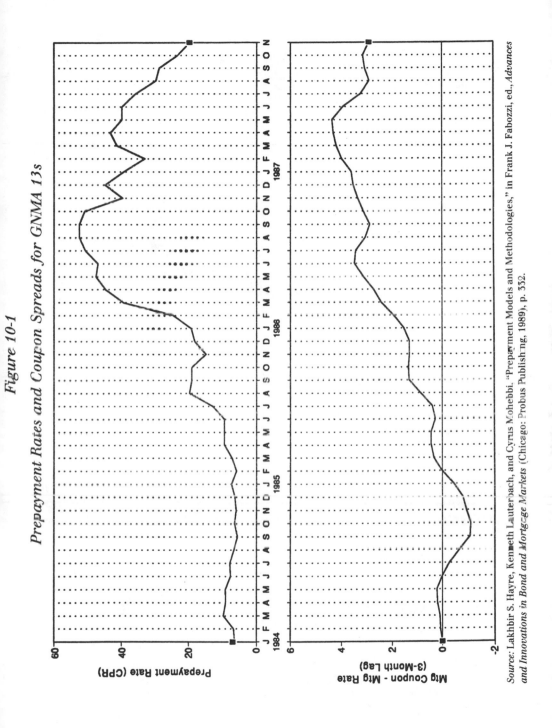

Source: Lakhbir S. Hayre, Kenneth Lauterbach, and Cyrus Mohebbi. "Prepayment Models and Methodologies," in Frank J. Fabozzi, ed., *Advances and Innovations in Bond and Mortgage Markets* (Chicago: Probus Publishing, 1989), p. 332.

Figure 10-2

SMM and Multiplicative Interest Rate Differential for GNMA 30-Year MBSs

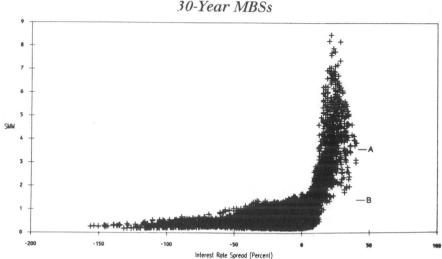

Source: Charles N. Schorin, "Fixed-Rate MBS Prepayment Models," in Frank J. Fabozzi, ed., *The Handbook of Mortgage-Backed Securities,* 3d ed. (Chicago: Probus Publishing, 1992).

refinancing rate is lagged because it takes time for the home-owner to obtain financing.

The present value of the benefits from refinancing depends on the initial level of the contract rate. Specifically, the present value of the benefits of a 200 basis point decline from an initial contract rate of 8% is greater than for a 200 basis point decline from an initial contract rate of 17%. Consequently, in modeling prepayment behavior one would expect that prepayments caused by refinancing might be more highly correlated with a percentage change in the rates rather than a spread. Figure 10-2 provides a scatter diagram that relates the monthly prepayment rate (as measured by the SMM) for 30-year GNMAs and percentage interest rate differentials.[2] Prepayments are small and have little dispersion for negative

---

[2] Charles N. Schorin, "Fixed-Rate MBS Prepayment Models," in Frank J. Fabozzi, ed., *The Handbook of Mortgage-Backed Securities*, 3d ed. (Chicago: Probus Publishing, 1992).

interest rate spreads (measured in percentage terms) and for spreads that are positive but less than 10%. Prepayments increase for interest rate spreads greater than 10%. Moreover, the dispersion of prepayments is greater. This phenomenon is explained later when we discuss the effect of the path of mortgage rates.

Because of the lack of observations in a wide range of mortgage rate environments, it has not been possible to evaluate empirically whether a spread measured in basis points or in percentage terms better explains prepayment behavior. As a result, refinancing opportunities can be measured in a variety of ways. In the Goldman, Sachs prepayment model, for example, refinancing opportunities are measured by the ratio of the contract rate to the mortgage refinancing rate.[3] For a specific pool, the contract rate is the weighted average of the contract rates for the underlying mortgage loans. To reflect the lags in the refinancing process, the Goldman, Sachs prepayment model uses a weighted average of the past five-month ratio of the contract rate to the mortgage refinancing rate. Figure 10-3 shows the results of the Goldman, Sachs prepayment model for 30-year GNMA and FNMA/FHLMC pass-throughs, where prepayments are measured in terms of CPR.

Path of Mortgage Rates

The historical pattern of prepayments and economic theory suggests that it is not only the level of mortgage rates that affects prepayment behavior but also the path that mortgage rates take to get to the current level.

To illustrate why, suppose the underlying contract rate for a pool of mortgage loans is 11% and that three years after origination, the prevailing mortgage rate declines to 8%. Let's consider two possible paths of the mortgage rate in get-

[3]The Goldman, Sachs prepayment model is described in Scott F. Richard and Richard Roll, "Prepayments on Fixed-Rate Mortgage-Backed Securities," *The Journal of Portfolio Management* (Spring 1989), pp. 73–74, and Scott F. Richard, "Relative Prepayment Rates on Thirty-Year FNMA, FHLMC and GNMA Fixed Rate Mortgage-Backed Securities," in Fabozzi, ed., *Advances and Innovations in the Bond and Mortgage Markets*, pp. 351–369.

Figure 10-3

GNMA vs. FNMA/FHLMC Refinancing Incentive
(without Path Dependency)

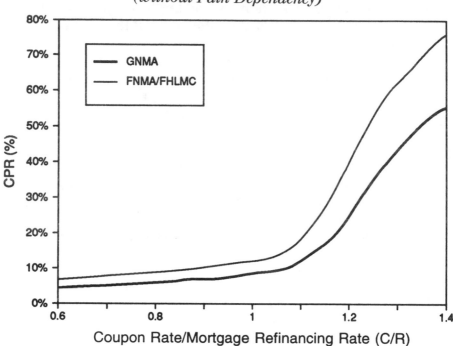

Source: Scott F. Richard, "Relative Prepayment Rates on Thirty-Year FNMA, FHLMC and GNMA Fixed Rate Mortgage-Backed Securities," in Fabozzi, ed., *Advances and Innovations in the Bond and Mortgage Markets*, p. 354.

ting to the 8% level. In the first path, the mortgage rate declines to 8% at the end of the first year, then rises to 13% at the end of the second year, and then falls to 8% at the end of the third year. In the second path, the mortgage rate rises to 12% at the end of the first year, continues its rise to 13% at the end of the second year, and then falls to 8% at the end of the third year.

  If the mortgage rate follows the first path, those who can benefit from refinancing will more than likely take advantage of this opportunity when the mortgage rate drops to 8% in the first year. When the mortgage rate drops again to 8%

at the end of the third year, the likelihood is that prepayments because of refinancing will not surge; those who can benefit by taking advantage of the refinancing opportunity will have done so already when the mortgage rate declined for the first time. This is the prepayment behavior referred to as the refinancing burnout (or simply, burnout) phenomenon.

In contrast, the expected prepayment behavior when the mortgage rate follows the second path is quite different. Prepayment rates are expected to be low in the first two years. When the mortgage rate declines to 8% in the third year, refinancing activity and therefore prepayments are expected to surge.

Consequently, the burnout phenomenon is related to the path of mortgage rates. This might help explain the results in Figure 10-2, which show the greater dispersion of prepayments for GNMA 30-year MBSs when the interest rate spread is greater than about 10%. Observations below B in the figure may be from pools that have burned out, while those above A in the figure may be from pools that previously had the opportunity to take advantage of refinancing.

Notice that in Figure 10-3, the refinancing incentive based on the Goldman, Sachs prepayment model is shown without path dependency. Figure 10-4 shows the Goldman, Sachs prepayment model adjustment for burnout for newly issued GNMA and FNMA/FHLMC passthroughs with different coupon rates in a 10% refinancing rate environment. Notice that for the 11.5% passthroughs, there is no adjustment for burnout in a 10% refinancing rate environment. However, for the premium passthroughs—the 12%, 12.5%, and 13% passthroughs—the higher the coupon rate, the faster the expected burnout.

The difficulty in modeling prepayments has been to quantify path dependency. Some researchers have used the ratio of the remaining mortgage balance outstanding for the pool to the original mortgage balance. This ratio is called the *pool factor*. The argument is that the lower the pool factor, the greater prepayments have been historically and therefore the more likely it is that burnout will occur. One researcher who has tested various measures of path dependency

Figure 10-4

GNMA vs. FNMA/FHLMC Burnout for New Issues
(Refinancing Rate = 10%)

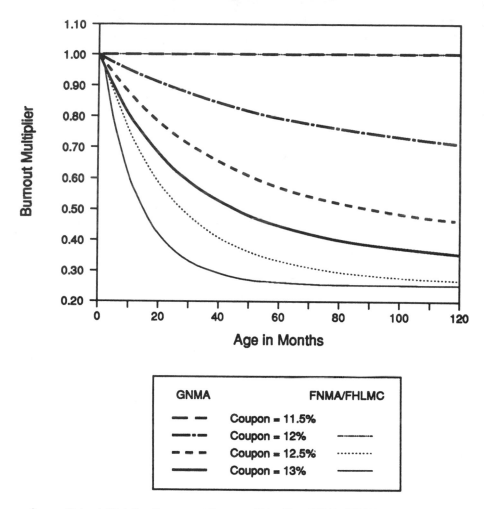

Source: Richard, "Relative Prepayment Rates on Thirty-Year FNMA, FHLMC and GNMA Fixed Rate Mortgage-Backed Securities," in *Advances and Innovations in the Bond and Mortgage Markets,* p. 358.

reports that the pool factor is the best measure.[4] In contrast, the Goldman, Sachs prepayment model adjustment for burnout shown in Figure 10-4 is a nonlinear function generated from the entire history of the ratio of the contract rate to the mortgage refinancing rate since the mortgage was issued.

Level of Mortgage Rates

As we discussed earlier, prepayments occur because of housing turnover and refinancing. Our focus so far has been on the factors that affect prepayments caused by refinancing. The level of mortgage rates affects housing turnover to the extent that a lower rate increases the affordability of homes. Such rate environments provide an opportune time to purchase a more expensive home (trade up) or to change location for other reasons.

The effect of the level of mortgage rates on prepayments can be seen in Figure 10-5, which shows for the period January 1984 to November 1987 the relationship between prepayment rates for GNMA 8.5% (contract rate of 9%) and mortgage rates. Over this period, mortgage rates exceeded the 9% contract rate, so there was no incentive to refinance. Yet, as can be seen in the figure, when mortgage rates were high and then dropped, prepayments increased.

CHARACTERISTICS OF THE UNDERLYING MORTGAGE LOANS

The following characteristics of the underlying mortgage loans affect prepayments: (1) the contract rate, (2) whether the loans are FHA/VA-guaranteed or conventional, (3) the amount of seasoning, (4) whether the mortgage loans have a fixed rate or an adjustable rate, (5) the pool factor, and (6) the geographical location of the underlying properties. We have already discussed how the contract rate affects prepayment behavior and how the pool factor has been used by

[4]Schorin, "Fixed-Rate MBS Prepayment Models."

Figure 10-5

Prepayment Rates GNMA 8.5s and Mortgage Rates

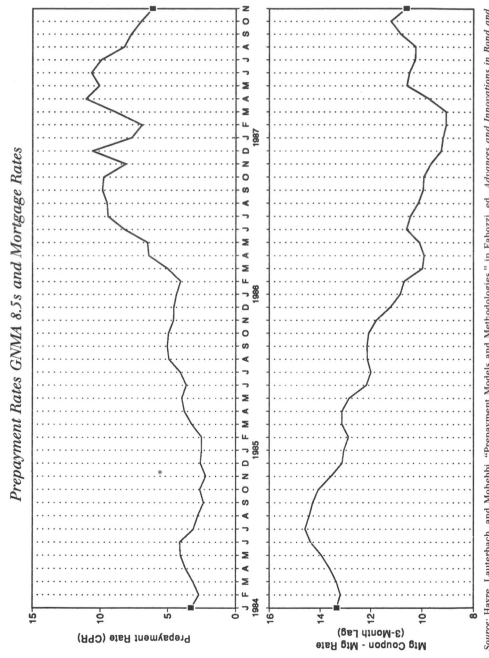

Source: Hayre, Lauterbach, and Mohebbi, "Prepayment Models and Methodologies," in Fabozzi, ed., *Advances and Innovations in Bond and Mortgage Markets*, p. 777.

some researchers as a measure to proxy for path dependency. Below we focus on the other four characteristics.

FHA/VA Mortgages versus Conventional Mortgages

The underlying mortgage loans for GNMA pass-throughs are guaranteed by either the FHA or VA. Most FNMA and FHLMC passthroughs are conventional loans. There are four characteristics of FHA- and VA-guaranteed loans that cause their prepayment characteristics to differ from those of conventional loans. First, FHA- and VA-guaranteed loans are assumable. Consequently, prepayments should be lower than for otherwise comparable conventional loans when the contract rate is less than the current mortgage rate. This is because purchasers will assume the seller's mortgage loan in order to acquire the below-market interest rate and, as a result, there will be no prepayment resulting from the sale of the property. Second, the amount of the mortgage loan is typically small, reducing the incentive to refinance as mortgage rates decline and thereby producing a rate of prepayment because of refinancing that is less than for conventional loans. Third, the income level of those who must obtain a mortgage loan guaranteed by the FHA or VA is typically less than that of borrowers with conventional loans. Their ability to take advantage of a refinancing opportunity is limited because they often do not have the funds to pay the costs associated with refinancing. While these three characteristics suggest that prepayments for these loans will be less than for conventional loans, the last characteristic also suggests faster prepayments. As explained in Chapter 4, default rates are greater for FHA- and VA-guaranteed loans compared to conventional loans. Defaults result in prepayments. However, the factor of faster prepayments because of default is swamped by the other characteristics that cause slower prepayments.

The difference in prepayment rates can be seen by comparing prepayments for GNMA and FNMA/FHLMC passthroughs. Figure 10-3 shows that for a given refinancing incentive, the prepayment rate is greater for FNMA/FHLMC passthroughs relative to GNMA passthroughs. Figure 10-4 shows that FNMA/FHLMC passthroughs burn out faster than GNMA passthroughs.

Seasoning

Seasoning refers to the aging of the mortgage loans. Empirical evidence suggests that prepayment rates are low after the loan is originated and increase after the loan is somewhat seasoned. Then prepayment rates tend to level off, in which case the loans are referred to as fully seasoned. This is the underlying theory for the PSA prepayment benchmark discussed in Chapter 9. Recall that the PSA prepayment benchmark is based on prepayment rates of .2% CPR for the first month, increasing by .2% per month until the 30th month, when prepayment rates are assumed to be 6% CPR for the remainder of the mortgage term.

While empirical evidence does support the theory that prepayment rates follow the general pattern described above, the seasoning process has been found to take considerably longer than indicated by the PSA prepayment benchmark. For example, consider the CPRs for the 12-month period May 1989 to April 1990 reported in Table 10-1 for two GNMA 8.5% passthroughs issued at two different times, 1976 and 1986. Both of these issues should be fully seasoned according to the PSA prepayment benchmark and should both be paying at the same prepayment rate. As can be seen in the table, the 12-month CPR for the GNMA issued in 1976 is 7%, while that for the GNMA issued in 1986 is only 3.6%.[5]

The explanation for the departure of actual prepayment behavior from the model suggested by the PSA prepayment benchmark is that other factors interact with seasoning and affect prepayment behavior. Figure 10-6 shows how the rate of seasoning depends on the type of passthrough (GNMA versus FNMA/FHLMC) and the refinancing incentive (discount pool, C/R = .8; par pool, C/R = 1.0; and premium pool, C/R = 1.2). GNMA discount, par, and premium pools take about 9 years, 5 years, and 30 months, respectively, to

[5]David Jacob et al., "The Seasoning of Prepayment Speeds and Its Effect on the Average Lives and Values of MBS," in Fabozzi, ed., *The Handbook of Mortgage-Backed Securities*, 3d ed.

Table 10-1

CPR for Two Fully Seasoned GNMA 8.5%,
May 1989–April 1990

Month	GNMA 8.5 1976	GNMA 8.5 1986
April 1990	6.8%	4.3%
March 1990	6.8	3.3
February 1990	6.4	3.1
January 1990	7.6	3.8
December 1989	6.5	3.8
November 1989	7.7	3.8
October 1989	7.5	3.8
September 1989	7.8	4.2
August 1989	6.3	3.1
July 1989	7.2	3.7
June 1989	6.8	3.8
May 1989	6.7	3.3
12 months	7.0	3.6

Source: David Jacob et al., "The Seasoning of Prepayment Speeds and Its Effect on the Average Lives and Values of MBS," in Fabozzi, ed., *The Handbook of Mortgage-Backed Securities,* 3d ed.

fully season. For FNMA/FHLMC passthroughs the corresponding time for the pools to fully season is just less than 9 years, 4 years, and 20 months. Thus, par and premium FNMA/FHLMC passthroughs season considerably faster than GNMA passthroughs.

Notice that GNMA premium pools appear to fully season in the time frame set forth by the PSA prepayment benchmark, while FNMA/FHLMC pools do so faster. Although the PSA prepayment benchmark sets forth the same prepayment rate until the final mortgage loan is paid off, there is no end-of-data prepayment behavior history to verify this conjecture statistically.

Fixed-Rate versus Adjustable-Rate Mortgages

Our focus up to this point has been on pools in which the underlying mortgage loans have a fixed rate.[6] The pre-

[6] ARM products are discussed in Chapter 6.

Figure 10-6

GNMA vs. FNMA/FHLMC Seasoning

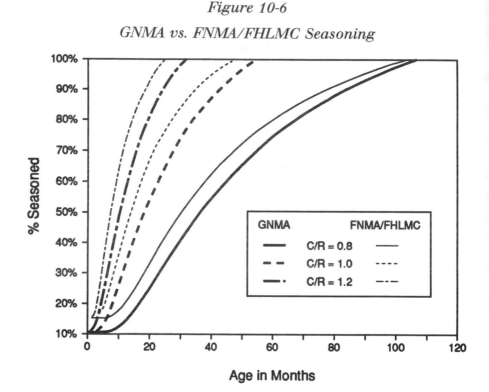

Source: Richard, "Relative Prepayment Rates on Thirty-Year FNMA, FHLMC and GNMA Fixed Rate Mortgage-Backed Securities," in Fabozzi, ed., *Advances and Innovations in the Bond and Mortgage Markets*, p. 355.

payment behavior of ARMs has recently been investigated.[7] The prepayment rates of ARM pools tend to be different from those of fixed-rate mortgages in several important ways. First, as can be seen in Figure 10-7, the seasoning process differs. As in the case of fixed-rate mortgages, ARM prepayments increase in the earlier years. The time it takes to fully season, however, is shorter than for ARMs. Unlike fixed-rate mortgage pools where one plateau for prepayments is reached and then prepayments level off, there are two plateaus observed for ARM pools, the first being at a higher CPR than the second,

[7]Scott F. Richard and Lynn M. Edens, "Prepayment and Valuation Modeling for Adjustable Rate Mortgage-Backed Securities," in Frank J. Fabozzi, ed., *The Handbook of Mortgage-Backed Securities*, 3d ed.

Figure 10-7

Seasonally Adjusted Prepayment Rates for One-Year CMT ARMs

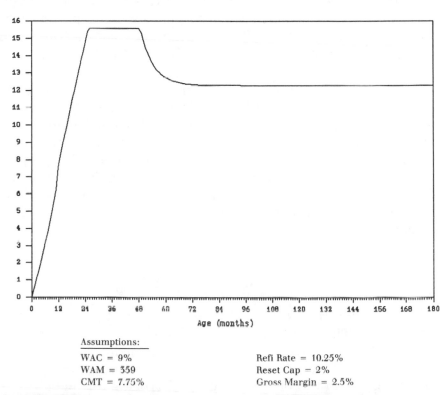

CPR (%)

Age (months)

Assumptions:

WAC = 9%	Refi Rate = 10.25%
WAM = 359	Reset Cap = 2%
CMT = 7.75%	Gross Margin = 2.5%

Source: Scott F. Richard and Lynn M. Edens, "Prepayment and Valuation Modeling for Adjustable Rate Mortgage-Backed Securities," in Frank J. Fabozzi, ed., *The Handbook of Mortgage-Backed Securities,* 3d ed. (Chicago: Probus Publishing, 1992).

which is reached about two years later.[8] Second, the annual reset caps affect prepayments, causing them to slow when mortgage rates rise.

Geographical Location of the Underlying Properties

The prepayment behavior described thus far is for generic pools. In some regions of the country the prepayment

[8]Richard and Edens refer to this phenomenon of a lower CPR as "deseasoning."

behavior tends to be faster than the average national prepayment rate, while other regions exhibit slower prepayment rates. This is caused by differences in local economies that affect housing turnover. Historically, prepayment rates for pools with properties concentrated in Los Angeles, for example, have been much faster than for pools with properties concentrated in Houston. The geographical concentration of properties appears to be particularly important in projecting prepayment rates for ARM pools.[9]

An investor may invest in a specific pool when he believes he is more capable of projecting prepayments for that pool than for a generic pool. A microanalysis of specific pools requires information on the prepayment history of that pool and on the prepayment behavior of other pools with properties concentrated in the same geographical region and by the same lender. The Wall Street firm that has developed a data base to analyze prepayment behavior for specific pools is Bear Stearns.[10]

SEASONAL FACTORS

There is a well-documented seasonal pattern in prepayments. This pattern is related to activity in the primary housing market, with home buying increasing in the spring and gradually reaching a peak in the late summer. Home buying declines in the fall and winter. Mirroring this activity are the prepayments that result from the turnover of housing as home buyers sell their existing homes and purchase new ones. Prepayments are low in the winter months and begin to rise in the spring, reaching a peak in the summer months. However, probably because of delays in passing through prepayments, the peak may not be observed until early fall. The seasonal effect appears to be true for pools in which the underlying loans are ARMs.[11]

---

[9]Richard and Edens, "Prepayment and Valuation Modeling for Adjustable Rate Mortgage-Backed Securities."

[10]For illustrations of the type of information provided, see Chuck Ramsey and J. Michael Henderson, "Investing in Specified Pools," in Fabozzi, ed., The Handbook of Mortgage-Backed Securities rev. ed. (Chicago: Probus Publishing, 1988), pp. 115–130.

[11]Richard and Edens, "Prepayment and Valuation Modeling for Adjustable Rate Mortgage-Backed Securities."

GENERAL ECONOMIC ACTIVITY

Economic theory would suggest that general economic activity affects prepayment behavior through its effect on housing turnover. The link is as follows: a growing economy results in a rise in personal income and in opportunities for worker migration; this increases family mobility and as a result increases housing turnover. The opposite holds for a weak economy. One researcher suggests that prepayments can be projected by identifying and forecasting the turnover rate of the single-family housing stock.[12]

Although some modelers of prepayment behavior may incorporate macroeconomic measures of economic activity such as gross national product, industrial production, or housing starts, the trend has been to ignore them or limit their use to specific applications. There are two reasons why macroeconomic measures have been ignored. First, empirical tests suggest that the relationship between residuals of a prepayment forecasting model that does not include macroeconomic measures and various macroeconomic measures is either statistically insignificant or, if it is statistically significant, its explanatory power is low.[13] Second, as explained later, prepayment models are based on a projection of a path for future mortgage rates. The inclusion of macroeconomic variables in a prepayment model would require the forecasting of the value of these variables over long time periods.

Macroeconomic variables, however, have been used by some researchers in prepayment models in two ways. One way is to capture the effect of housing turnover on prepayments by specifying a relationship between interest rates and housing turnover. This is the approach used in the Prudential-Bache Prepayment Model.[14] A second way is to incorporate macroeconomic variables and their forecasts in projecting short-term rather than long-term prepayments. As will be explained in Chapter 13, in assessing the potential total return from investing in mortgage-backed securities, short-term prepayment forecasts are required.

---

[12] Joseph C. Hu, "An Alternative Prepayment Projection Based on Housing Activity," in Fabozzi, ed., *The Handbook of Mortgage-Backed Securities*, rev. ed., pp. 639–648.

[13] Richard and Roll, "Prepayments on Fixed-Rate Mortgage-Backed Securities," pp. 78–79.

[14] Hayre, Lauterbach, and Mohebbi, "Prepayment Models and Methodologies," p. 338.

PREPAYMENT MODELS AND PROJECTIONS

A prepayment model begins by modeling the statistical relationships among the factors that are expected to affect prepayments. One study suggests that the following four factors (already discussed above) explain about 95% of the variation in prepayment rates: refinancing incentives, burnout, seasoning, and seasonality.[15] These factors are then combined into one model. For example, in the Goldman, Sachs prepayment model the effects interact proportionally through the following multiplicative function, which is used to project prepayments:

> monthly prepayment rate =
> (refinancing incentive) × (seasoning multiplier) ×
> (month multiplier) × (burnout multiplier)

where the various multipliers are adjustments for the effects we discussed earlier in this chapter.

For two of the effects, the only information that is needed is the amount of seasoning and the month. For the refinancing incentive and burnout, it is necessary to know the contract rate on the underlying pool and the refinancing mortgage rate. While the former is known and is unchanged over the life of the mortgage pool, the latter will change. The practice in prepayment modeling has been to generate a path of monthly mortgage rates as follows. First, a path for monthly short-term interest rates that is consistent with the prevailing term structure of interest rates is generated. Based on an assumed relationship between short-term interest rates and long-term interest rates, a path for monthly mortgage rates can be obtained. From these monthly mortgage rates, prepayment rates caused by refinancing incentives and burnout are projected. Consequently, the prepayment projection is contingent on the interest rate path projected.

The product of a prepayment forecast is not one prepayment rate but a set of prepayment rates for each month of

---

[15]Richard, "Relative Prepayment Rates on Thirty-Year FNMA, FHLMC and GNMA Fixed Rate Mortgage-Backed Securities," pp. 359–360.

the remaining term of a mortgage pool. The set of monthly prepayment rates, however, is not reported by Wall Street firms or vendors. Instead, a single CPR or PSA figure is reported. One way to convert a set of monthly prepayment rates into a single prepayment rate is to calculate a simple average of the prepayment rates. The obvious drawback to this approach is that it does not take into consideration the outstanding balance each month. An alternative approach is to use some type of weighted average, selecting the weights to reflect the amount of the monthly cash flow corresponding to a monthly prepayment rate. This is done by first computing the cash flow yield for a passthrough given its market price and the set of monthly prepayment rates. Then a single prepayment rate (CPR or PSA multiple) that gives the same cash flow yield is found.

PREPAYMENT RISKS ASSOCIATED WITH PASSTHROUGHS

Because of prepayments, the cash flow of a passthrough is not known. To understand prepayment risk, suppose an investor buys a 10% coupon GNMA at a time when mortgage rates are 10%. Let's consider what will happen to prepayments if mortgage rates decline to, say, 6%. There will be two adverse consequences. First, we know from the fundamental property of an option-free bond that its price will rise, since the present value of the expected cash flow will be greater when the bond is discounted at a lower rate. The new valuation will be such that the owner of the security could secure the initial cash flow by selling his instrument despite the lower returns now available in the market. But in the case of a passthrough the rise will not be as large as that of an option-free bond, because a fall in interest rates will increase the probability that the market rate will fall below the rate currently paid by the borrower, thus giving him an incentive to prepay his loan and refinance his debt at a lower rate. To the extent that this happens, the owner of the security will be repaid, not at a price incorporating the premium, but at the par value of the debt. The investor therefore risks capital loss, which also reflects the fact that the anticipated reimbursements at par will not enable him to maintain the initial cash flow.

When mortgage rates decline, the adverse consequences for investors in a passthrough are the same as those faced by holders of a callable bond. In both cases the upside price potential of the instrument is truncated because of the embedded call option granted to the borrower. This should not be surprising since a mortgage loan effectively grants the borrower the right to call the loan at par value. Thus, the adverse consequences when mortgage rates decline are referred to as *call risk* or *contraction risk*.

Now let's look at what happens if mortgage rates rise to, say, 15%. The price of the passthrough, like that of any bond, will decline. But again it will decline more because the higher rates will tend to slow down the rate of prepayment, in effect increasing the amount invested at the pool coupon rate, which is lower than the market rate. Prepayments will slow down because homeowners will not refinance or partially prepay their mortgages when mortgage rates are higher than their contractual rate of 10%. Yet this is just the time when investors want prepayments to speed up so that they can reinvest the prepayments at the higher market interest rate. This adverse consequence of rising mortgage rates is called *extension risk*.

Therefore, prepayment risk encompasses contraction risk and extension risk. These risks associated with passthroughs help us understand the reason for the creation of the collateralized mortgage obligation, which we discuss in Chapter 11.

11

Derivative Products: CMO and Stripped MBS

In this chapter we will discuss collateralized mortgage obligations and stripped mortgage-backed securities and examine the motivation for their creation. Because these securities derive their cash flow from underlying mortgage collateral such as passthroughs or a pool of whole loans, they are referred to as "derivative" products. All of these trade in the over-the-counter market with different degrees of liquidity.

COLLATERALIZED MORTGAGE OBLIGATIONS

At the close of the previous chapter, we discussed the prepayment risks associated with investing in passthroughs (contraction risk and extension risk). Collateralized mortgage obligations are instruments created by redirecting the cash flows of mortgage-related products (whole loans, passthroughs, and stripped MBSs) so as to mitigate prepayment risk. The creation of a CMO cannot eliminate prepayment risk; it can only distribute the various forms of this risk among different classes of bondholders. In addition, the redistribution of the coupon interest from the underlying mortgage-related products to different classes—so that a CMO class has a different coupon rate than the underlying collateral—results in instruments with different convexity characteristics (discussed in Chapters 12 and 13) that may be more suitable to the needs and expectations of investors.

Motivation for the Development of the CMO Structure

From an asset/liability perspective, passthroughs are an unattractive investment for many institutional investors because of prepayment risk. The CMO structure was developed to broaden the appeal of mortgage-backed products to traditional fixed-income investors. Consider commercial banks and thrifts (S&Ls, savings banks, and credit unions). The objective of these financial institutions is to lock in a spread over their cost of funds. Their funds are raised on a short-term basis either through the issuance of short-term money market obligations or the issuance of certificates of deposit. If they invest the proceeds in fixed-rate passthroughs, they will be mismatched because a passthrough is a long-term security. We discussed the mismatch problem in Chapter 6.

Passthroughs may not be useful for satisfying certain obligations of insurance companies. More specifically, consider a life insurance company that has issued a four-year *guaranteed investment contract* (GIC). A GIC is an insurance product in which the insurance company agrees to pay a specified interest rate over a predetermined time period in return for a specified sum of money, the premium. If the insurance company purchases a passthrough with the premium received, the security could have a life considerably longer than four years or any other maturity that was anticipated when the passthrough was purchased. That is, the insurance company is exposed to extension risk.

Finally, consider a pension fund or a life insurance company with a predetermined set of liabilities that must be paid over the next 15 years. In the case of a pension fund, this would be the defined benefit payments it must make to beneficiaries; for the life insurance company, it might be obligations resulting from an annuity policy that it has sold. By buying a passthrough, these institutional investors are exposed to the risk that prepayments will speed up and, as a result, the passthrough's maturity will shorten to considerably less than 15 years. Prepayments will speed up if interest rates decline, thereby forcing reinvestment of prepayments at a lower interest rate. In this case, the pension fund and the life insurance company are exposed to contraction risk.

As can be seen, some institutional investors are concerned with extension risk and others with contraction risk when they invest in a passthrough. By redirecting cash flows, CMOs allow the redistribution of prepayment risk among investors that want to reduce their exposure to one form of prepayment risk. Since the total prepayment risk of a passthrough is not changed by altering the cash flows, other investors must be willing to accept the unwanted prepayment risk.

The CMO Structure

A CMO reduces the uncertainty concerning the maturity of a mortgage-backed security, thereby providing a risk/return pattern not available with passthroughs or whole loans. Below we describe the basic or plain vanilla CMO structure. Later we talk about other types of classes that have been included in a CMO structure. Figure 11-1 shows a time line indicating when the various CMO structures we will discuss in this chapter were introduced.

A CMO is a security backed by a pool of passthroughs, whole loans, or stripped mortgage-backed securities (dis-

Figure 11-1

CMO Time Line

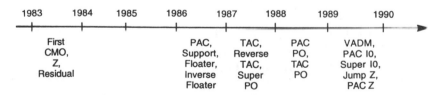

Source: Presented by Robert Kulason of Salomon Brothers Inc at the Collateralized Mortgage Obligations tutorial sponsored by Frank J. Fabozzi Associates, September 27, 1991.

cussed later in the chapter). CMOs are structured so that there are several classes of bondholders with varying *stated* maturities. The principal payments from the underlying collateral are used to retire the bonds on a priority basis as specified in the prospectus. The first generation of CMOs were structured so that each class of bond would be retired sequentially, and hence such structures are referred to as *sequential-pay* CMOs. Later we describe classes included in CMO structures that result in the simultaneous paydown of more than one class of bondholders based on a set of priority rules.

In a plain vanilla CMO structure, there may be four classes of bonds, which we shall refer to as Class A, Class B, Class C and Class Z. (The classes are commonly referred to as *tranches*.) The first three classes, with Class A representing the shortest maturity bond, receive periodic interest payments from the underlying collateral; Class Z is an accrual bond that receives no periodic interest until the other three classes are retired. When principal payments, both scheduled and prepayments, are received by the trustee for the CMO, they are applied to retire the Class A bonds. After all the Class A bonds are retired, all principal payments received are applied to retire the Class B bonds. Once all the Class B bonds are retired, Class C bonds are paid off from all principal payments. Finally, after the first three classes of bonds are retired, the cash flow payments from the remaining underlying collateral are used to satisfy the obligations on the Z-bonds (original principal plus accrued interest). These bonds are referred to as *accrual or Z-bonds*.

As an example, consider one of the early CMO issues, which had four classes: the MDC Mortgage Funding Corporation, Series J CMO, a $100 million issue priced on July 7, 1986.[1] The underlying collateral are GNMA passthroughs with a weighted average coupon of 9.5% and 297 months remaining to maturity. The original maturity for the GNMA passthroughs was 360 months. Basic information for each class is summarized in the upper panel of Table 11-1.

---

[1]This information is taken from Lakhbir S. Hayre, David Foulds, and Lisa Pendergast, "Introduction to Collateralized Mortgage Obligations," in Frank J. Fabozzi, ed., *The Handbook of Mortgage-Backed Securities*, rev. ed. (Chicago: Probus Publishing, 1988).

Table 11-1

Summary Information for MDC Mortgage Funding, Series J

Class	Par (in $ millions)	Stated Maturity	Coupon	Price
A	$35.5	5/99	8.05%	99.87500
B	15.5	2/02	8.75	99.84575
C	40.5	2/07	9.35	99.71875
Z	9.0	8/16	9.50	93.15625

Class	Expected Maturity	Average Life (years)	Duration	Projected Yield	Benchmark Treasury	Spread over Treasury (in basis points)
A	5/91	2.30	2.10	7.87%	2 year	120
B	8/93	5.80	4.61	8.72	5	160
C	11/99	10.10	6.58	9.38	10	210
Z	8/11	18.50	17.05	10.00	20	235

Source: Lakhbir S. Hayre, David Foulds, and Lisa Pendergast, "Introduction to Collateralized Mortgage Obligations," in Frank J. Fabozzi, ed., *The Handbook of Mortgage-Backed Securities,* rev. ed. (Chicago: Probus Publishing, 1988), p. 346.

Cash flow of a CMO. The cash flow for each class can only be derived by assuming some prepayment rate for the underlying mortgage collateral. The yield cited for each class of a CMO is the cash flow yield, a measure that depends on a prepayment assumption, as we explained in Chapter 9. The prepayment benchmark used by mortgage-backed securities dealers to quote CMO cash flow yields is the PSA standard prepayment model. The issuer of the CMO illustrated in Table 11-1 priced it based on a prepayment rate of 110% PSA. The expected maturity, average life, duration, projected yield, and spread to Treasuries based on 110% PSA are summarized in the lower panel of Table 11-1. The cash flows (separated by interest and principal) for each of the four classes assuming 110% PSA are shown in Figure 11-2.

Considerations in structuring a CMO. In structuring a CMO, the issuer must consider the following. First, the CMO must be structured to ensure that the cash flow will satisfy the bond obligations even under adverse prepayment

Figure 11-2

Cash Flow Distribution to MDC J Bonds at 110% PSA

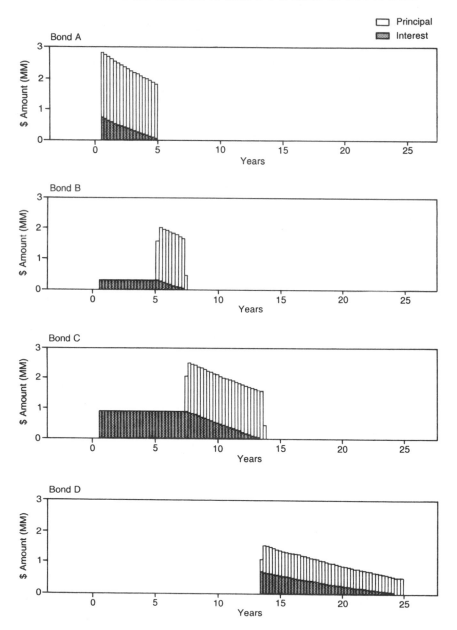

Source: Hayre, Foulds, and Pendergast, "Introduction to Collateralized Mortgage Obligations," in Fabozzi, ed., *The Handbook of Mortgage-Backed Securities,* rev. ed., p. 343.

conditions. This is necessary so that a high quality rating can be obtained from commercial rating companies. We'll discuss this later in the chapter. Second, to avoid adverse tax consequences, the issue must be structured so that the trust is not treated as a taxable entity. This enables it to avoid double taxation—a tax at both the trust and security holder levels; that is, it removes the possibility that the distributions made to security holders are treated as dividends and therefore not tax-deductible by the trust. The third point is that the issuer wants the CMO to be considered as a sale of assets so that it will not appear as debt on its balance sheet. Last—but certainly not least—is the arbitrage available to the issuer in the transaction. The issuer must be able to acquire the collateral for the transaction at a price that will permit a profit. The factors that affect the arbitrage profit are the yield curve shape, general prepayment levels, client demand for CMOs, and the demand for the underlying collateral.

With respect to taxation, recall from our discussion in Chapter 2 that an entity issuing a passthrough structured as a grantor trust is not treated as a taxable entity. However, prior to the Tax Reform Act of 1986, the IRS ruled that multiple-class passthroughs such as CMOs were taxable entities even if structured as a grantor trust. To circumvent this provision in the tax code, so that the issuer of a CMO would not be treated as the issuer of a multiple-class passthrough and therefore be treated as a taxable entity, issuers designed CMO structures so that they would be classified as debt payments for tax purposes. This, however, meant that the CMO would be treated as debt on the balance sheet, thereby failing to satisfy the issuer's objective of avoiding this adverse financial reporting consequence.

The Real Estate Mortgage Investment Conduits provision in the Tax Reform Act of 1986 allows issuers to issue a multiple-class passthrough without being treated as a taxable entity. This means that a CMO can now be structured so that the issuer can treat it as a sale of assets for tax purposes, and the transaction will not be treated as debt for financial reporting purposes. The issuer does this by electing to have the CMO treated as a REMIC. Thus a REMIC CMO is not a new security but a tax election made by an issuer.

Credit risk. The credit quality for most CMOs is high enough to be rated triple A by the major commercial rating agencies. The credit risk is determined by the way in which the CMO is structured and the quality of the underlying mortgage collateral, and generally not by the creditworthiness of the CMO's issuer.

With respect to the collateral, for CMOs backed by agency passthroughs or FHA/VA-guaranteed mortgage loans, credit risk is minimal. The CMOs issued by Freddie Mac and Fannie Mae carry their guarantee and are perceived to have low credit risk. CMOs that do not fall into one of these two categories typically carry pool insurance that guarantees the timely payment of interest and principal.

The other key element in determining the credit quality of the CMO is the manner in which the cash flows are structured. In order to receive a triple-A quality rating, the cash flows must be sufficient to meet all of the obligations under any prepayment scenario. Also, the reinvestment rate assumed to be earned on the cash flow until it is distributed to bondholders must be low.

Because of the safeguards built into a CMO structure, a CMO with a triple-A rating is generally viewed as having less credit risk than a corporate bond with the same rating.

CMO Classes

There have been numerous innovations in structuring CMOs, which have resulted in the creation of classes of bonds with one or more of the following characteristics: (1) greater stability of cash flows over a wide range of prepayment speeds, (2) better matching of floating-rate liabilities, (3) substantial upside potential in a declining interest rate environment but less downside risk in a rising interest rate environment,[2] or (4) properties that allow them to be used for hedging mortgage-related products such as mortgage servicing. Below we discuss the various classes.

Accrual bonds. In the CMO structure shown in Table

---

[2] In the parlance of the analytical framework discussed in Chapter 12, these classes have substantial positive convexity.

11-1, the Z-bond class is the accrual bond. In most of the earlier CMO structures, the accrual bond was the last class to be paid off and therefore the class with the longest stated maturity. This bond appealed to long-term investors that sought to mitigate the risk associated with the reinvestment of coupon and principal payments. As we shall explain when we discuss PAC bonds later, accrual bonds with intermediate stated maturities have been introduced.

The inclusion of an accrual bond in a CMO structure is important because it is this class of bondholders that protects earlier classes from extension risk. Moreover, the greater the principal amount of the accrual class, the greater the amount of bonds with a short stated maturity that can be included in a structure. In terms of the economics of the transaction, the inclusion of a larger amount of bonds with a short stated maturity leads to greater arbitrage profits for the issuer in a positive sloping yield curve environment.

We'll have more to say about the role of accrual bonds in some deal structures later in this chapter as we describe certain CMO classes.

Floating-rate CMOs. In September 1986, Shearson Lehman Brothers introduced a CMO (SLB CMO Trust D, $150 million) in which the first class received interest that was reset quarterly at a spread of 37.5 basis points over the three-month London Interbank Offered Rate (LIBOR). This CMO structure, referred to as a floating-rate CMO, appealed to financial institutions and foreign investors that sought investments in which investment yields varied with the rate paid on their liabilities. As an indication of the popularity of this structure, almost one-half of the 150 CMOs issued in the six-month period following the introduction of the floating-rate CMO included a floating-rate class.[3] The design of the floating-rate CMO subsequently changed to make the floating-rate class comparable in investment characteristics to other short-term instruments that attract funds from financial institutions.

One feature of the floating-rate CMO necessary to ensure that the collateral would be sufficient to meet all obliga-

---

[3]Ravi Dattatreya and Lakhbir S. Hayre, "Floating-Rate Collateralized Mortgage Obligations," in Fabozzi, ed., *The Handbook of Mortgage-Backed Securities,* rev. ed.

tions of the CMO issue was a cap placed on the maximum lifetime interest rate that could be paid to the floating-rate class. This feature made floating-rate CMOs a less attractive vehicle for financial institutions and foreign investors seeking instruments for asset/liability management. To overcome this drawback, an inverse floating-rate class was introduced.

Inverse floater. In October 1986, a CMO class was introduced in which the coupon rate floated in the direction opposite to the change in interest rates. This CMO class is called an *inverse floating-rate* class, or simply, *inverse floater.* When an inverse floater is included in a CMO structure along with a floating-rate class, the maximum coupon rate that can be paid to the floating-rate class is higher than in the absence of an inverse floater.

To illustrate the inverse floater and how it affects the cap on a floating-rate class, we will use an actual CMO deal. The FHLMC Series 128 CMO was issued in January 1990. The coupon rate on the underlying collateral was 9% and the principal amount at the time of issuance was $1 billion. As part of the CMO structure there was a floating-rate class with a principal of $64 million and an inverse floater with a principal of $16 million. Therefore, the floater and inverse floater represented $80 million of the $1 billion structure.

The coupon rate for the floating-rate class is:

$$LIBOR + 0.65$$

For the inverse floater the coupon rate is:

$$42.4 - 4 \times LIBOR$$

The weighted average coupon rate is:

$$\frac{64}{80} \text{ (Floater coupon rate) } +$$

$$\frac{16}{80} \text{ (Inverse floater coupon rate)}$$

The weighted average coupon rate is 9% regardless of the level of LIBOR. For example, if LIBOR is 10%, then

floater coupon rate = 10 + 0.65 = 10.65
inverse floater coupon rate = 42.4 − 4 × 10 = 2.4

The weighted average coupon rate is:

$$\frac{64}{80}\,(10.65) + \frac{16}{80}\,(2.4) = 9$$

Consequently, the coupon rate on the underlying collateral, 9%, can support the aggregate interest payments that must be made to these two classes.

Since LIBOR is always positive, the coupon rate paid to the floating-rate class cannot be negative. However, if there are no restrictions placed on the coupon rate for the inverse floater, it is possible for the coupon rate for that class to be negative. To prevent this, a floor is set on the coupon rate for the inverse floater. In this deal, the floor is set at zero. By imposing this floor, a restriction is placed on the maximum coupon rate that can be paid to the floating-rate class. The maximum coupon rate is 11.25%. This is found by substituting zero for the coupon rate of the inverse floater in the formula for the weighted average coupon rate and then setting the formula equal to 9.

Notice also that in the absence of the inverse floater, the coupon rate that the floating-rate class can be paid cannot go to far above 9%, the coupon rate on the underlying collateral. The reason that it can be slightly above 9% will be explained later when we discuss the CMO residual.

The multiple by which the coupon interest rate on the inverse floater will change is called the *coupon leverage*. In our illustration, the multiple is 4. The larger the coupon leverage, the more the inverse floater's coupon interest rate will change for a given change in LIBOR. For example, a coupon leverage of 4 means that a 100 basis point change in LIBOR will change the coupon interest rate on the inverse floater by 400 basis points; a coupon leverage of 0.7 means that the coupon interest rate will change by 70 basis points for a 100 basis point change in LIBOR. Inverse floaters with a wide variety of coupon leverages are available in the market. Participants refer to low-leverage inverse floaters as those with a coupon leverage between 0.5 and 2.1; medium leverage as those with a coupon leverage greater than 2.1 but not exceeding 4.5; and high leverage as those with a coupon leverage greater than 4.5.

An inverse floater can be used to hedge portfolios with fixed-rate assets that mature sooner than fixed-rate liabilities. For example, if an asset matures in two years but the corresponding liability matures in three years, this asset/liability mismatch makes the investor vulnerable to a fall in market interest rates, which causes the value of liabilities to rise more than that of the asset and creates the danger that when the asset matures the proceeds will be reinvested at a lower rate. The spread between the yield on the asset and the liability will then narrow and possibly become negative. By purchasing an inverse floater, the investor can protect himself against this risk. Should interest rates decrease, the investor will receive a higher rate on the inverse floater, which can be used to offset the lower rate earned when the proceeds are reinvested.

A special type of inverse floater is the *two-tiered index bond*. With this bond, the coupon is fixed within a specified range for the reference rate. Once the upper range for the reference rate is reached (called the strike rate), the coupon resets based on a specified formula so that as the reference rate rises, the coupon rate falls. The rate at which the coupon is fixed represents the cap on the bond; a floor is set at a coupon rate of 0%. For example, a two-tiered index bond may be structured as follows: (1) for one-month LIBOR (the reference rate) between 0% and 9%, the coupon rate is fixed at 9.3%, and (2) if one-month LIBOR is greater than 9% (the strike rate), the coupon rate is set by the following formula:

$$\text{coupon rate} = 69 - 6 \times \text{one-month LIBOR}$$

with a floor of 0% which is reached when LIBOR is 11.5% or greater.

With floater and inverse floater classes in a CMO structure, a fixed-rate instrument is converted into two instruments that satisfy two different asset/liability objectives.

Superfloater. In September 1987, a new type of floating-rate bond class was introduced. This bond class, developed by PaineWebber and Franklin Savings Bank, has a coupon rate that changes by a multiple of the change in LIBOR and is referred to as a *super floater*.[4] In a conventional floating-rate class, the coupon rate resets at a fixed spread above LIBOR. For example, the coupon rate may be LIBOR plus 60 basis points. In contrast, a superfloater has a coupon rate that is initially set below LIBOR but that changes by some multiple of the change in LIBOR. For example, the initial coupon rate for a superfloater may be:

initial LIBOR − 50 basis points +
2 X (change in LIBOR)

To illustrate, suppose that initial LIBOR is 8%. Then the coupon rate for a conventional floater of, say, LIBOR plus 60 basis points and the superfloater with a coupon rate based on the above formula is as follows if LIBOR changes:

	coupon rate (in basis points) if LIBOR changes by:						
	−300	−200	−100	0	+100	+200	+300
conventional floater	5.6	6.6	7.6	8.6	9.6	10.6	11.6
superfloater	1.5	3.5	5.5	7.5	9.5	11.5	13.5

The spread to LIBOR if LIBOR changes is then:

	spread (in basis points) to LIBOR if LIBOR changes by:						
	−300	−200	−100	0	+100	+200	+300
conventional floater	60	60	60	60	60	60	60
superfloater	−350	−250	150	−50	50	150	250

From the above table, notice that the spread to LIBOR (1) provides a substantially higher yield than a conventional floater when interest rates are rising, and (2) provides a substantially lower yield than a conventional floater when interest rates are falling or stable.

To see the potential use for this instrument, consider a thrift that (1) has invested funds in a fixed-rate mortgage

[4]The first superfloater was called Floating LIBOR Indexed Coupon Security or FLICS.

portfolio with a yield of 10.5% and (2) has a short-term funding cost that is on average equal to LIBOR plus 20 basis points. LIBOR we shall assume is currently 8%. Suppose that the thrift's objective is to lock in an interest rate spread of 80 basis points. The table below shows the interest rate spread as LIBOR changes:

	change in LIBOR in basis points						
	− 300	− 200	− 100	0	+ 100	+ 200	+ 300
mortgage yield (%)	10.5	10.5	10.5	10.5	10.5	10.5	10.5
ST funding cost (%)	5.2	6.2	7.2	8.2	9.2	10.2	11.2
interest spread (%)	5.3	4.3	3.3	2.3	1.3	0.3	− 0.7

Notice that the thrift will not be able to meet its interest rate spread objective if LIBOR changes by more than 200 basis points. Now suppose that the thrift purchases the superfloater that we used in our illustration. In particular, assume that the thrift is able to restructure its asset portfolio so that it has an equal amount of 10.5% mortgages and superfloaters. The thrift's portfolio return is the average of the mortgage yield and the superfloater rate. The average portfolio yield as LIBOR changes is then:

	change in LIBOR in basis points						
	− 300	− 200	− 100	0	+ 100	+ 200	+ 300
mortgage yield (%)	10.5	10.5	10.5	10.5	10.5	10.5	10.5
superfloater (%)	1.5	3.5	5.5	7.5	9.5	11.5	13.5
avg. port. yield (%)	6.0	7.0	8.0	9.0	10.0	11.0	12.0

The interest rate spread is then:

	change in LIBOR in basis points						
	− 300	− 200	− 100	0	+ 100	+ 200	+ 300
avg. port. yield (%)	6.0	7.0	8.0	9.0	10.0	11.0	12.0
ST funding cost (%)	5.2	6.2	7.2	8.2	9.2	10.2	11.2
interest spread (%)	0.8	0.8	0.8	0.8	0.8	0.8	0.8

Notice that regardless of how LIBOR changes, the thrift will meet its investment objective of an 80 basis point interest rate spread. This does not come without a cost. The thrift has given up the opportunity to realize an interest rate spread greater than 80 basis points if LIBOR decreases.

This simple illustration demonstrates how a thrift can use a superfloater to hedge its interest rate spread. The actual hedge is more complicated to construct but the basic principle is the same.[5]

The same hedge can be constructed using existing instruments. The return pattern of a superfloater can be replicated by purchasing (1) a conventional floater and (2) LIBOR-based caps that are paid for with a combination of cash and premium income received from writing both in- and out-of-the-money LIBOR-based options.[6] Sounds complicated, doesn't it? The superfloater is much simpler; that's why it was created.

PAC bonds. While many traditional corporate bond buyers shifted their allocation to CMOs, there were still investors on the sidelines reluctant to invest in an instrument that they continued to perceive as having significant prepayment risk despite the innovations discussed above. Potential demand for a CMO product with greater stability for the cash flow was increasing because of two trends in the corporate bond market. First was the increased event risk faced by investors, highlighted by the RJR Nabisco leveraged buyout in 1988.[7] The second trend was the decline in the number of triple-A rated corporate issues. Traditional corporate bond buyers sought a structure that had high credit quality and the characteristics of a corporate bond. While CMOs satisfied the first condition, they did not satisfy the second.

In March 1987, the M.D.C. Mortgage Funding Corporation issued a class of bonds in its CMO series O referred to as *stabilized mortgage reduction term* (SMRT) bonds and in its CMO Series P a class referred to as *planned amortization class* (PAC) bonds. The Oxford Acceptance Corporation III, Series C

---

[5]For a discussion of these complications, see Michael Smirlock, "Superfloaters: A CMO Innovation," *MBS Letter,* March 21, 1988, pp. 7, 10.

[6]Ibid, p. 7.

[7]Event risk refers to the unexpected impairment of an issuer's ability to make interest and principal payments as the result of a takeover, corporate restructuring, or a natural or industrial accident.

CMOs included a class of bonds referred to as *planned redemption obligation* (PRO) bonds. The common characteristic shared by these three bonds is that, within a specified range of prepayment rates, the cash flow pattern is known.

The greater predictability of the cash flow for these classes of bonds, now referred to exclusively as PAC bonds, occurs because there is a principal repayment schedule that must be satisfied. The PAC bondholders, therefore, have priority over all other classes in the CMO issue in receiving principal payments from the underlying collateral. The greater certainty of the cash flow for the PAC bonds comes at the expense of the non-PAC classes, called the *companion* or *support* classes. Should the actual prepayment speed be faster than the upper limit of the PAC range, then the companion bonds receive the excess. This means that the companion bonds absorb the contraction risk. Should the actual prepayment speed be slower than the lower limit of the range, then in subsequent periods the PAC bondholders have priority on principal payments (both scheduled and prepayments). This reduces extension risk, which is absorbed by the companion bondholders. Because there may be more than one class of bonds receiving principal payments at the same time, structures with PAC bonds are called *simultaneous-pay* CMOs.

Figure 11-3 illustrates how a PAC bond can be constructed from underlying collateral. Figure 11-3a shows the principal payments that will result if the prepayment speed for the life of some hypothetical collateral is 80% PSA. Therefore, if the prepayment speed does in fact turn out to be 80% PSA, the solid curve in Figure 11-3a represents a principal payment schedule that can be satisfied by the underlying collateral. Next consider Figure 11-3b. This figure shows the principal payments if the prepayment speed is considerably faster, 300% PSA. Thus, the broken line in Figure 11-3b represents a principal payment schedule that can be satisfied by the underlying collateral if the prepayment speed is in fact 300% PSA. Notice that the principal payments are higher in the earlier years in comparison to Figure 11-3a but in later years the principal payments are lower because of the faster prepayments.

Figure 11-3c combines the solid line in Figure 11-3a and the broken line in Figure 11-3b. The shaded area in Figure

Figure 11-3
Principal Cash Flow at 80% PSA and 300% PSA

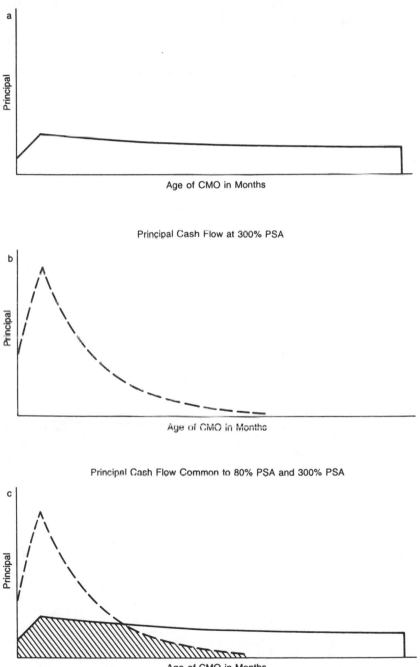

Principal Cash Flow at 80% PSA

a

Principal

Age of CMO in Months

Principal Cash Flow at 300% PSA

b

Principal

Age of CMO in Months

Principal Cash Flow Common to 80% PSA and 300% PSA

c

Principal

Age of CMO in Months

11-3c represents the principal payments that will be available to pay bondholders as long as the prepayment rate is either 80% or 300% PSA.[8] In fact, it tells us even more. The shaded area represents the principal payment schedule that will be available to pay bondholders at every possible PSA rate between 80% and 300% PSA.

The upper and lower PSA levels used to construct the principal payment schedule shown in Figure 11-3c are called the *initial PAC collar*. The key is that prepayment protection is ensured as long as the companion bonds are not fully paid off. Consequently, the degree of prepayment protection changes over time as actual prepayments occur. For example, if prepayments over the first few years are at the lower end of the initial PAC collar, there will be a greater amount of companion bonds remaining. This will result in greater prepayment protection for the PAC bonds. A new collar can be determined that will allow PAC bondholders to realize their original principal payment schedule as long as prepayments are within the collar. This new collar is called the *effective collar*.

The breaking of the initial collar does not mean that the principal payment schedule will not be met. It depends on when the initial collar is broken, the amount of the deviation from the collar, and how long the collar is broken. For example, if for the PAC bond in Figure 11-3 the prepayment rate is within the initial PAC collar for the first three years but then speeds up to, say, 350% PSA for two months, this will not affect the principal payment schedule. The reason is that since the prepayments in the first three years were within the initial PAC collar, there will be a greater amount of companion bonds at the end of three years than originally anticipated. The faster prepayment for two months will be easily absorbed by the companion bonds. In contrast, if the prepayment rate for the first 10 months is 400% PSA, there is a good chance that the principal payment schedule will not be satisfied, since the companion bonds will be paid off, thereby offering less prepayment protection.

---

[8]The length of time over which the scheduled principal payments are expected to be made is referred to as the PAC *window*. From an investor's perspective, the preferred length of the window depends on the liability stream. Market participants, however, appear to prefer tight windows, as if all institutional investors face a bullet liability.

Figure 11-4

Creation of a Sequence of PAC Bonds

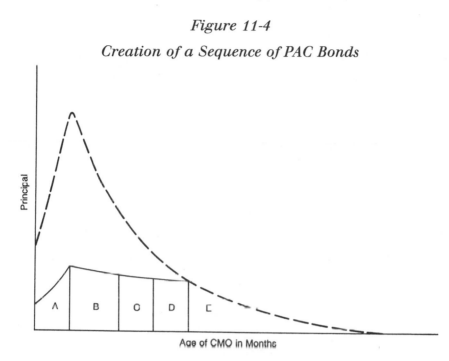

Age of CMO in Months

In practice, there is more than one class of PAC bonds in a CMO structure. How this can be done with the collateral in Figure 11-3 is illustrated in Figure 11-4, where five sequential PACs (labeled A, B, C, D, and E) are shown. If the prepayment rate is between 80% and 300% PSA, the principal payment schedule indicated in the figure can be made for each of these PACs. The average life for the PACs is short term, A, to long term, E. In fact, the protection for the later PACs is even greater than the 80% and 300% PSA initial collar suggests. This can be seen in Figure 11-5, which shows two additional curves with prepayment rates faster than 300% PSA. Notice that the principal payment schedule for C will be satisfied if the prepayment rate is between 80% and 370% PSA and for B 80% and 390% PSA.

    Beginning in 1989, CMO PAC structures were created with a sequential series of accrual PAC (or Z-PAC) bond classes.[9] The Z-PAC bonds had a variety of average lives, from

---

[9] Also in 1989, structurers included some unusual features for turning the accrual mechanism on and off. Under certain conditions—either relating to a particular date, the level of interest rates, or the amount of principal available to pay other classes in the CMO structure—a Z-PAC bond can be converted into a coupon-paying bond. Such bonds are referred to as "jump Z-bonds."

Figure 11-5

Greater Protection for a Sequence of PAC Bonds

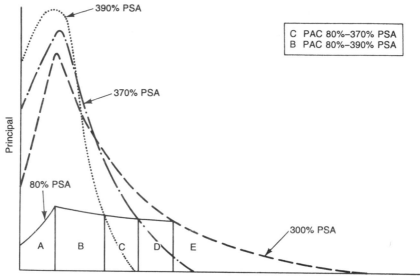

Age of CMO in Months

intermediate term to long term. Moreover, unlike the traditional accrual bond, Z-PAC bonds have less uncertainty about cash flow. The Z-PAC bonds broaden the interest of traditional zero-coupon bond buyers in CMOs.

The selection of the PACs to be created will depend on investor demand for classes with certain average lives and windows. The procedure for calculating the average life of a mortgage-backed security is described in the next chapter. As we have already noted, the window for a PAC refers to the time between the first payment of principal and the estimated final principal payment. The tighter the PAC window, the more a PAC resembles a corporate bond with a bullet payment (i.e., a corporate term bond).

The market seems to have settled upon initial PAC collars from 80 to 250 PSA or 90 to 275 PSA. Structurers of CMOs find that such ranges allow them to increase arbitrage profits.

A few more wrinkles in the subject of PAC bonds. In some CMO structures, structurers have found it more profitable to exclude some of the shorter maturity PACs. For example, for the CMO structure in Figure 11-3, only the last three PACs (C, D, and E), might be included. The exclusion of A and B is referred to as a *lockout*. When there is a lockout, it increases the prepayment protection offered to the PAC bonds included in the structure. For example, at slow prepayment speeds, there will be no earlier PAC bonds (A and B in our example) that are entitled to receive priority on future principal payments when there is a shortfall in the amount due. Thus, the risk of extension for the PACs included in the structure is reduced.

Some structures have been designed to give certain PAC bonds greater prepayment protection than other PAC bonds. This can be done by reversing the order of priority of the distribution of principal payments when prepayment speeds increase. Turning once again to our earlier PAC with five tranches, the CMO can be structured so that if, say, the PAC A bond is paid its scheduled principal and all the companion bonds have been paid off completely, then instead of paying PAC A bondholders more than their scheduled amount, the last PAC bond, E, begins receiving principal payments. Thus, the PAC A bond is protected from contraction risk by the PAC E bonds. A structure in which the priority of PACs with respect to the distribution of principal is reversed is known as a *reverse PAC* structure.

Earlier we discussed floating-rate and inverse floating-rate classes. In the more recent CMO structures, these bonds typically have been created from the companion bonds in a CMO deal with PAC bonds. Since they are companion bonds, floaters and inverse floaters have greater prepayment risk.

Companions with schedules. The creation of a floater and inverse floater from a companion bond is but one example of how a companion bond's cash flow can be distributed in order to create a bond or bonds that can be used for better asset/liability matching or hedging. The companion bonds absorb prepayment risk, thereby protecting the PAC bonds. However, companion bonds themselves can have cash flows prioritized so as to reduce prepayment risk. Companion bonds with schedules resulting from the prioritization of cash flows still have greater prepayment risk than the PAC bonds they support. However, prepayment risk is less than in the absence of a schedule.

Companion bonds with schedules, also referred to as *PAC II level bonds,* are supported by other companion bonds without schedules. (PACs in a structure in which there are PAC II level bonds are called PAC I level bonds.) There have been CMO structures with PAC III level bonds, these being bonds in which the companion (support) bonds for the level II PAC bonds have schedules.

TAC bonds. In 1988, PaineWebber introduced a variant of the PAC bond in its PaineWebber CMO Trust Series L. This CMO had a class called the Targeted Amortization Class (TAC) bond. As with PAC bonds, a TAC bond has priority over companion bonds. The prepayment protection afforded TAC bonds, however, is less than that of PAC bonds. It is designed to provide protection against contraction risk but exposes the investor to extension risk. This is accomplished by specifying a narrower PSA prepayment range or just a single PSA prepayment rate over which the principal is guaranteed.[10]

Some institutional investors are interested in protection against extension risk but are willing to accept contraction risk. This is the opposite protection that is sought by TAC bondholders. The structures that have been created to provide such protection are referred to as *reverse TAC* bonds.

The use of TAC bonds in a CMO structure in the earlier deals is quite different from its use today. Today TAC and reverse TAC bonds are created from companion bonds. As such, they provide support for PAC bondholders.

VADM bonds. Accrual or Z-bonds have been used in CMO structures as support for bonds called *very accurately defined maturity* (VADM) or *guaranteed final maturity* bonds. Specifically, the interest accruing (i.e., not being paid out) on a Z-bond is used to pay the interest and principal on a VADM bond. What this effectively does is provide protection against extension risk even if prepayments slow down, since the interest accruing on the Z-bond will be sufficient to pay off the

---

[10]For a more detailed explanation of TACs see William J. Curtin and Paul T. Van Valkenburg, "CMO PAC and TAC Bonds: Call Protected Mortgage Securities," in Frank J. Fabozzi, ed., *Managing Institutional Assets* (New York: Harper & Row, 1990).

scheduled principal and interest on the VADM bond. Thus, the *maximum* final maturity can be determined with a high degree of certainty. However, if prepayments are high, resulting in the supporting Z-bond being paid off faster, a VADM bond can shorten.

A VADM is similar in character to a reverse TAC. For structures with similar collateral, however, a VADM bond offers greater protection against extension risk. Moreover, most VADMs that have been created will not shorten significantly if prepayments speed up. Thus, they offer greater protection against contraction risk compared to a reverse TAC with the same underlying collateral. Compared to PACs, VADM bonds have greater absolute protection against extension risk, and though VADM bonds do not have as much protection against contraction risk, as just noted the structures that have included these bonds are such that contraction risk is generally not significant.

CMO residuals. The excess of the cash flow generated by the underlying collateral over the amount needed to pay interest, retire the bonds, and pay administrative expenses is called the *CMO residual.* Investors can purchase an equity position in the residual cash flow as it accumulates over time. The excess cash flow is not known with certainty. It depends on several factors: (1) current and future interest rates, (2) the coupon rate on the underlying mortgage collateral, (3) the type of collateral, (4) the prepayment rate on the underlying collateral, and (5) the structure of the CMO issue.

The three most common sources of CMO residual cash flow are (1) premium interest, (2) bond coupon differential, and (3) reinvestment income.[11] The first and most important component is the cash flow generated from premium interest. This represents the difference between the coupon rate on the collateral and the coupon rate paid on the highest coupon rate bond in the CMO structure. For example, if the coupon rate on the collateral is 9.5% and 9.125% is the highest coupon rate paid on a bond class, the premium interest is 0.375%. The bond coupon differential arises because a CMO

---

[11]Mark Stanley, Helene Halperin, Robert Kulason, and William Calan, *CMO Residuals: Structure and Performance* (Merrill Lynch Capital Markets, January 1988).

structure is designed to support bond payments assuming that each bond class has a coupon rate equal to the highest coupon rate bond class. For example, if the coupon rate on the highest coupon rate bond is 9.125% and there are three other classes with coupon rates of 7.75%, 8.0%, and 8.9%, the bond coupon differential would be generated from 137.5, 112.5, and 22.5 basis point differentials, respectively. The third source of residual cash flow is the income generated by the reinvestment of cash flow payments from the collateral between the time received and the time payments must be made to bondholders.

The CMO residual is an interesting instrument because its value should move in the same direction as the change in interest rates and not in the opposite direction, assuming that there is no floating-rate class in the structure. To understand why, consider what happens when interest rates/mortgage rates fall. There are two adverse affects. First, prepayments are expected to speed up. The result is that the classes receiving the lower coupon rate will be paid off faster, thereby reducing the cash flow for the investor in the CMO residual resulting from the premium income and bond coupon differential. Second, the cash flow that is reinvested until it is paid to each CMO class will be invested at a lower interest rate. Together, these two effects will result in a lower expected cash flow for the CMO residual owners and a lower price for the CMO residual.[12] If interest rates/mortgage rates rise, the expected cash flow for the CMO residual will increase, because prepayments will be expected to slow down and cash flow before payout to CMO bondholders will be reinvested at a higher interest rate. The result should be an increase in the price of the CMO residual.

Because the price of a CMO residual moves in the same direction as the change in interest rates, it can be used by institutions for hedging portfolios of passthroughs.

IOettes and PAC IOs. In the earlier structures, the premium interest and the coupon bond differential accrued to the benefit of the residual class. This is no longer the practice in structuring CMOs. Instead, the premium income is now

---

[12] The cash flow will be discounted at a lower interest rate but typically the overall effect means a lower price.

stripped off and used to pay a class known as the *interest only* (IO) class, and the coupon bond differential is stripped off to create a class known as a *PAC IO*.

This can be illustrated with the FHLMC 1044 CMO. This deal included five PAC I level bonds and one PAC II level bond. The coupon rate for each of these bonds is:

A PAC I level 7.75%
B PAC I level 8.00
C PAC I level 8.60
D PAC I level 8.90
E PAC I level 8.50
F PAC II level 8.40

The coupon rate for the underlying collateral for this structure was 9.5%. The residual class was given a fixed coupon rate of 9.125%. A bond class was created, called the Class L, which was given the difference between the collateral coupon rate of 9.5% and the maximum coupon rate of the PACs and residual class; that is, it was the premium income. Since the maximum coupon rate was 9.125%, the coupon rate of the residual class, Class L received 37.5 basis points. Since this class was only entitled to receive interest, it was called an IO. However, a provision in the tax law does not permit a CMO structure to have a class that receives no principal. Consequently, structurers must include a nominal principal for an IO class included in a CMO structure, effectively making the class a bond with an extremely high coupon rate. Because of this nominal principal, an IO included in a CMO is referred to as an *IOette*.

Notice also that in the FHLMC 1044 CMO there is still excess coupon interest available, since only 9.125% of the 9.5% is paid out to the IOette and the residual class (which we earlier called bond coupon differential). The difference between the coupon interest rate that had to be paid to the PAC I level and PAC II level bonds given the level of interest rates at the time this structure was created allowed for the additional stripping of interest. In this structure, the bond coupon differential between 9.125% and the coupon rate on PAC bonds A, B, and C was used to create an IO bond, Class I. Since this IO class is created out of the stripped interest from PACs, it is called a PAC IO. In fact, in the FHLMC 1044 deal a second PAC IO, Class J, was created by stripping off the interest from the two PAC Classes D and E. By stripping off the interest between 9.125% and the coupon interest of 8.4% on the PAC II level bond (Class F), a PAC II level IO was created (Class K).

Number of Classes in CMO Structures

Given the vast number of CMO classes that can be included in a deal structure, it is not surprising to see structures issued today with as many as 70 classes. Prior to 1988, the average number of classes in a CMO deal was four. With the introduction of PACs, the average number of classes per deal increased to about six by 1988. The deals between 1986 (when PACs were introduced) and 1988 typically included only one or two PAC classes. By 1989, there was an average of nine classes per deal, and in 1990 and 1991, there were about 11 classes per deal.

STRIPPED MORTGAGE-BACKED SECURITIES

Stripped mortgage-backed securities, introduced by Fannie Mae in 1986, are another example of derivative products. A passthrough assigns the cash flow from the underlying pool of mortgages on a pro rata basis to the security holders. A stripped MBS is created by altering the distribution of principal and interest from a pro rata distribution to an *unequal* distribution. The securities thus created will have a price/yield relationship that is different from the price/yield relationship of the underlying mortgage pool.

Types of Stripped MBS

There are three types of stripped MBS: (1) synthetic-coupon passthroughs, (2) interest only/principal only securities, and (3) CMO strips.

Synthetic-coupon passthroughs. The first generation of stripped mortgage-backed securities are called synthetic-coupon passthroughs. This is because the unequal distribution of coupon and principal resulted in a synthetic coupon rate that is different from the underlying collateral. We can illustrate this development by looking at the stripped MBSs issued by Fannie Mae in mid-1986.[13] The Class B stripped mortgage-backed securities were backed by FNMA 9% graduated payment mortgage pools. (The mortgages were seasoned such that the monthly payments were no longer graduated but level.) The mortgage payments from the underlying mortgage pool are distributed to Class B-1 and Class B-2 in the following way. Both classes receive an equal amount of the principal. However, the interest payments are divided so that Class B-1 receives one-third while Class B-2 receives two-thirds. Thus, for every $100 of principal cash flow from the collateral, both Class B-1 and Class B-2 receive $50. For every $9 of coupon interest, the distribution is as follows: $3 to Class B-1 and $6 to Class B-2. The synthetic coupon for Class B-1 is 6% ($3/$50) and for Class B-2 it is 12% ($6/$50). In a 9% interest rate environment, Class B-1 would effectively be a discount security and Class B-2 a premium security.

In a subsequent issue, Fannie Mae distributed the cash flow from the underlying mortgage pool in a far different way. Using FNMA 11% coupon pools, Fannie Mae created Class A-1 and Class A-2. Class A-1 is given 4.95% of the 11% coupon interest while Class A-2 receives the other 6.05%. However, Class A-1 is given almost all of the principal payments, 99%, while Class A-2 is given only 1% of the principal payments.

Interest only/principal only strips. In early 1987, stripped MBSs began to be issued in which all of the interest is allocated to one class (the interest only or IO class) and all of the principal to the other class (called the *principal only* or PO class). The IO class receives no principal payments.

The PO security is purchased at a substantial discount

---

[13] For a further discussion, see Richard Roll, "Stripped Mortgage-Backed Securities," in Fabozzi, ed., *The Handbook of Mortgage-Backed Securities,* rev. ed.

from par value. The yield an investor will realize depends on the speed at which prepayments are made. The faster the prepayments, the higher the yield that will be realized by the investor. For example, suppose that there is a mortgage pool consisting of only 30-year mortgages with $400 million in principal and that investors can purchase POs backed by this mortgage pool for $175 million. The dollar return on this investment will be $225 million. How quickly that dollar return is recovered by PO investors determines the yield that will be realized. In the extreme case, if all homeowners in the underlying mortgage pool decide to prepay their mortgage loans immediately, PO investors will realize the $225 million immediately. At the other extreme, if all homeowners decide to remain in their home for 30 years and make no prepayments, the $225 million will be spread out over 30 years, which will result in a lower yield for PO investors.

Let's look at how the price of the PO can be expected to change as mortgage rates in the market change. When mortgage rates decline below the coupon rate, prepayments are expected to speed up, accelerating payments to the PO holder. Thus, the cash flow of a PO improves (in the sense that principal repayments are received earlier). The cash flow will be discounted at a lower interest rate since the mortgage rate in the market has declined. The result is that the price of a PO will increase when mortgage rates decline. When mortgage rates rise above the coupon rate, prepayments are expected to slow down. The cash flow deteriorates (in the sense of its taking longer to recover principal repayments). Coupled with a higher discount rate, the price of a PO will fall when mortgage rates rise.

When an IO is purchased there is no par value. In contrast to the PO investor, the IO investor wants prepayments to be slow. The reason is that the IO investor only receives interest on the amount of the principal outstanding. As prepayments are made, the outstanding principal declines and less dollar interest is received. In fact, if prepayments are too fast, the IO investor may not recover the amount paid for the IO.

Let's look at the expected price response of an IO to changes in mortgage rates. If mortgage rates decline below the coupon rate, the prepayments are expected to accelerate. This results in a deterioration of the expected cash flow for an IO. Although the cash flow will be discounted at a lower rate, the net effect is typically a decline in the price of an IO. If mortgage rates rise above the coupon rate the expected cash flow improves. However, the cash flow is discounted at a higher interest rate. The net effect may be either a rise or fall for the IO. Thus, we see an interesting characteristic of an IO: its price tends to move in the same direction as the change in mortgage rates. This effect occurs (1) when mortgage rates fall below the coupon rate and (2) for some range of mortgage rates above the coupon rate.

An example of this effect can be seen in Figure 11-6, which shows for various mortgage rates the price of (1) a 9% passthrough, (2) a PO created from this passthrough, and (3)

Figure 11-6

Relationship Between Price and Mortgage Rates for a Passthrough, PO and IO

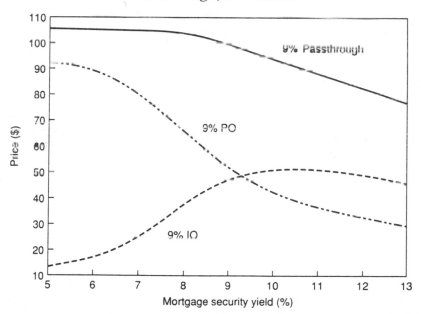

Source: Adapted from Steven J. Carlson and Timothy D. Sears, "Stripped Mortgage Pass-Throughs: New Tools for Investors," in Frank J. Fabozzi, ed., *The Handbook of Mortgage-Backed Securities*, rev. ed. (Chicago: Probus Publishing, 1988), p. 564.

an IO created from this passthrough. Notice that as mortgage rates decline below 9%, the price of the passthrough does not respond much. This is the negative convexity (or price compression) property of passthroughs, which we discuss in Chapters 12 and 13. For the PO security, the price falls monotonically as mortgage rates rise. For the IO security, at mortgage rates above approximately 10%, the price declines as mortgage rates rise; as mortgage rates fall below about 10%, the price of an IO falls as mortgage rates decline.

Both POs and IOs exhibit substantial price volatility when mortgage rates change. As we explain in Chapter 12, the greater price volatility of the IO and PO compared to the passthrough from which they were created can be seen by the steepness of a tangent line to the curves at any given mortgage rate.

As we noted in our discussion of CMOs, the collateral can be passthroughs or a pool of whole loans. There are also CMOs that are backed by POs, such structures being referred to as *PO-collateralized CMOs*.

CMO strips. One of the classes in a CMO structure can be a principal only or interest only class.[14] These are called CMO strips. A CMO strip may be a PAC or TAC. When a CMO strip is a PO class that is neither a PAC nor a TAC, it is called a *Super PO*. The reason for referring to such a class as a Super PO relates to its potential price performance if prepayments increase in speed as interest rates decline. When this occurs, the Super PO bondholders are paid off faster; since these bonds are issued at a substantial discount from par, the result is "super" price performance.[15]

Hedging Applications of Stripped MBSs

Traditional derivative products such as futures contracts can be used to hedge interest rate risk. Investors in

---

[14] Actually, the interest only classes structured as a REMIC must receive some nominal principal. Therefore, technically they are often referred to as high-coupon classes.

[15] For an illustration of the performance of Super POs, see Blaine Robert, Sarah Keil Wolf, and Nancy Wilt, "Advances and Innovations in the CMO Market," in Frank J. Fabozzi, ed., *Advances and Innovations in the Bond and Mortgage Markets* (Chicago: Probus Publishing, 1989), pp. 437–456.

mortgage-related products are concerned with hedging both interest rate and prepayment risk. If properly handled, stripped MBSs can be used to hedge these two risks simultaneously. To understand how, we must first explain a concept that we discuss in more detail in Chapter 12. Duration is a measure of the price volatility of an interest-sensitive security. For a security to have a positive duration means that when interest rates move in one direction, the price moves in the opposite direction; for a security to have a negative duration means that when interest rates move in one direction, the price moves in the same direction. Hedging involves creating a position with a zero duration.

A PO's price changes in the direction opposite to the change in interest rates. Consequently, a PO has a positive duration. In addition, a PO can be purchased at a discount, thereby affording leveraging potential for hedging. A PO can be used to hedge a mortgage-related product with a negative duration. Two examples of such products are passthroughs selling at a premium and mortgage servicing.[16]

Since an IO tends to move in the same direction as the change in interest rates when mortgage rates are declining, an IO has negative duration. An IO is recommended for hedging the interest rate and prepayment risk for a portfolio of discount passthroughs.[17]

Thus, while IOs and POs are high-risk securities in terms of their potential price volatility, if properly used these securities can reduce a portfolio's interest rate and prepayment risk.

---

[16]For an illustration of how a PO can be used to hedge a premium passthrough, see Steven J. Carlson and Timothy D. Sears, "Stripped Mortgage Pass-Throughs: New Tools for Investors," in Fabozzi, ed., *The Handbook of Mortgage-Backed Securities,* rev. ed., pp. 553–584. An illustration of how a PO can be used to hedge mortgage servicing is given in Lakhbir Hayre and Errol Mustafa, "Stripped Mortgage-Backed Securities," in Fabozzi, ed., *The Handbook of Mortgage-Backed Securities,* 3d ed.

[17]Illustrations can be found in ibid.

12

Review of Fixed-Income Analysis

In this chapter we provide a review of the techniques for analyzing fixed-income securities. Our intent is not to set forth a rigorous discourse on this topic; instead, we highlight the key concepts needed to understand the valuation methodologies described in Chapter 13. Readers who are familiar with the price/yield properties of fixed-income securities (option-free bonds and callable bonds) and their price volatility characteristics (duration and convexity) can skip this chapter.

FUNDAMENTAL PRINCIPLE OF VALUATION

The value or price of any financial instrument is equal to the present (discounted) value of its *expected* cash flow. By discounting the cash flows, allowance is made for their timing. Consequently, determining the price requires that an investor estimate (1) the expected cash flow and (2) the appropriate required yield.

The expected cash flow for some financial instruments is simple to determine; for others, the task may be quite complex. Assuming that the issuer does not default, determination of the cash flow for a fixed-rate, option-free (that is, a noncallable, nonputable, and nonconvertible) bond is straightforward. The cash flows are (1) coupon interest payments to the maturity date and (2) the par (or maturity) value at maturity. The required yield is determined by investigating the yields offered on comparable bonds in the market. By comparable, we mean issues of the same credit quality, features, and maturity.[1]

OPTION-FREE BONDS

Before discussing the more complex topic of callable securities, we will review the characteristics of option-free bonds.

Price/Yield Relationship for an Option-Free Bond

A fundamental property of a bond is that its price changes in the direction opposite to the change in the required yield. The reason is that the price of the bond is the present value of the cash flow. As the required yield increases, the present value of the cash flow decreases; hence, the price decreases. The opposite is true when the required yield decreases: the present value of the cash flow increases and, therefore, the price of the bond increases.

If we graphed the price/yield relationship for any option-free bond, we would find that it has the "bowed" shape shown in Figure 12-1. This shape is referred to as *convex*. The convexity of the price/yield relationship has important implications for the investment characteristics of a bond, as we will see.

The Relationship of Coupon Rate, Yield, and Price

As yields in the marketplace change, the only variable that market participants can alter to compensate for the new

---

[1]Later in this chapter we present a measure of interest rate risk known as duration. Instead of considering bonds with the same maturity to be comparable, we will recast the analysis in terms of duration.

Figure 12-1

Shape of Price/Yield Relationship for an Option-Free Bond

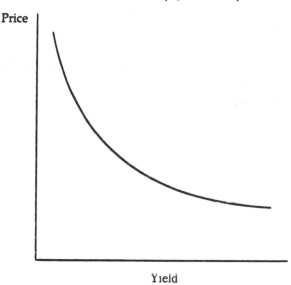

yield is the bond's price. When the coupon rate is equal to the required yield, the price of the bond will be equal to its par value.

When yields in the marketplace rise above the coupon rate, the market price of the bond adjusts downward—below par value—so that any investor that wishes to purchase the bond can realize additional interest. The capital appreciation realized by holding the bond to maturity represents a form of interest payment to the investor, compensating for a coupon rate that is less than the yield required in the market. A bond selling below its par value is said to be selling at a *discount*. When the yield required in the market is below the coupon rate, the price of the bond must sell above its par value. This occurs because investors with the opportunity to purchase the bond at par will be getting a coupon rate in excess of what the market requires. Because its yield is attractive, investors will bid up the price of the bond to a level at which it offers the required yield in the market. A bond priced above its par value is said to be selling at a *premium*.

Sources of a Bond's Return

An investor that purchases a bond can expect to receive a dollar return from one or more of the following sources:

- the coupon interest payments made by the issuer,
- any capital gain (or capital loss—negative dollar return) when the bond matures or is sold, and
- income from reinvestment of the coupon interest payments.

The last source of dollar return is referred to as *interest on interest.*

Yield to Maturity

The most popular measure of yield in the bond market is the yield to maturity. The yield to maturity is the interest rate that will make the present value of the cash flow stream from a bond equal to its price.[2] The yield to maturity considers the coupon income and any capital gain or loss that the investor will realize *by holding the bond to maturity.* The yield to maturity also considers the timing of the cash flows. It does consider interest on interest; *however, it assumes that the coupon payments can be reinvested at an interest rate equal to the yield to maturity.* So, if the yield to maturity for a bond is 10%, for example, to earn that yield the coupon payments must be reinvested at an interest rate equal to 10%. The following illustration clearly demonstrates this.[3]

Suppose an investor has $74.26 and could place the funds in a certificate of deposit that pays 5% every six months for 20 years or 10% per year (on a bond equivalent basis). At the end of 20 years, the $74.26 investment would have grown

---

[2] Letting C_t denote the semiannual coupon interest for the t-th six-month period, M the maturity value, n the number of six-month periods remaining to maturity, P the price of the bond, and y_{SA} the semiannual yield to maturity, then y_{SA} is found by solving the following equation using a trial-and-error process:

$$P = \sum_{t=1}^{n} \frac{C_t}{(1 + y_{SA})^t} + \frac{M}{(1 + y_{SA})^n}$$

[3] This can also be demonstrated by multiplying the formula in the previous footnote by $(1 + y_{SA})^n$.

to $522.79. Instead, the investor buys a 7%, 20-year bond with par value of $100 and a price of $74.26. The yield to maturity for this bond is 10%. The investor expects that at the end of 20 years, the total dollars from the investment will be, like the bank certificate of deposit, $522.79.

Let's look at what the investor will receive. There will be 40 semiannual interest payments of $3.50, which will total $280. When the bond matures, the investor will receive $100. Thus, the total amount that the investor will receive if he holds the bond to maturity is $240. But this is $282.79 less than the $522.79 necessary to produce a yield of 10% on a bond equivalent yield basis. How is this deficiency supposed to be made up? If the investor reinvests the coupon payments at a semiannual interest rate of 5% until the maturity date (or 10% annual rate on a bond equivalent yield basis), then the interest earned on the coupon payments will be $282.79. Consequently, of the $448.53 total dollar return necessary to produce a yield of 10%, about 63% ($282.79 divided by $448.53) must be generated by reinvesting the coupon payments.

Clearly, the investor will only realize the yield to maturity that is stated at the time of purchase if (1) the coupon payments can be reinvested at the yield to maturity, and (2) the bond is held to maturity. With respect to the first assumption, an investor faces the risk that future reinvestment rates will be less than the yield to maturity at the time the bond is purchased. This risk is referred to as *reinvestment risk*. If the bond is not held to maturity, the bond may have to be sold for less than its purchase price, resulting in a return that is less than the yield to maturity. The risk that a bond will have to be sold at a loss is referred to as *interest rate risk* or *price risk*.

Reinvestment risk. There are two characteristics of a bond that determine the degree of reinvestment risk. First, for a given yield to maturity and a given coupon rate, the longer the maturity the more the bond's total dollar return is dependent on the interest on interest to realize the yield to maturity at the time of purchase. That is, the longer the maturity, the greater the reinvestment risk. The implication is that the yield to maturity measure for long-term coupon bonds tells little about the potential yield an investor may realize if the bond is actually held to maturity. For long-term bonds in high-interest rate environments, the interest-on-interest component may be as high as 80% of the bond's potential total dollar return.

The second characteristic that determines the degree of reinvestment risk is the coupon rate. For a given maturity and a given yield to maturity, the higher the coupon rate, the more dependent the bond's total dollar return will be on the reinvestment of the coupon payments in order to produce the yield to maturity at the time of purchase. This means that holding maturity and yield to maturity constant, premium bonds will be more dependent on interest on interest than bonds selling at par. In contrast, discount bonds will be less dependent on interest on interest than bonds selling at par.[4]

Interest rate risk. As explained earlier in this chapter, a bond's price moves in the direction opposite to the change in interest rates. For an investor that plans to hold a bond to maturity, the change in the bond's price prior to maturity is of no concern unless the investor is an institution that must mark its position to market. However, for an investor that may have to sell the bond prior to the maturity date, an increase in interest rates subsequent to the time the bond was purchased will mean the realization of a capital loss. Not all bonds have the same degree of interest rate risk. Later we will explain the characteristics of a bond that determine its interest rate risk.

Given these assumptions underlying yield to maturity, we now can illustrate why yield to maturity has limited value in assessing the relative value of bonds. Suppose that an investor with a five-year investment horizon is considering the following four option-free bonds:

Bond	Coupon	Maturity	Yield to Maturity
W	5%	3 years	9.0%
X	6%	20 years	8.6%
Y	11%	15 years	9.2%
Z	8%	5 years	8.0%

Assuming that all four bonds are of the same credit quality, which one is the most attractive to this investor? An investor that selects the Y bond because it offers the highest yield to

---

[4]For zero-coupon bonds, none of the total dollar return is dependent on interest on interest. So, a zero-coupon bond has no reinvestment risk if held to maturity.

maturity is failing to recognize that the bond must be sold after five years, the price of the bond depending on the yield required in the market for 10-year, 11% coupon bonds at the time of sale. Hence, a capital gain or capital loss may make the return higher or lower than the yield to maturity promised now. Moreover, the higher coupon rate on the Y bond relative to the other three bonds means that more of this bond's return will be dependent on the reinvestment of coupon interest payments.

The W bond offers the second-highest yield to maturity. On the surface, it seems to be particularly attractive because it eliminates the Y bond's problem of realizing a possible capital loss when the bond must be sold prior to the maturity date. In addition, the reinvestment risk seems to be less than for the other three bonds because the coupon rate is the lowest. However, the investor would not be eliminating reinvestment risk, since after three years he must reinvest the proceeds received at maturity for two more years. The yield that the investor will realize will depend on interest rates three years from now, when the investor must reinvest the proceeds received from the maturing bond.

Which is the best bond? The yield to maturity doesn't seem to help us identify the best bond. Instead the answer depends on the investor's expectations. Specifically, it depends on the interest rate at which the coupon interest payments can be reinvested until the end of the investor's investment horizon. Also, for bonds with a maturity longer than the investment horizon, it depends on the investor's expectations about interest rates at the end of the investment horizon. Consequently, any of these bonds can be the best investment vehicle under various scenarios for the reinvestment rate and future interest rate at the end of the investment horizon. Later we will present a framework for assessing the potential performance of a bond over some investment horizon.

BONDS WITH EMBEDDED CALL OPTIONS

Given the foregoing background for option-free bonds, we can now move on to the valuation of callable bonds (i.e., bonds with an embedded call option). Our focus is on callable bonds since passthroughs are effectively securities with embedded call options. The reason, as we have stressed several times throughout this book, is that homeowners have a call option on the mortgage loan and these loans are the underlying pool for a passthrough.

Yield to Call

When a bond is callable, the practice has been to calculate a yield to call as well as a yield to maturity. The former yield calculation assumes that the issuer will call the bond at the first call date. The procedure for calculating the yield to call is the same as for any yield calculation: determine the interest rate that will make the present value of the expected cash flow equal to the price. In the case of yield to call, the expected cash flow includes the coupon payments to the first call date and the call price.

The conventional practice for valuing callable bonds is to compute the yield to call and yield to maturity for a callable bond, and then select the lower of the two as a conservative estimate of potential return. This need only be done for bonds selling at a premium.

The yield to call does consider all three sources of potential return from owning a bond. However, as in the case of the yield to maturity, it assumes that all cash flows can be reinvested at the computed yield—in this case the yield to call—until the assumed call date. As we noted earlier, this assumption may be inappropriate. Moreover, the yield to call assumes that (1) the investor will hold the bond to the assumed call date and (2) the issuer will call the bond on that date.

These assumptions underlying the yield to call are often unrealistic. They do not take into account how an investor will reinvest the proceeds if the issue is called. For example, consider two bonds: the M bond is a five-year noncallable bond and the N bond a five-year bond callable in three years. Suppose that the yield to maturity for the M bond is 10% and the yield to call for the N bond, assuming the bond will be called in three years, is 10.5%. Which bond is better for an investor with a five-year investment horizon? It's not possible to tell from the yields cited. If the investor intends to hold the bond for five years and the issuer calls the bond after three years, the total dollars that will be available at the end of five years will depend on the interest rate that can be earned from investing funds from the call date to the end of the investment horizon.

Disadvantages of Callable Bonds

The holder of a callable bond has given the issuer the right to call the issue prior to the expiration date. This results in two disadvantages to the bondholder. First, an issuer will call a bond when the yield on bonds in the market is lower than the issue's coupon rate. For example, if the coupon rate on a callable bond is 13% and prevailing market yields are 7%, the issuer will find it economic to call the 13% issue and refund it with a 7% issue. From the investor's perspective, the proceeds received will have to be reinvested at a lower interest rate. Thus, callable bonds expose bondholders to reinvestment risk.

Second, as we will explain later in this section, the price appreciation potential for a bond in a declining interest rate environment is limited when it is callable. The price of the callable bond will remain near its call price, rather than rising to the higher price that would result for an otherwise comparable noncallable bond. This phenomenon for a callable bond is referred to as *price compression*.

Given these disadvantages of a callable bond, an investor must receive sufficient compensation in the form of higher potential yield (lower price for the bond) in order to accept call risk.

Price/Yield Relationship for a Callable Bond

We stated earlier that the price/yield relationship for an option-free (i.e., noncallable) bond is convex. Figure 12-2 shows the price/yield relationship for both a noncallable bond and the same bond if it is callable. The convex curve a-a' is

Figure 12-2

Price/Yield Relationship for a Noncallable and a Callable Bond

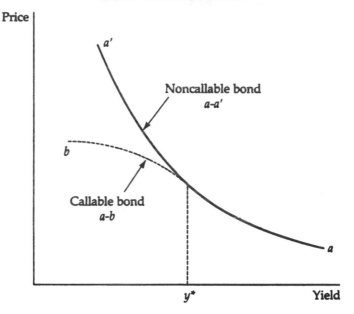

the price/yield relationship for the noncallable (option-free) bond. The unusually shaped curve denoted by a-b is the price/yield relationship for the callable bond.

The reason for the shape of the price/yield relationship for the callable bond is as follows. When the prevailing market yield for comparable bonds is higher than the bond's coupon rate, it is unlikely that the issuer will call the bond. For example, if the coupon rate on a bond is 8% and the prevailing yield on comparable bonds is 16%, it is highly improbable that the issuer will call an 8% bond so that it can issue a 16% bond. Since the bond is unlikely to be called, the callable bond will have the same price/yield relationship as a noncallable bond. However, even when the coupon rate is just below the market yield, investors may not pay the same price for the bond as they would for a noncallable bond. There is still the chance that the market yield may drop further and that the issuer may then call the bond.

As yields in the market decline, the likelihood increases that yields will fall to a level at which the issuer will benefit from calling the bond. We may not know the exact yield level at which investors begin to consider the issue a good candidate for calling, but we do know that there is some level. In Figure 12-2, at yield levels below y*, the price/yield relationship for the callable bond departs from the price/yield relationship for the noncallable bond. If, for example, the market yield is such that a noncallable bond would be selling for 109 but since it is callable would be called at 104, investors will not pay 109. If they did and the bond were called, investors would receive 104 (the call price) for a bond they purchased for 109. Notice that for a range of yields below y*, there is price compression—that is, there is limited price appreciation as yields decline. For the reasons discussed later in this chapter, the portion of the callable bond price/yield relationship below y* is said to be *negatively convex* (another term for price compression).

Decomposition of a Callable Bond

To develop an analytical framework for assessing relative value and evaluating the potential performance of callable bonds over some investment horizon, it is necessary to understand the components of a callable bond. A callable bond is a bond in which the bondholder has sold the issuer an option (more specifically, a call option) that allows the issuer to repurchase the contractual cash flow of the bond, from the time the bond is first callable until the maturity date.

Consider the following two bonds: (1) a 20-year 8% coupon bond callable in five years at 104 and (2) a 10-year 9% coupon bond callable immediately at par. For the first bond, the bondholder owns a five-year noncallable bond and has sold a call option granting the issuer the right to call away from the bondholder 15 years of cash flows five years from now for a price of 104. The investor who owns the second bond has a 10-year noncallable bond and has sold a call option granting the issuer the right to immediately call the entire

10-year contractual cash flows or any cash flows remaining at the time the issue is called for 100.

Effectively, the owner of a callable bond is entering into two separate transactions. First, he buys a noncallable bond from the issuer for which he pays some price. Then, he sells the issuer a call option for which he receives the option price from the issuer. Therefore, we can summarize the position of a callable bondholder as follows:

long a callable bond = long a noncallable bond
+ short a call option

In terms of price, the price of a callable bond is therefore equal to the price of the two components. That is,

callable bond price = noncallable bond price
− call option price

The call option price is subtracted from the price of the noncallable bond. The reason is that when the bondholder sells a call option, he receives the option price. Graphically this can be seen in Figure 12-2. At a given yield on the horizontal axis, the vertical difference between the noncallable bond price and the callable bond price is the embedded call option price.

Actually, the position is more complicated than the above description suggests. The issuer may be entitled to call the bond at the first call date and anytime thereafter, or at the first call date and any subsequent coupon anniversary. Thus the investor has effectively sold a strip (or package) of call options to the issuer. The call price may vary with the date the issue may be called. The underlying bond for the call option is the remaining coupon payments that would have been made by the issuer had the bond not been called. For exposition purposes, it is easier to clarify the principles associated with the investment characteristics of callable bonds by describing the investor's position as long a noncallable bond and short a call option.

BOND PRICE VOLATILITY

To evaluate the potential price performance of a bond, we need to know about its price volatility characteristics. We know that the price of a bond moves in the direction opposite to the change in interest rates. But some bonds rise or fall more than others when interest rates change. In this section we will review the price volatility characteristics of bonds, looking first at option-free bonds.

Bond Price Volatility Properties

There are two fundamental properties of price volatility:

- For small changes in yield, the absolute change in price is approximately the same regardless of whether yields increase or decrease.
- When yields change by a large amount, a given change in basis points will produce a noticeably greater price increase if yield declines than it will produce a price decrease if yield increases.

This last property is illustrated in Figure 12-3.

An investment implication of the property illustrated here is that if an investor owns a bond, the capital gain that will be realized if yield decreases is greater than the capital loss that will be realized if yield increases by the same number of basis points.

Two characteristics of an option-free bond determine its price volatility: coupon and term to maturity.

- For a given term to maturity and initial yield, the lower the coupon rate, the greater the price volatility.
- For a given coupon rate and initial yield, the longer the term to maturity, the greater the price volatility.

Figure 12-3

Illustration of Bond Price Volatility Properties

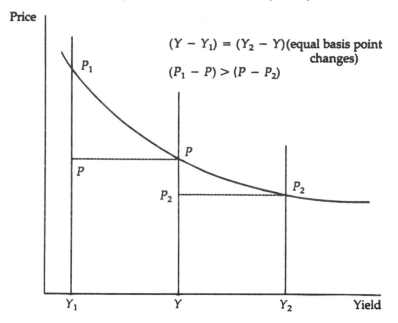

An investment implication of the first characteristic is that bonds selling at a deep discount will have greater price volatility than bonds selling near or above par. Zero-coupon bonds thus have the greatest price volatility for a given maturity.

Measuring Price Volatility

There are various measures of price volatility: price value of a basis point, the yield value of a 32nd, duration, and convexity. The last two are the measures more commonly used by practitioners. All of these measures, however, are related.[5]

Modified and Macaulay duration. Mathematically, modified duration is measured as follows for a bond that pays

---

[5]See Mark Pitts and Frank J. Fabozzi, *Interest Rate Futures and Options* (Chicago: Probus Publishing, 1990), p. 63.

interest semiannually:[6]

$$\text{modified duration} = \frac{\text{Macaulay duration (in years)}}{(1 + \text{yield to maturity}/2)}$$

where Macaulay duration is a weighted average term to maturity of the components of a bond's cash flows, in which the time of receipt of each payment is weighted by the present value of that component. The denominator of Macaulay duration is the sum of the weights, which is precisely the price of the bond. It is named in honor of Frederick Macaulay, who used this measure in a study published in 1938.[7]

Except at high yield levels, there is very little difference between Macaulay duration and modified duration. Consequently, we use these terms interchangeably in this book.

Duration is commonly used as a measure of the term of a bond; what makes it a valuable indicator is that it is related to the price volatility of a bond. More specifically, the relationship between modified duration and percentage price change

---

[6]Mathematically, modified duration is derived from the price of a bond, which can be expressed as follows (ignoring the subscript *sa* denoting semiannual yield):

$$P = \frac{C}{(1 + y)} + \frac{C}{(1 + y)^2} + \frac{C}{(1 + y)^3} + \dots + \frac{C + M}{(1 + y)^n}$$

Taking the first derivative of the price with respect to yield, y, and dividing both sides by P, we get

$$\frac{dP}{dy}\frac{1}{P} = -\frac{1}{(1 + y)}D$$

where

$$D = \frac{\dfrac{(1)C}{(1 + y)} + \dfrac{(2)C}{(1 + y)^2} + \dfrac{(3)C}{(1 + y)^3} + \dots + \dfrac{(n)\,(C + M)}{(1 + y)^n}}{P}$$

D is Macaulay duration.

[7]Frederick R. Macaulay, *Some Theoretical Problems Suggested by the Movement of Interest Rates, Bond Yields, and Stock Prices in the U.S. Since 1856* (New York: National Bureau of Economic Research, 1938). Hicks used the same measure in his study of the properties of cash flows that made the ratio of their values invariant with respect to changes in interest. He called his measure *average maturity*. See John R. Hicks, *Value and Capital*, 2d ed. (Oxford: Clarendon Press, 1946). In a study of the impact of a rise in interest rates on the banking system, Samuelson used a similar concept, which he called the *average time period* of the cash flow. See Paul A. Samuelson, "The Effects of Interest Rate Increases on the Banking System," *American Economic Review* (March 1945), pp. 16–27.

can be shown to be equal to:[8]

$$- \text{modified duration} \times (\text{yield change}) \times 100$$

The larger the duration, the greater the price sensitivity of a bond to a change in yield. From the above relationship, modified duration can be seen to equal the approximate percentage change in the price of a bond if yield changes by 100 basis points. For example, if the modified duration of a bond is 5, this means that a 100 basis point change in yield will change the bond's price by approximately 5%.

Dollar duration. Dollar duration is the approximate dollar price change of a bond per $100 of par value if yield changes by 100 basis points. It is calculated as follows:

$$\text{Dollar duration} = \frac{\text{modified duration} \times \text{price}}{100}$$

Convexity. For small changes in yield, duration does a good job of estimating the actual percentage price change. However, for large changes in yield it does not. In fact, the larger the yield change, the poorer the approximation. The reason is that duration is a linear approximation to the convex price/yield relationship. The increase in the error in projecting the new price when yields change by a large amount (which is equivalent to projecting the percentage price change), can be seen in Figure 12-4. The line tangent to the price/yield relationship at y^* represents the approximation using duration.[9]

---

[8]This can be seen from the previous footnote by solving for dP/P:

$$\frac{dP}{P} = -\frac{D}{(1+y)}(dy)$$

where dP/P is the percentage change in price, D is Macaulay duration, $D/(1+y)$ is modified duration, and dy is the change in yield. Multiplying by 100 as in the text casts the change in yield in terms of basis points. Mathematically, duration is a first approximation of the change in the price function using the first term of a Taylor series.

[9]Actually, the tangent line is the dollar duration estimate. However, there is no loss of generality in our discussion if we refer to the tangent line as the modified duration estimate.

The approximation can be improved by supplementing duration with another measure, convexity.[10] The relationship between percentage price change and convexity is as follows:[11]

$$.5 \times (\text{convexity}) \times (\text{yield change})^2 \times 100$$

Modified duration and convexity are combined to estimate the percentage price change. This is done by simply summing the estimated percentage price changes as a result of duration and convexity.

An important property of the convexity of an option-free bond is that as the yield increases (decreases), the modified duration of a bond decreases (increases). This property of convexity has interesting implications for bond investors. As yield declines, an investor that owns a bond will want its price to increase as much as possible—hence, an investor wants duration to increase. The opposite is true if yield increases, when an investor wants the duration to decline. For

---

[10]The formula for convexity is:

$$\frac{\dfrac{(1)(2)C}{(1 + y)} + \dfrac{(2)(3)C}{(1 + y)^2} + \dfrac{(3)(4)C}{(1 + y)^3} + \ldots + \dfrac{(n)(n+1)(C+M)}{(1 + y)^n}}{(1 + y)^2 P}$$

where the symbols are as defined in previous footnotes.

[11]This is a simple application of a fundamental property of calculus: a mathematical function can be approximated by a Taylor series. The more terms of a Taylor series used, the better the approximation. For example, the first two terms of a Taylor series for the price function are:

$$\frac{dP}{P} = \frac{dP}{dy}\frac{1}{P}dy + \frac{1}{2}\frac{d^2P}{dy^2}\frac{1}{P}dy^2$$

The first term of the Taylor series is the duration estimate of the price change. The second term of the Taylor series requires the calculation of the second derivative of the price function. The second derivative normalized by price (i.e., divided by price) is

$$\frac{d^2P}{dy^2}\frac{1}{P} = \frac{\dfrac{(1)(2)C}{(1 + y)} + \dfrac{(2)(3)C}{(1 + y)^2} + \dfrac{(3)(4)C}{(1 + y)^3} + \ldots + \dfrac{(n)(n+1)(C+M)}{(1 + y)^n}}{(1 + y)^2 P}$$

which is the convexity measure given in the previous footnote.

This is an unfortunate misuse of terminology since it suggests that the convexity measure above measures the curvature of the convex shape of the price/yield relationship for a bond. It does not. It is simply an approximation of the curvature.

Figure 12-4

Error in Estimating Price with Duration

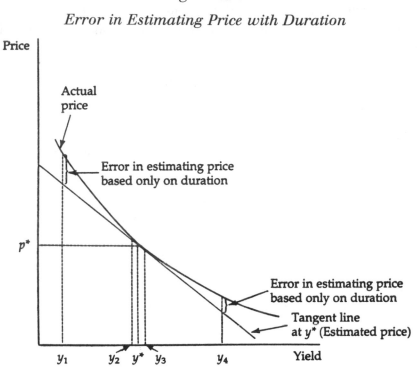

this reason, investors commonly refer to the shape of the price/yield relationship for an option-free bond as having "positive" convexity—"positive" indicating that it is a good attribute of a bond. Later in this chapter, we will find that callable bonds exhibit "negative" convexity, which means duration may not change in the desired direction as yield declines. Without going into details, let us state that convexity measures the rate of change of dollar duration as yield changes. The greater the rate of change of dollar duration, the greater the convexity of a bond. Since the dollar duration of all option-free bonds always changes in the right direction, greater convexity is a desirable property. Consequently, two bonds may have the same dollar duration but different convexities. They will not perform alike.

It is often thought that for two bonds with the same dollar duration, the one with the higher convexity will outperform the other. This is not true, because the market prices convexity. The bond with the higher convexity will sell at a higher price and therefore offer a lower yield. Consequently, to obtain greater convexity, the investor must pay for it. The performance of a bond over some investment horizon will depend on actual market volatility. The greater the actual market volatility, the greater the benefit from improving convexity. Thus, the yield giveup that an investor will be ready to pay to obtain higher convexity depends on the investor's expectations of future interest rate volatility.

Formulas for Approximating Duration and Convexity

Duration and convexity measures for option-free bonds are inappropriate for callable bonds such as pass-throughs or derivative mortgage-backed securities. Here we present formulas for approximating duration and convexity that can be used for any bond.

Since duration is a measure of the change in price for small changes in interest rates, the following formula, known as *effective duration,* can be used to approximate duration:

$$\text{effective duration} = \frac{\begin{array}{c}\text{Price if yield decreases} \\ \text{by } x \text{ basis points}\end{array} - \begin{array}{c}\text{Price if yield increases} \\ \text{by } x \text{ basis points}\end{array}}{\text{Initial price } (2x)}$$

For example, consider a 20-year 7% coupon bond selling at 74.26 to yield 10%. Suppose we evaluate the price changes for a 20 basis point change up and down. Then,

Initial price = 74.26
For $x = .002$
Price if yield decreases by 20 basis points = 75.64
Price if yield increases by 20 basis points = 72.92

$$\text{effective duration} = \frac{75.64 - 72.92}{(74.26)\,2\,(.002)} = 9.16$$

The modified duration for this bond is 9.18. The effective duration is 9.16, indicating a good approximation.

To approximate convexity, the following formula, called *effective convexity,* can be used:

effective convexity =

$$\frac{\text{Price if yield decreases by } x \text{ basis points} + \text{Price if yield increases by } x \text{ basis points} - 2(\text{Initial price})}{2(\text{Initial price}) (x)^2}$$

Consider the 20-year 7% coupon bond selling at 74.26 to yield 10%. Effective convexity is:

$$\frac{75.64 + 72.92 - 2 (74.26)}{(74.26) (.002)^2} = 134.66$$

The convexity is equal to 132.08. The effective convexity (134.66) has proven itself to be a good approximation of convexity (132.08).

Limitations of Duration and Convexity Measures

We presented the basics concerning duration and convexity as a measure of price volatility. Three assumptions underlie their use. First, it is assumed that the yield curve is flat. This means that all interest rates—short, intermediate, and long—are equal. Second, it is assumed that when the yield curve shifts, the shift is parallel. That is, all interest rates rise and fall by the same rate. Thus, the flattening, steepening, or twisting of the yield curve is not consistent with the use of duration and convexity. Third, it is assumed that the expected cash flow of the bond does not change when interest rates change. When a bond is callable, this assumption may be violated because as interest rates change, the likelihood that the issuer will call the bond changes. Therefore, the expected cash flows change when interest rates change.

Price Volatility of Callable Bonds

Earlier in this chapter, we explained that the price of a callable bond can be viewed as follows:

price of a callable bond =
price of a noncallable bond − call option price

This means that the price volatility of a callable bond will depend on (1) the price volatility of the noncallable bond when interest rates change and (2) the price volatility of the call option when interest rates change. For example, if interest rates decline, the price of a noncallable bond will rise. The amount it will rise by depends on the duration of the noncallable bond. But, when interest rates decline, the call option the bondholder sold to the issuer increases in value. Since the call option price is subtracted from the noncallable bond price, this reduces the price appreciation of the callable bond. This is why the callable bond exhibits the negative convexity or price compression we discussed earlier.

TOTAL RETURN FRAMEWORK

We have highlighted the limitations of yield measures such as yield to maturity and yield to call. The proper measure of the potential return is one that considers all three sources of potential dollar return over the investor's investment horizon. The return is then the interest rate that will make the price grow to the projected total dollar return. The yield computed in this manner is referred to as the *total return* or *horizon return*.

The total return requires that the investor specify:

- an investment horizon
- a reinvestment rate
- a selling price for the bond at the end of the investment horizon (which depends on the assumed yield to maturity that the bond will sell for at the end of the investment horizon)

More formally, the steps for computing a total return over some investment horizon for a semiannual pay bond are as follows:

Step 1: Compute the total coupon payments plus the interest on interest based on the assumed reinvestment rate.
Step 2: Determine the projected sale price at the end of the

investment horizon. The projected sale price will depend on the projected yield on comparable bonds at the end of the investment horizon.

Step 3: Add the values computed in steps 1 and 2. The sum is the total future dollars that will be received from the investment, given the assumed reinvestment rate and projected required yield at the end of the investment horizon.

Step 4: To obtain the semiannual total return, use the following formula:

$$\left(\frac{\text{total future dollars}}{\text{purchase price of bond}}\right)^{1/\text{length of horizon}} - 1$$

Step 5: Since coupon interest is assumed to be paid semiannually, double the interest rate found in step 4. The resulting interest rate is the total return expressed on a bond equivalent basis. Instead, the total return can be expressed on an effective interest rate basis by using the following formula:

$$(1 + \text{semiannual total return})^2 - 1$$

Objections to the total return framework cited by some portfolio managers are: (1) it requires assumptions about reinvestment rates and future yields; and (2) it forces a portfolio manager to think in terms of an investment horizon. Unfortunately, some portfolio managers find comfort in meaningless measures such as the yield to maturity because it is not necessary to incorporate expectations. Total return enables the portfolio manager to analyze the performance of a bond based on different interest rate scenarios for reinvestment rates and future market yields. By investigating multiple scenarios, the portfolio manager can see how sensitive the bond's performance is to each scenario. There is no need to assume that the reinvestment rate will be constant for the entire investment horizon.

The principles reviewed in this chapter apply to all fixed-income securities. In the next chapter, these principles are applied to the valuation of mortgage-backed securities.

13

Methodologies for Valuing Mortgage-Backed Securities

Market participants employ several methodologies to analyze mortgage-backed securities. These include (1) the static cash-flow yield methodology, (2) the option pricing methodology, and (3) the option-adjusted spread methodology. At the end of this chapter, we will discuss how an investor with a specific investment horizon should assess the potential performance of an MBS using the total return framework discussed at the end of Chapter 12.

STATIC CASH-FLOW YIELD METHODOLOGY

The static cash-flow yield methodology is the simplest to use, but, as we shall see, it offers little insight into the relative value of an MBS.

Cash Flow Yield

The methodology is based on the cash flow yield measure that we described for passthroughs in Chapter 9. The cash flow yield is based on some prepayment assumption.

As we explained in Chapter 12, there are two short-comings of the yield to maturity as a measure of a bond's potential return: (1) the coupon payments must be reinvested at a rate equal to the yield to maturity, and (2) the bond must be held to maturity. These shortcomings are equally applicable to the cash flow yield measure: (1) the projected cash flows are assumed to be reinvested at the cash flow yield, and (2) the passthrough is assumed to be held until the entire pool of mortgage loans is paid off. The importance of reinvestment risk—the risk that the cash flow will be reinvested at a rate less than the cash flow yield—is particularly great for pass-throughs because payments are monthly. In addition, the cash flow yield is dependent on the realization of the projected cash flow based on some prepayment rate. If the prepayment experience is different from the prepayment rate assumed, the cash flow yield will not be realized.

Spread to Treasuries

It should be clear that at the time of purchase it is not possible to determine an exact yield for a passthrough; the yield depends on the actual prepayment experience of the mortgages in the pool. Nevertheless, the convention in all fixed-income markets is to measure the yield on a non-Treasury security against that of a "comparable" Treasury security.

In comparing the yield of a passthrough to a comparable Treasury security, prepayments make it inappropriate to use the stated maturity of the passthrough. Instead, market participants have used two measures: Macaulay duration and average life. We have already seen the use of these two measures for just this purpose in Chapter 11 when we discussed CMOs (see Table 11-1).

Macaulay Duration. In Chapter 12, we explained the role of Macaulay duration as a measure of the interest rate sensitivity of a fixed-income security, not as a measure of its life. As we will see later, Macaulay duration is not a good measure of the interest rate sensitivity of a passthrough security. Nevertheless, it is commonly used as a measure of its life.

The procedure for calculating the Macaulay duration requires a projection of the cash flow, which, in turn, requires a prepayment rate assumption. As we explained in Chapter 12, Macaulay duration can be determined using the projected cash flow, the price of the passthrough, and the monthly interest rate (computed from the yield on a bond equivalent basis). Macaulay duration is converted into years by dividing the Macaulay duration in months by 12.

To illustrate the calculation, suppose that a passthrough with a gross coupon rate of 9.5%, a servicing fee of 0.5%, 360 months remaining to maturity, and a mortgage balance of $100,000 is selling for $94,521. Assuming a prepayment rate of 100% PSA, the cash flow yield for this passthrough would be 10.21%. This is the same passthrough and prepayment assumption for which the projected cash flow is shown in Table 9-3 of Chapter 9. The Macaulay duration is 6.17 as explained below.

The numerator of the Macaulay duration is the present value of the projected cash flow using a monthly interest rate of 0.8333% times the time period (the month). For our passthrough, the numerator is $6,998,347. Macaulay duration is then found by dividing by the price of the passthrough. Thus,

$$\text{Macaulay duration (in months)} = \frac{\$6,998,347}{\$94,521} = 74.04$$

To convert the Macaulay duration in months to Macaulay duration in years:

$$\text{Macaulay duration (in years)} = \frac{74.04}{12} = 6.17$$

Average life. A second measure commonly used to determine a comparable Treasury security is the average life, which is the average time to receipt of principal payments (projected scheduled principal and projected principal prepayments), weighted by the amount of principal expected divided by the total principal to be repaid.

Mathematically, the average life is expressed as follows:

$$\text{average life} = \frac{1}{12} \sum_{t=1}^{n} \frac{t\,(\text{principal expected at time t})}{\text{total principal}}$$

where n is the number of months remaining.

For the passthrough in the previous illustration, assuming the same prepayment rate (100% PSA), the principal payments are shown in columns 6 and 8 of Table 9-3 of Chapter 9. Adding the principal payments in these two columns and applying the above formula, the average life is 12.18 years.

Price Volatility: Duration

Duration is a measure of the volatility of a bond's price to interest rate changes assuming that the expected cash flow does not change with interest rates. Macaulay duration is not an appropriate measure for passthroughs because as a result of prepayments the projected cash flow does change as interest rates change. When interest rates decline (rise), prepayments are expected to rise (fall). As a result, when interest rates decrease (increase), duration may decrease (increase) rather than increase (decrease). This property, as we explained in Chapter 12, is referred to as negative convexity.

To illustrate this characteristic, consider the Macaulay duration for the 9.5% passthrough assuming 100% PSA and selling to offer a cash flow yield of 10.21%. If the required yield decreases to 8.14% instantaneously and the prepayment rate is not assumed to change, Macaulay duration will increase from 6.17 to 6.80. However, suppose that when the yield declines to 8.14%, the assumed prepayment rate changes to 150% PSA. The Macaulay duration will decline to 5.91 rather than increase.

The impact of negative convexity on the price performance of a passthrough security is the same as for the callable bond discussed in Chapter 12. When interest rates decline, a bond with an embedded call option such as a passthrough will not perform as well as an option-free bond. For example, if the required yield decreases instantaneously from 10.21% to 8.14%, the price for our hypothetical passthrough will increase from \$94,521 to \$107,596. However, if the prepayment rate increases to 150% PSA, the price will rise to only \$106,710.

For passthroughs selling at a discount or par, duration will be positive. Passthroughs selling at a premium will exhibit negative convexity; however, whether the duration is positive or negative depends on how high the coupon rate is relative to the prevailing mortgage rate. If the coupon rate falls sufficiently for below the mortgage rate, it is possible that the price of a passthrough will fall as mortgage rates decline. Thus, duration will be negative. This is illustrated in Figure 13-1.

As explained in Chapter 11, the prioritization of classes in a CMO structure will affect the average life of a class so that the average life will not be the same as that of the underlying collateral. This is also true for the convexity of a CMO, since the average life affects a bond's convexity.

Figure 13-1

Price/Yield Relationship for a Passthrough

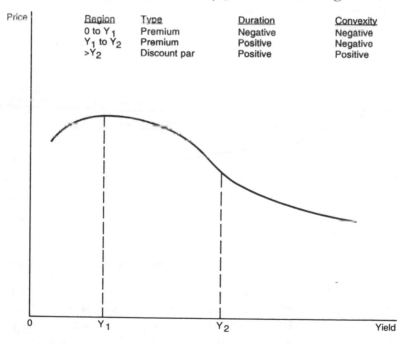

Region	Type	Duration	Convexity
0 to Y_1	Premium	Negative	Negative
Y_1 to Y_2	Premium	Positive	Negative
>Y_2	Discount par	Positive	Positive

Figure 13-2

CMO Yield/Convexity Trade-off

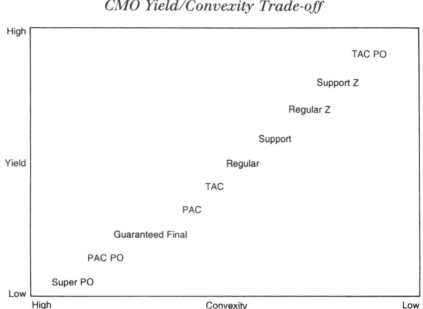

Source: This diagram is adapted from a presentation by Robert Kulason of Salomon Brothers Inc at the Collateralized Mortgage Obligations tutorial sponsored by Frank J. Fabozzi Associates, September 26, 1991.

Moreover, the redistribution of the collateral coupon interest rate to the classes may result in classes with a wide range of coupon rates. Since the convexity of a bond is also affected by the coupon rate, the convexity of the classes may be very different from that of the collateral. Consequently, while the collateral may exhibit negative convexity, many of the classes may not exhibit this characteristic. Figure 13-2 shows the yield/convexity characteristics of the CMO classes we discussed in Chapter 11.

Formulas for Approximating Duration and Convexity

Although Macaulay duration and modified duration are inappropriate as measures of interest rate sensitivity, it is possible to revise these measures to allow for changing prepayment rates as interest rates change. This can be done by using the approximation formulas for duration and convexity that we discussed in Chapter 12. We referred to these measures as effective duration and effective convexity.

Effective duration. The formula for effective duration is:

$$\text{effective duration} = \frac{\begin{array}{c}\text{Price if yield decreases} \\ \text{by } x \text{ basis points}\end{array} - \begin{array}{c}\text{Price if yield increases} \\ \text{by } x \text{ basis points}\end{array}}{\text{Initial price } (2x)}$$

where price is per \$100 of par.

When computing effective duration, the price at the higher and lower interest rates will depend on the prepayment rate assumed. A lower prepayment rate is typically assumed at the lower interest rate rather than at a higher interest rate.

Consider once again the passthrough that we have used in our previous illustrations. The price assuming 100% PSA and a yield of 10.21% is \$94,521 or \$94.521 per \$100 of par value. Let's look at what will happen to the price if the yield changes by 50 basis points. Suppose that if the yield decreases by 50 basis points to 9.71%, the prepayment rate is assumed to be unchanged at 100% PSA. However, if the yield increases by 50 basis points to 10.71%, the prepayment rate is assumed to decrease to 75% PSA. The price at 9.71% and 10.71% would be \$97,520 and \$90,992, respectively, or \$97.520 and \$90.992 per \$100 of par value. Therefore,

Initial price = 94,521
For x = .005
Price if yield decreases by 50 basis points = 97.520
Price if yield increases by 50 basis points = 90.992

$$\text{effective duration} = \frac{97.520 - 90.992}{(94.521)\, 2\, (.005)} = 6.91$$

Effective convexity. The formula for effective convexity is:

$$\text{effective convexity} = \frac{\begin{array}{c}\text{Price if yield decreases} \\ \text{by } x \text{ basis points}\end{array} + \begin{array}{c}\text{Price if yield increases} \\ \text{by } x \text{ basis points}\end{array} - \begin{array}{c}2(\text{Initial} \\ \text{price})\end{array}}{(\text{Initial price})\, (x)^2}$$

For the passthrough in our previous illustration:

$$\text{effective convexity} = \frac{90.992 + 97.520 - 2\,(94.521)}{(94.521)(.005)^2}$$

$$= \frac{-.53}{.004726} = -224.29$$

Notice that the convexity of this passthrough is negative.

THE OPTION PRICING METHODOLOGY

The option pricing methodology is based on the principle that the price of a callable bond can be decomposed into two component parts—a noncallable bond and a call option. That is,

> callable bond price =
> noncallable bond price − call option price

We discussed this principle in Chapter 12. The call option price is subtracted from the price of the noncallable bond because the bondholder has sold a call option to the issuer.

The above relationship can be recast as follows for a passthrough:

> passthrough price =
> noncallable passthrough price − call option price

By a noncallable passthrough we mean a hypothetical passthrough in which prepayments are not permitted. Thus, the cash flow is known with certainty. The call option price can be estimated using an option pricing model. Because the analysis proceeds based on the estimated option price, we refer to this approach as the options methodology.

Given the above relationship for a passthrough, an investor wants to know if the noncallable passthrough is correctly priced in the sense that he is being adequately compensated after adjusting for the embedded call option. Of course, the market price of the noncallable passthrough is not observable. It can be estimated, however, by rewriting the relationship as:

> noncallable passthrough price =
> passthrough price + call option price

From the estimated call option price based on some option pricing model and the observed market price of the passthrough, the estimated price of the noncallable passthrough can be calculated. Given the estimated price of the noncallable passthrough, it is then simple to compute the yield on this theoretical security if there are no prepayments permitted. This yield, referred to as the *option-adjusted yield*, is the interest rate that will make the present value of the cash flow for the passthrough assuming no prepayments equal to the price.

The difficulty with applying the option pricing methodology is the problem of estimating the call option price.[1] The complications are several. First, unlike options on common stock, options on a fixed-income security are much more complicated to estimate. The application of the Black-Scholes model (even a modified Black-Scholes) is inappropriate.[2] Second, the prepayment options may be irrationally exercised,

---

[1] One of the earliest attempts to apply option-pricing technology to the valuation of passthroughs is found in Kenneth B. Dunn and John J. McConnell, "Valuation of GNMA Mortgage-Backed Securities," *Journal of Finance* (June 1901), pp. 599–010. A later attempt is found in Fung Shine Pan, "The Pricing of GNMA Mortgage Backed Securities and Futures Contracts," unpublished Ph.D diss., University of California at Berkeley, 1986. More recent efforts are found in H. Gifford Fong, Ki-Young Chung, and Eric M.P. Tang, "The Valuation of Mortgage-Backed Securities: A Contingent Claims Approach," in Frank J. Fabozzi, ed., *The Handbook of Mortgage-Backed Securities*, rev. ed. (Chicago: Probus Publishing, 1988), pp. 833–854, and Andrew S. Davidson, Michael D. Herskovitz, and Leonard D. Van Drunen, "The Refinancing Threshold Pricing Model: An Economic Approach to Valuing MBS," *The Journal of Real Estate Finance and Economics* (June 1988), pp. 117–130. The first three studies develop a valuation model based on the generic model for pricing interest rate claims developed by Brennan and Schwartz (Michael Brennan and Eduardo Schwartz, "Savings Bonds, Retractable Bonds, and Callable Bonds," *Journal of Financial Economics* [August 1977], pp. 67–88), and Cox, Ingersoll, and Ross (John C. Cox, Jonathan E. Ingersoll, and Stephen A. Ross, "A Theory of the Term Structure of Interest Rates," *Econometrica* [March 1985], pp. 385–407).

[2] For a discussion of these problems, see Lawrence J. Dyer and David P. Jacob, "Guide to Fixed Income Option Pricing Models," in Frank J. Fabozzi, ed., *The Handbook of Fixed Income Options* (Chicago: Probus Publishing 1989), pp. 63–110.

making the pricing of the option even more complicated to estimate. Third, a partial exercise is possible since the homeowner can prepay a portion of the mortgage loan. The fourth problem is that there is not one option for one borrower but an option granted to each homeowner in the pool of underlying mortgage loans. Finally, in the case of a CMO class, valuation of the call option becomes exceedingly complicated.

An option-adjusted yield spread can be calculated by computing the difference between the yield on a comparable Treasury and the option-adjusted yield. Herein lies another problem with the options methodology—the difficulty of selecting the appropriate benchmark that the noncallable passthrough should be compared to.

With the options methodology, effective duration and convexity can also be estimated. An alternative approach is to use the option-adjusted duration and option-adjusted convexity measures discussed in Chapter 12. The input for these measures (delta and gamma) must be obtained from an option pricing model.

OPTION-ADJUSTED SPREAD METHODOLOGY

In the static cash-flow yield methodology, the yield spread for a passthrough is the difference between the cash flow yield and the yield to maturity of a comparable Treasury. The latter is obtained from the yield curve. The drawback of this procedure is that the cash flow yield is not calculated properly for either the passthrough or Treasury security because it fails to take into consideration (1) the term structure of interest rates for Treasuries (i.e., the theoretical spot rate curve), and (2) expected interest rate volatility that will alter the expected cash flow for the passthrough. In contrast, based on some assumed interest rate volatility the option-adjusted spread (OAS) methodology[3] determines the average incremental return over the term structure of interest rates.

---

[3] In a critical review of this methodology, Finnerty and Rose (John D. Finnerty and Michael Rose, "Arbitrage-Free Spread: A Consistent Measure of Relative Value," *Journal of Portfolio Management* [Spring 1991], pp. 65–81) state that the earliest published work involving this methodology

We will begin our explanation of the OAS methodology by focusing on the first problem: failure to incorporate the term structure of interest rates.

Static Spread

In the static cash-flow yield methodology, an investor compares the cash flow yield of a passthrough with the yield to maturity of a similar duration on-the-run Treasury security. This means that the cash flow yield of a high and low coupon passthrough with a duration of seven years would be compared to the on-the-run seven-year Treasury security. Such a comparison makes little sense, since the cash flow characteristics of the two passthroughs will not be the same as that of the benchmark Treasury.

The proper procedure to compare passthroughs of the same duration but with different coupon rates is to compare the passthrough with a portfolio of zero-coupon Treasury securities that have the same cash flow stream as projected for the passthrough. Assuming the passthrough's cash flow is riskless, its value is equal to the portfolio value of all of the zero-coupon Treasuries. In turn, these cash flows are valued at the spot rates. A passthrough's value will be less than the portfolio of zero-coupon Treasury securities because investors are demanding a spread for the risk associated with holding a passthrough rather than a riskless (in the sense of default risk and certainty of the cash flow) package of Treasury securities.

The spread to Treasuries is determined as follows. It is the spread that will make the present value of the projected cash flow from the passthrough when discounted at the spot rate plus a spread equal to the passthrough's market price. A trial-and-error procedure is required to determine the spread.

This procedure assumes that the cash flows will not change because interest rates do not change. Hence, the spread calculated on this assumption is referred to as a *static*

appeared in Michael Waldman and Stephen Modzelewski, "A Framework for Evaluating Treasury-Based Adjustable Rate Mortgages," in Frank J. Fabozzi, ed., *The Handbook of Mortgage-Backed Securities* (Chicago: Probus Publishing, 1985), pp. 307–346.

spread. Next we look at how to incorporate expected interest rate volatility into the analysis.

Option-Adjusted Spread

We stated earlier that there are two drawbacks to the static cash-flow yield methodology. Previously, we explained how to overcome the first problem: failure to incorporate the term structure of interest rates. This leads to the static spread. Now we'll look at the second drawback: failure to take into account future interest rate volatility. The greater the volatility of interest rates, the higher the uncertainty about prepayments.

Not only is the direction of interest rates important but so is the path of interest rates. The following example illustrates their importance. We will simplify our discussion by assuming that cash flows are annual rather than monthly and that there are 10 years remaining to the stated maturity of a passthrough. Consider the following three possible interest rate paths, in which the interest rate begins at 10% and ends at 9.1% at the end of 10 years assuming that interest rates can rise or fall by 10% every year:

Year	Path 1	Path 2	Path 3
1	10.0%	10.0%	10.0%
2	11.0	9.1	11.0
3	12.1	8.3	10.0
4	10.9	7.5	9.1
5	9.8	6.8	8.3
6	8.8	6.2	7.5
7	8.3	6.8	8.3
8	9.1	7.5	9.1
9	10.0	8.3	10.0
10	9.1	9.1	9.1

For a given passthrough and based on a prepayment model, prepayments for each year on each path can be projected. Thus, a cash flow (interest plus scheduled principal repayment plus prepayments) for each year on each path can be projected. The cash flow for a given passthrough will differ for each path, depending on the coupon rate of the passthrough.

There are obviously an enormous number of possible interest rate paths. Let's imagine for the moment that we can analyze each path for a given passthrough. For each path, the present value of the cash flow of the passthrough can be calculated. The discount rate used to calculate the present value of each annual cash flow on each path is determined from the term structure that results on an interest rate path plus a spread. Therefore, for each path a total present value can be calculated. An average of the total present values from all the paths can be computed. If the average total present value is equal to the market price of the passthrough, then the spread used is the option-adjusted spread. If it is not, the present value of the cash flow along each path is calculated again using a different spread, and another total present value can be calculated. An average total present value is then calculated. Once again, if the average total present value is equal to the market price of the passthrough, this new spread is the option-adjusted spread. If not, the process continues until a spread is found that satisfies this condition.[4]

Thus far, we have skirted the question of the complexity of evaluating all paths. In practice, techniques such as Monte Carlo simulation can be employed to estimate the option-adjusted spread. To do this, it is necessary to specify how the term structure will shift during each period. This is accomplished by specifying a probability distribution for the short-term Treasury rate. A change in the short-term Treasury rate will determine how the entire term structure will shift. The assumed probability distribution must be consistent with the existing term structure of interest rates. These nuances are beyond the scope of this chapter.

---

[4]Mathematically, the option-adjusted spread is the spread that satisfies the following condition:

$$PV_j = \frac{CF_{1j}}{(1 + r_1 + OAS)} + \frac{CF_{2j}}{(1 + r_2 + OAS)^2} + \ldots + \frac{CF_{Tj}}{(1 + r_T + OAS)^T}$$

Price = $(1/J) [PV_1 + PV_2 + \ldots + PV_J]$

where CF_{tj} = projected cash flow at month t for path j

r_t = spot rate for month t
PV_j = present value on path j
Price = observed market price
T = number of months remaining for the passthrough
J = number of paths

The procedure to calculate the option-adjusted spread is summarized below:

1. From the Treasury yield curve, estimate the term structure of interest rates (spot rates) and the implied forward rates.
2. Select a probability distribution for short-term Treasury spot rates. The probability distribution should be selected such that it is consistent with (a) the current term structure of interest rates and (b) the historical behavior of interest rates. This will prevent the possibility of arbitrage along the yield curve.
3. Use the probability distribution and Monte Carlo simulation to determine randomly a large number of interest rate paths (say, 2,000).[5]
4. Use a prepayment model to project prepayments.
5. For each path found in (3), determine the cash flows given information about the passthrough and the prepayment model.
6. For an assumed spread and term structure, calculate a total present value for each path.
7. Calculate the average total present value for all paths.
8. Compare the average total present value to the market price of the passthrough. If they are equal, the assumed spread used in (6) is the option-adjusted spread. If they are not, try another spread and repeat (7) and (8).

The volatility of interest rates assumed in the procedure will have an impact on the option-adjusted spread. The volatility assumption is introduced when a probability distribution for the short-term Treasury securities must be selected. One parameter that must be specified in selecting a probability distribution is the variance (or standard deviation). The larger the variance assumed, the greater the volatility assumed for interest rates.

---

[5]There are rules developed in the operations research literature for selecting the number of paths.

The OAS framework can easily be extended to the valuation of passthroughs backed by ARMs, CMO classes, the CMO residual, and other mortgage-related products such as mortgage servicing. The limitation to applying the OAS methodology to CMO classes and its residual is the high computing costs. This is because each class must be analyzed, not just the one particular class that might be of interest to an investor.

Option Cost

Based on the decomposition principle for a callable bond discussed earlier, the implied cost of the option of a passthrough can be obtained by calculating the difference between the static spread and the option-adjusted spread at the assumed volatility of interest rates. That is,

Option cost = Static spread − Option-adjusted spread

The option cost measures the prepayment (or option) risk embedded in the passthrough. Notice that the cost of the option is a byproduct of the option-adjusted spread methodology and is not valued explicitly with an option pricing model as in the option pricing methodology.

Illustrations

In this section we will show how the OAS has been applied to various mortgage-backed securities products.

Application to passthroughs. The concepts discussed above will be made clearer with the following illustrations from the OASs reported by Lakhbir Hayre and Kenneth Lauterbach of Prudential-Bache for six GNMAs, which we have reproduced as Table 13-1.[6] The analysis is based on closing prices as of May 5, 1988. The cash flow yield is shown in the fifth column based on a projected PSA prepayment rate shown in the fourth column. The Prudential-Bache prepayment model was used to project the PSA prepayment rate.

---

[6]See Lakhbir S. Hayre and Kenneth Lauterbach, "Stochastic Valuation of Debt Securities," in Frank J. Fabozzi, ed., *Managing Institutional Assets* (New York: Harper & Row, 1990), pp. 321–364.

Table 13-1

Yield Spreads and OASs for GNMAs

Coupon	Price[a]	Rem. Term	Proj. PSA[b]	Yield	Avg. Life	Spread[c]	OAS[d]
GNMA 8	91-18	18-09	100	9.84	8.0	106	88
GNMA 9	96-08	20-08	108	9.87	8.5	105	80
GNMA 10	99-31	28-02	130	10.14	9.6	123	80
GNMA 11	105-21	26-00	199	9.77	6.9	108	48
GNMA 12	109-00	26-03	331	9.19	4.4	88	33
GNMA 13	111-12	25-00	396	8.89	3.6	70	50

a. Prices and prepayment projections as of May 5, 1988.
b. Projected prepayment rate is expressed as a percentage of the benchmark Public Securities Association (PSA) curve.
c. Spread is the difference between the yield of the GNMA and the Treasury curve yield at the average life.
d. OAS is calculated using a volatility of 15%.
Source: Lakhbir S. Hayre and Kenneth Lauterbach, "Option-Adjusted Spread Analysis of Mortgage-Backed Securities," in Frank J. Fabozzi, ed., The Handbook of Mortgage-Backed Securities, 3d ed. (Chicago: Probus Publishing, 1992).

The spreads shown in the next-to-last column of the table are the difference between the GNMA (cash flow) yield and the yield to maturity of a Treasury with a maturity equal to the same average life as the GNMA. (The average life is shown in the sixth column.) The last column shows the OAS.

Based on the static cash-flow yield methodology, since the spread for the GNMA 8 and GNMA 11 is 108 and 106 basis points, respectively, this suggests that both have similar spreads over a comparable Treasury security. However, the OAS methodology indicates that the GNMA 8 is more attractive than the GNMA 11 because of the higher OAS (48 basis points versus 8 basis points). This reflects the negative convexity of the higher coupon GNMA and its higher prepayment volatility as interest rates change.

The sensitivity of the OAS to the interest rate volatility assumption for each of the GNMA passthroughs shown in Table 13-1 is shown in Table 13-2. Four annual interest rate volatilities are shown. As expected, the higher the expected interest rate volatility, the lower the OAS. The difference between the OAS at a nonzero interest rate volatility and the OAS

Table 13-2

Sensitivity of GNMA OASs to Volatility Changes

	OAS at Volatility of:			
	0%	10%	15%	20%
GNMA 8	105	96	88	79
GNMA 9	106	94	80	64
GNMA 10	130	106	80	55
GNMA 11	119	82	48	17
GNMA 12	116	68	33	3
GNMA 13	115	77	50	26

Source: Hayre and Lauterbach, "Option-Adjusted Spread Analysis of Mortgage-Backed Securities," in Fabozzi, ed., *The Handbook of Mortgage-Backed Securities,* 3d ed.

at a zero interest rate volatility (that is, the static spread) is the option cost. As can be seen from Table 13-2, the lower the coupon rate, the lower the option cost.

CMO applications. The two illustrations below show how CMOs can be analyzed using the OAS methodology. The analysis was provided by Scott Richard of Goldman, Sachs.[7] Table 13-3 shows the OAS for a plain vanilla sequential-pay structure, FNMA 89–97. The structure included five bond classes, A, B, C, D, and Z, and a residual class. Class Z is an accrual bond and the D class is an IOette. The focus of the analysis is on the A, B, C, and Z classes. The top panel of Table 13-3 shows the OAS and the option cost for the collateral and the five classes in the CMO structure. The OAS for the collateral is 70 basis points. Since the option cost is 45 basis points, the static spread is 115 basis points (70 basis points plus 45 basis points). Notice that the classes did not share the OAS equally. Class A did not receive a significant portion of the OAS, but only 23 basis points. The longer maturity structures, particularly Class Z, received much of the OAS. The option cost was also distributed unequally among the four classes. The Z class, which was exposed to the greatest prepayment risk, had the highest option cost, a cost that was greater than for the collateral.

---

[7]The illustrations were presented by Scott Richard at the Collateralized Mortgage Obligations tutorial sponsored by Frank J. Fabozzi Associates, September 27, 1991.

Table 13-3

OAS Analysis of FNMA 89–97 Classes A, B, C, and Z (as of 4/27/90)

Base case (assumes 12% interest rate volatility)

	Option-adjusted Spread (in basis points)	Option Cost (in basis points)
Collateral	70	45
Class		
A	23	29
B	46	41
C	59	36
Z	74	50

Prepayments at 80% and 120% of Prepayment Model (assumes 12% interest rate volatility)

	New Option-adjusted Spread (in basis points)		Change in Price per $100 Par (holding OAS constant)	
	80%	120%	80%	120%
Collateral	70	71	$0.00	$0.04
Class				
A	8	40	−0.43	0.48
B	31	65	−0.86	1.10
C	53	73	−0.41	0.95
Z	72	93	−0.28	2.70

Interest rate volatility of 8% and 16%

	New Option-adjusted Spread (in basis points)		Change in Price per $100 Par (holding OAS constant)	
	8%	16%	80%	16%
Collateral	92	46	$1.03	−$1.01
Class				
A	38	5	0.42	−0.51
B	67	21	1.22	−0.45
C	77	39	1.22	−1.45
Z	99	50	3.55	−3.41

Source: Data provided by Scott Richard of Goldman, Sachs.

The next panel in the table shows for the collateral and the four classes (1) how the OAS changes if prepayments are 80% and 120% of the prepayment speed employed in estimating the OAS in the base case (the top panel), and (2) the change in the dollar price if the prepayments are 80% and 120% of the prepayment speed assuming that the OAS is constant. For example, consider the collateral. If the prepayment speed is 80% of the assumed prepayment speed in the base case, then the OAS will not change and there will be no change in the collateral price. In contrast, note the dramatic change for the four classes.

To see how an investor might use the information in the second panel, consider the A class. At 80% of the prepayment speed, the OAS for this class declines from 23 basis points to 8 basis points. For a buyer of a Class A bond, if the OAS is held constant, the panel also indicates that the bondholder would lose $0.43 per $100 par value. The reason for the adverse effect of a slowdown in prepayment speed on the Class A is obvious. If prepayments slow down, Class A (the class with the shortest stated maturity) extends. The OAS for the two longer classes (C and Z) does not change materially.

Should the prepayment speed be 120% greater than in the base case, the second panel in Table 13-3 indicates that the collateral's OAS will increase only slightly (one basis point), but that the OAS for the classes does not change equally. As can be seen, if prepayments are faster, the OAS of Class Z rises dramatically and its price increases substantially ($2.80 per $100 par) assuming OAS is held constant at the base case of 74 basis points.

The second panel also indicates that while the OAS and change in collateral price are not sensitive to the prepayment assumption (for plus and minus 20%), the same cannot be said for the classes in the structure.

The third panel shows what happens if interest rate volatility is less and greater than assumed in the base case, respectively. In the base case, it is assumed that interest rate volatility is 12%. Lower interest rate volatility (8%) results in an increase in the OAS for the collateral to 92 basis points and an increase in the collateral price (assuming a constant OAS of 70 basis points) by $1.03 per $100 par value. Thus, if actual

Table 13-4

OAS Analysis of FHLMC 120

Base case (assumes 12% interest rate volatility)

	Option-adjusted Spread (in basis points)	Option Cost (in basis points)
Collateral	72	34
Class		
A	52	4
B	48	− 1
C	64	− 7
D	67	5
E	68	8
F	73	9
G	75	9
H	85	9
J	17	62
K	61	58
Z	78	83

Prepayments at 80% and 120% of Prepayment Model (assumes 12% interest rate volatility)

	New Option-adjusted Spread (in basis points)		Change in Price per $100 Par (holding OAS constant)	
	80%	120%	80%	120%
Collateral	69	77	$0.15	$0.22
Class				
A	65	42	0.43	− 0.35
B	17	54	− 0.71	0.12
C	14	86	− 1.52	0.67
D	61	62	− 0.24	− 0.20
E	65	61	− 0.13	− 0.37
F	76	63	0.16	− 0.59
G	80	64	0.33	− 0.68
H	93	75	0.56	− 0.69
J	4	56	− 0.43	1.34
K	64	75	0.17·	0.82
Z	85	114	0.75	3.77

Interest rate volatility of 8% and 16%

	New Option-adjusted Spread (in basis points)		Change in Price per $100 Par (holding OAS constant)	
	8%	16%	8%	16%
Collateral	91	51	$0.88	− $0.91
Class				
A	57	43	0.14	− 0.31
B	47	51	− 0.02	0.07
C	57	75	− 0.15	0.35
D	72	59	0.13	− 0.34
E	74	56	0.21	− 0.59
F	80	60	0.26	− 0.80
G	82	60	0.26	− 0.88
H	92	75	0.27	− 0.69
J	47	− 17	0.54	− 0.31
K	94	26	0.95	− 1.98
Z	126	28	2.58	− 5.30

Source: Data provided by Scott Richard of Goldman, Sachs.

volatility is less than that used to model this deal (the base case of 12%), the collateral and the classes would be priced cheaply. The greatest increase in value resulting from an underestimation of future market volatility would be for Class Z.

If volatility is greater (16%), instead of lower, there will be more scenarios in which the homeowner will be likely to prepay. Consequently, the OAS and the change in price (holding OAS constant) will decline for the collateral and the four classes.

Table 13-4 shows how the OAS methodology can be applied to a more complicated CMO structure, FHLMC Series 120. There are 14 classes in this structure. There are nine PAC bonds (including two PAC PO bonds and a PAC IO bond), a TAC support bond, an accrual support bond, a coupon-paying support bond, and a residual bond. Basic information about this structure is summarized in Table 13-5.[8] Figure 13-3 is a

---

[8] Notice that for the PAC IO (the I bond) the coupon rate shown is 857%. As we explained in Chapter 11, there must be some principal allocated to all classes in a CMO structure. In this case, the original balance for the PAC IO class is $100,000.

Table 13-5

Information about FHLMC 120 Classes

Total issue: $300 million
Issue date: 1/15/90
Collateral composition: 100% FHMLC
Weighted average coupon: 9.5%
Weighted average gross coupon: 10.1186%
Weighted average maturity: 29.4 years

Tranche	Original Balance	Coupon	Stated Maturity
120-A (PAC Bond)	$37,968,750	16.000%	11/15/13
120-B (PAC Bond)	$20,500,000	0.000%	2/15/11
120-C (PAC Bond)	$9,031,250	0.000%	11/16/13
120-D (PAC Bond)	$12,000,000	9.000%	2/15/15
120-E (PAC Bond)	$40,500,000	9.000%	5/15/18
120-F (PAC Bond)	$10,000,000	9.000%	1/15/19
120-G (PAC Bond)	$6,500,000	9.000%	6/16/19
120-H (PAC Bond)	$33,000,000	9.000%	2/15/21
120-I (PAC Bond)	$100,000	857.000%	2/15/21
120-J (TAC Bond)	$99,600,000	9.500%	2/15/21
120-K	$15,700,000	9.500%	7/15/15
120-R	$90,000	9.500%	2/15/21
120-S	$10,000	9.500%	2/15/21
120-Z (Accrual Bond)	$15,000,000	9.500%	2/16/21

diagram showing the principal allocation structure. Such a diagram is useful in order to obtain a quick grasp of the priority of principal allocation distribution. Moving from the bottom to the top of the diagram indicates the structural priority; moving from left to right shows the time priority.

In the base case, the top panel of Table 13-4 shows the OAS and the option cost for the collateral and all but the residual and PAC IO classes. The collateral OAS and the option

Figure 13-3

Diagram of Principal Allocation Structure for FHLMC 120

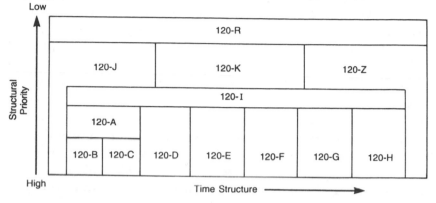

are 72 and 34 basis points, respectively. Thus the spread of the collateral to the Treasury curve is 106 basis points.

Several interesting observations about this structure can be made. First, notice that Class J, a support TAC bond, did not realize a good OAS allocation. It has a low OAS and a high option cost. It would be expected that, given the prepayment uncertainty associated with this support bond, its OAS would be higher. The reason is that at issuance the bond was priced so that its static cash-flow yield was high. Consequently, market participants that are "yield buyers" were probably willing to bid aggressively for this bond and thereby drive down its OAS, despite our warning in this chapter and the previous chapter that yield is not a meaningful measure of potential return. Such buyers are willing to trade off "yield" for OAS. The support K bond did not get a good OAS allocation either; however, its allocation was more than three times greater than the J bond's. The K bond was also offered at a price that provided a high relative yield. This analysis indicates that the OAS for the K bond was higher than that for the J bond.

Second, notice that the B and C bonds have a negative option cost. These two bonds are PAC POs. Greater prepayment risk would mean a speeding up of prepayments, resulting in faster repayment of principal. Since PAC POs benefit from fast prepayments, they benefit from such a scenario, re-sulting in a negative option cost.

The next two panels in Table 13-4 show the sensitivity of the OAS and the price (holding OAS constant at the base case) to changes in the prepayment speed (80% and 120% of the base case speed of 180% PSA) and to changes in volatility (8% and 16%). From this analysis it can be seen once again that the change in the prepayment speed does not affect the collateral significantly; however, the change in the OAS and price (holding OAS constant) for each class is significant. For example, a slower prepayment speed, which increases the time period over which a PAC PO bondholder can recover the principal, significantly reduces the OAS and price. The opposite effect results if prepayments are faster than the base case. The A class, which is a high coupon bond (as can be seen from the information in Table 13-5), benefits from a slowing of prepayments, since the bondholder will receive the higher coupon for a longer period of time. In contrast, faster pre-payments represent an adverse scenario. This is supported by the results reported in the last panel of the table.[9]

Other Illustrations. Additional applications of the OAS methodology to mortgage-backed securities are shown in Tables 13-6, 13-7, and 13-8. Table 13-6 shows the OAS method-ology applied to a four-class sequential-pay CMO structure, as well as to the underlying collateral (a GNMA 9%). The effect of interest rate volatility can be seen in the last three columns of the table. Notice that the OAS for the CMO classes is much more sensitive to changes in interest rate volatility than the GNMA passthrough. Thus, while a CMO class may have less prepayment risk than a passthrough, it is exposed to greater risk because of changes in interest rate volatility. Table 13-7 shows the OAS methodology applied to IOs, POs, PACs, and plain vanilla CMO classes. This table shows not only what might happen to the OAS and price if there is a 20% change in expected interest rate volatility, but what will happen if

---

[9] A somewhat surprising result involves the effect that the change in prepayments has on the accrual bond (the Z-bond). Notice that regardless of whether prepayment speeds are slower or faster, the OAS and the price increase. Without the use of an OAS framework this would not be intuitively obvious.

Table 13-6

OASs for a GNMA 9 CMO

Class	Par Amt. ($)	Price[a]	Cpn.	Avg. Life (Yrs.)	B-E Yield	Trsy. Spread	OAS at Volatility of:		
							10%	15%	20%
GNMA 9[b]	100.0	92.65625	9.0	11	10.48	123	104	88	71
A	35.1	98.37792	8.0	2	9.10	100	67	48	21
B	19.0	95.50843	8.5	5	9.85	115	83	59	25
C	18.0	94.74840	9.0	7	10.27	125	103	80	52
Z	27.9	80.99880	0.0	17	10.87	150	102	79	52

a. All prices shown in decimal form.
b. The GNMA 9 is assumed to have a remaining term of 28-00 years; the CMO is priced assuming a projected prepayment speed of 100% PSA.
Source: Hayre and Lauterbach, "Option-Adjusted Spread Analysis of Mortgage-Backed Securities," in Fabozzi, ed., *The Handbook of Mortgage-Backed Securities,* 3d ed.

the yield curve changes and the spread between MBSs and Treasuries widens.

Table 13-8 shows the application of the OAS methodology to ARMs and floating-rate CMOs. The OAS methodology can easily accommodate the valuation of floating-rate products. The interest rate path determines what the reset rate will be, based on the contractual spread to the benchmark rate and caps and floors (both periodic and lifetime). The OAS methodology has also been applied to the analysis of mortgage servicing rights.[10]

Industry Acceptance of the OAS Methodology

Despite the limitations of the OAS methodology that we will discuss later, it is far superior to the static cash-flow yield methodology. Every dealer firm has its own OAS model

[10] For an illustration, see Scott Brown et al., *Analysis of Mortgage Servicing Portfolios* (New York: Financial Strategies Group, Prudential-Bache Capital Funding, December 1990), pp. 14–16.

Table 13-7

OASs for Several Types of MBSs

Issue	Base Case Assumptions				20% Increase in Vol.		Yld. Curve Steepens	Mtg. Spreads Widen 20%
	Price	Yield	Eff. Dur.	OAS	OAS	% Change in Price	% Change in Price	% Change in Price
FNST731O (GNMA 9 1/2)	51.875	9.57	−7.9	175	145	−1.51	3.49	1.27
FNST151O (FNMA 9 15-yr)	31.000	10.12	−4.4	173	153	−0.60	0.60	0.60
FNST521O (FNMA 9)	43.625	9.21	−4.7	40	15	−1.07	1.72	1.72
FNST6PO (FNMA 9)	55.250	10.23	11.9	114	117	0.17	−2.66	−2.66

FN90108-3 PAC 5-yr	97.344	9.12	4.5	58	55	-0.16	0.55	-0.51
FN90108-5 PAC 10-yr	95.500	9.54	6.8	72	68	-0.23	-0.47	-0.90
PN90108-6 PAC 18-yr	177.438	9.77	8.5	89	88	-0.12	-0.97	-1.49
FHR 171-2 Plain Van 5-yr	98.531	9.37	5.6	58	46	-0.44	0.22	-0.48
FHR 169-3 Plain Van 10-yr	94.406	9.94	6.4	71	59	-0.73	-0.60	-0.93

Maturity	Base Case	50% Steeper
2-yr	7.91%	7.59%
3-yr	8.07	7.85
4-yr	8.23	8.07
5-yr	8.32	8.20
7-yr	8.56	8.55
10-yr	8.69	8.75
30-yr	8.82	8.95

Source: "Comments on Relative Value," presentation by Greg Parseghian of the First Boston Corporation at the Executive Enterprise's Fixed-Income Conference in New York City, November 1, 1990.

Table 13-8

OAS of Various Floating-Rate MBSs

Pool #	Coupon	Months to Next Reset	Reset Frequency	Index/Margin	Life/Periodic Caps	Price	Yield	OAS
Treasury ARMs:								
FNMA #66417	9.961	3	S	6-mo T-BILL (D) + 250*	12.88/0.50	102-00	9.32%	116 bp
FHLMC #350090	9.125	8	A	1-year CMT + 200	13.12/2.00	101-20	8.78	85
Glendale 90-01 "AA"	9.400	3	S	1-year CMT + 175	13.75/1.00	100-16	9.23	134
COFI ARMs:								
FNMA TBA	9.845	1	M	COFI + 125	13.00	101-28	8.77%	82 bp
Citi 89-19	10.000	1	M	COFI + 125	12.65	100-23	9.17	117
Floating Rate CMOs:								
CMSC S	9.075	3	Q	LIBOR + 70	12.00	100-24	8.88%	61 bp
TOMMIE 4	9.025	3	Q	LIBOR + 65	13.00	100-08	8.84	71

Source: Robert Gerber, "Adjustable-Rate Mortgages: Products, Markets, and Valuation," in Frank J. Fabozzi, ed., *The Handbook of Mortgage-Backed Securities*, 3d ed. (Chicago: Probus Publishing, 1992).

and there are a dozen or so software vendors that sell an OAS model. The more sophisticated institutional investors have developed their own OAS models. There are differences in the various models developed, but today their similarities appear to be greater than their differences.

In a recent editorial in the *Financial Analyst Journal,* Alden Toevs has documented the growing parity since 1986 in market pricing based on OAS.[11] Table 13-9 summarizes one of his tests for all three agency passthroughs. The top panel shows information for the period 1986 and 1987, a time span in which the OAS methodology was not widely used by market participants in the mortgage-backed securities market; the lower panel shows the same information for the period 1988 and 1989, in which Toevs argues there was greater acceptance of the OAS methodology.

For each time period, all the issues of an agency were divided into four quartiles based on their OAS at the time of purchase. Three-month total returns were calculated for the agency issues in each quartile. The same was done for a duration-matched Treasury security. The average performance differential was then calculated for each quartile. This is the value reported in the second column of Table 13-9. For example, consider the FNMAs in the second quartile in the 1986–1987 period. On average, the three-month total return for the issues in this quartile outperformed duration-based Treasuries by 68 basis points.

The relative performance is affected by how the OAS changed over the three-month investment horizons. The last column in each panel shows the average change in the OAS over a three-month period for each quartile. For example, look at the first and last quartile for the FHLMC issues in the first period. For the first quartile, the average change in the OAS was a decline of 37 basis points. That is, on average the OAS became richer by 37 basis points. For the last quartile, the OAS became cheaper by 38 basis points on average.

As Toevs argues, one indication of how the OAS methodology has influenced the pricing of passthroughs can be

---

[11] Alden Toevs, "Laser Brains Rejoice: Analytical Methods Can Help Shape Market Equilibrium Prices," *Financial Analysts Journal* (November–December 1990), pp. 8–10.

Table 13-9

Mortgage-Backed Securities Segmented by OAS Quartiles: Three-Month Total-Return Characteristics Relative to Duration-Matched Treasuries

	1986 through 1987	
Quartile	Average Outperformance (basis points)	Average Change in OAS (basis points)
	GNMAs	
1	135	−25
2	94	−11
3	−18	15
4	−152	43
	FNMAs	
1	150	−33
2	68	−8
3	7	6
4	−83	42
	FHLMCs	
1	158	−37
2	55	−5
3	−11	12
4	−70	38
	1988 through 1989	
Quartile	Average Outperformance (basis points)	Average Change in OAS (basis points)
	GNMAs	
1	40	0
2	46	−2
3	26	4
4	29	8
	FNMAs	
1	65	−9
2	38	−1
3	33	4
4	40	9
	FHLMCs	
1	69	−7
2	32	1
3	27	4
4	40	8

Source: Alden Toevs, "Laser Brains Rejoice: Analytical Methods Can Help Shape Market Equilibrium Prices," *Financial Analysts Journal* (November–December 1990), p. 9 (based on information provided by Morgan Stanley).

seen by comparing the results for the two time periods. A comparison indicates several things. First, unlike the first time period, investing based on the OAS methodology resulted in an average performance for each quartile that was greater than that of a comparable duration-based Treasury security in the second time period. Second, the range of the average performance differential was less in the second time period compared to the first time period. Finally, the average change in the OAS was insignificant in the second time period. Taken together, the evidence in Table 13-9 seems to support Toevs's view that "misvaluations of mortgage prepayment options have been increasingly priced away."[12]

Effective Duration and Convexity

Within the OAS methodology, effective duration and convexity can be computed by increasing and decreasing short-term Treasury rates by a small amount. When changing interest rates, the option-adjusted spread is kept constant. This produces two average total present values: one when short-term interest rates are increased and one when short-term interest rates are decreased. These average total present values can be viewed as the theoretical prices under small interest rate changes. These prices are then substituted into the formula for effective duration and convexity given in Chapter 12 and reproduced earlier in this chapter.

Limitations of the OAS Methodology

Although the OAS methodology is clearly superior to traditional analysis, it does have its limitations. The option-adjusted spread analysis helps us identify securities that *promise* to pay a spread over the Treasury term structure after adjusting for the embedded option if (1) the bond is held to the effective maturity date and (2) the cash flows can be reinvested in investment vehicles with an equivalent OAS. Thus, all the limitations of yield measures are applicable to a spread

[12] Ibid., p. 8.

measure.[13] Moreover, because dealer firms make different assumptions about the parameters of an OAS model, there is considerable variance in the OASs reported among firms for the same mortgage-backed security.

TOTAL RETURN FRAMEWORK

The total return framework discussed in Chapter 12 can be used to assess the performance of a passthrough security over some investment horizon. The total dollars received from investing in a passthrough consist of:

1. the projected cash flow of the passthrough from (a) the projected interest payments (net of servicing fee) and (b) the projected principal repayment (scheduled plus prepayments),
2. the interest earned on the reinvestment of the projected interest payments and the projected principal prepayments, and
3. the projected price of the passthrough at the end of the investment horizon.

To obtain (1), a prepayment rate over the investment horizon must be assumed. To calculate (2), a reinvestment rate must be assumed. Finally, any three of the methodologies described earlier can be used to calculate (3) under a particular set of scenarios. The two most common methodologies used are the static cash-flow yield and option-adjusted spread. Using either approach, it is necessary to assume a specific level for the prepayment rate and the Treasury rates at the end of the investment horizon. Using the static cash-flow yield approach, an assumed spread to a comparable Treasury determines the required cash flow yield, which then is used to compute the projected price. The OAS methodology requires an assumption of what the OAS will be at the investment horizon. Based on this assumption, the OAS methodology can work in

---

[13]For theoretical issues concerning the OAS methodology, see Finnerty and Rose, "Arbitrage-Free Spread: A Consistent Measure of Relative Value," pp. 65–81. See also the response by Lakhbir S. Hayre in the same issue, pp. 78–79.

reverse to obtain the price. In practice, a constant OAS is assumed (i.e., it is assumed that the OAS will not change over the investment horizon).

An investor should not use one set of projections to determine the total return. Instead, an investor should assess the performance of a security over a range of likely assumptions. If it is possible to assign probabilities to these scenarios, an expected value for the total return can be calculated.

The total monthly return is then found using the following formula:

$$\left(\frac{\text{total future dollars}}{\text{price of the passthrough}} \right)^{1/\text{no. of mos. in horizon}} - 1$$

The total monthly return can be annualized on a bond equivalent yield basis or by computing the effective annual yield as follows:

$$(1 + \text{total monthly return})^{12} - 1$$

Illustrations

To illustrate the calculation of total return, suppose a portfolio manager is considering investing in a passthrough with a 9.5% mortgage rate, 0.5% servicing fee, 360 months remaining to maturity, and an original mortgage balance of $100,000. The price of this passthrough is $94,521. The cash flow yield assuming 100% PSA is 10.21%. The portfolio manager has a six-month investment horizon and believes the following:

1. for the next six months the prepayment rate will be 100% PSA,
2. the projected cash flow can be reinvested at 0.5% per month,
3. the passthrough will sell to yield 7.62% at the end of the investment horizon, and[14]

---

[14]Because of the complexities of calculating an OAS, in this illustration we will use the static cash-flow yield methodology to determine the price at the horizon date.

4. the projected PSA prepayment rate at the end of the investment horizon will be 185% PSA.

Based on the first assumption, the projected cash flow (projected interest net of servicing fee, projected scheduled principal, and projected principal prepayment) for the first six months is:

End of month	Projected cash flow
1	$816
2	832
3	849
4	865
5	881
6	897

The projected cash flow is obtained from Table 9-3 in Chapter 9.

The projected cash flow plus interest from reinvesting the cash flow at 0.5% per month is shown below:

End of month	Projected cash flow	Projected cash flow plus reinvestment income
1	$816	$ 837
2	832	849
3	849	862
4	865	874
5	881	885
6	897	897
	Total	$5,204

At the end of the investment horizon, this passthrough would have a remaining mortgage balance of $99,181 (see Table 9-3) and remaining maturity of 355 months. Assuming a required yield of 7.62% and a prepayment rate of 185% PSA, the projected price of this passthrough would be $106,210.

The total future dollars are then:

projected cash flow plus
reinvestment income   = $ 5,204
projected price   =   106,210
total future dollars   = $111,414

The total monthly return is:

$$\left(\frac{\$111,414}{\$\ 94,521}\right)^{1/6} - 1 = .02778$$

On a bond equivalent basis, the total return is:

$$2\left[(1.02778)^6 - 1\right] = .3574 = 35.74\%$$

On an effective annual yield basis, the total return is:

$$(1.02778)^{12} - 1 = .3893 = 38.93\%$$

Suppose that a portfolio manager wants to assess the performance of the passthrough in the previous illustration over a six-month investment horizon based on the following assumptions:

1. for the next six months the prepayment rate will be 100% PSA,
2. the projected cash flow can be reinvested at 0.75% per month,
3. the passthrough will sell to yield 12.30% at the end of the investment horizon, and
4. the projected PSA prepayment rate at the end of the investment horizon will be 50% PSA.

Based on the first assumption, the projected cash flow for the first six months is the same as in the previous illustration. The projected cash flow plus interest from reinvesting the cash flow at 0.75% per month is computed below:

End of month	Projected cash flow	Projected cash flow plus reinvestment income
1	$816	$ 847
2	832	857
3	849	868
4	865	878
5	881	888
6	897	897
	Total	$5,235

At the end of the investment horizon, this passthrough would have a remaining balance of $99,181 and remaining maturity of 355 months. Assuming a required yield of 12.30% and a prepayment rate of 50% PSA, the projected price of this passthrough would be $78,757.

The total future dollars are then:

projected cash flow plus reinvestment income	=	$ 5,235
projected price	=	78,757
total future dollars	=	$ 83,992

The total monthly return is:

$$\left(\frac{\$\ 83,992}{\$\ 94,521}\right)^{1/6} - 1 = -.019491$$

On a bond equivalent basis, the total return is:

$$2\left[(0.98051)^6 - 1\right] = -0.2228 = -22.28\%$$

On an effective annual yield basis, the total return is:

$$(0.98051)^{12} - 1 = -0.2104 = -21.04\%$$

Tying the Total Return and OAS Frameworks Together

The total return and OAS frameworks can be combined to determine the projected price at the horizon date. This requires an OAS model and a prepayment model. At the end of the investment horizon it is necessary to specify how the OAS is expected to change. Under a constant OAS scenario, the horizon price can be "backed out" of the OAS model. We saw an application of this earlier in the chapter in the use of the OAS analysis for CMOs in Tables 13-3 and 13-4. For example, we reported the price change in a class assuming a constant OAS under various assumptions about prepayments and interest rate volatility. This can be extended to the total return

Table 13-10

One-Year Total Return Analysis for the Trust 63 PO and a Treasury Strip

		Interest-Rate Move (Bps.)						
		-300	-200	-100	0	100	200	300
Trust 63 PO	Proj. PSA	441	310	185	150	152	126	120
Price: 54-09	YTM	29.55	18.96	11.08	9.27	8.42	8.13	7.88
	Hor. Price	79-30	71-29	62-23	55-27	50-28	47-05	44-05
	Total Return	50.40	38.45	21.40	10.10	1.77	-4.48	-9.69
Tsy. STRIP	YTM	9.14	9.14	9.14	9.14	9.14	9.14	9.14
of 5/15/01	Hor. Price	54.48	49.43	44.86	40.74	37.01	33.64	30.59
Price: 40.581	Total Return	41.96	30.47	19.57	9.24	-0.56	-9.86	-18.68
	PO Advantage (Bps.)	844	798	183	86	233	538	899

Note: A parallel shift in interest rates is assumed to occur gradually over one year. The PO prices are calculated assuming an OAS of 100 basis points and a short-rate volatility of 15%. The initial reinvestment rate is assumed to be 8.5%. Analysis based on prices and yield curve at close on April 23, 1990.

Source: Lakhbir Hayre and Errol Mustafa, "Stripped Mortgage-Backed Securities," in Fabozzi, ed., *The Handbook of Mortgage-Backed Securities*, 3d ed.

Table 13-11

One-Year Total Return Analysis for an FNMA 6-Month
Treasury Bill ARM and a 2-Year Treasury

Interest Rate Scenario	Average First-Year Coupon	Ending Coupon	Ending Price	Approximate Cash Flow SMM	Total Return
− 200 bp	9.92%	9.49%	104−00	2.50%	10.42 %
− 100	9.94	9.52	102−29	2.50	9.74
0	10.12	10.11	101−30	2.25	9.36
+ 100	10.34	10.80	100−28	2.25	8.85
+ 200	10.38	10.88	99−11	2.00	7.84

	Comparative Total Returns		
Interest Rate Scenario	FNMA #66415	2-Year Treasury	Difference
− 200 bp	10.42%	9.93%	+ 0.49%
− 100	9.74	8.98	+ 0.76
0	9.36	8.05	+ 1.31
+ 100	8.85	7.13	+ 1.72
+ 200	7.84	6.22	+ 1.62

Source: Robert Gerber, "Adjustable-Rate Mortgages: Products, Markets, and Valuation," in Fabozzi, ed., *The Handbook of Mortgage-Backed Securities,* 3d ed.

framework by making assumptions about these parameters at the horizon date.

Applications

Two applications of the total return framework are shown in Tables 13-10 and 13-11. The first of these tables shows a comparison of the one-year total return of a PO and a Treasury STRIP[15] under various interest rate moves based on prices and the yield curve at the end of April 1990.[16] Under the assumptions specified in the table for the PO—namely,

[15]A Treasury STRIP is a stripped Treasury security that is created by dealer firms under the Treasury's Separate Trading of Registered Interest and Principal program.
[16]Lakhbir Hayre and Errol Mustafa, "Stripped Mortgage-Backed Securities," in Frank J. Fabozzi, ed., *The Handbook of Mortgage-Backed Securities,* 3d ed. (Chicago: Probus Publishing, 1992).

based on the projected PSA for each interest rate movement, an OAS of 100 basis points, and a 15% volatility for interest rates—the PO shown would outperform the Treasury STRIP in each scenario.

Table 13-11 compares the performance of an FNMA six-month Treasury bill ARM and a two-year Treasury over a one-year investment horizon for various interest-rate movement scenarios.[17] Assuming a constant OAS at the end of the one-year investment horizon and the prepayment rate shown in the table, the ARM outperforms the two-year Treasury in each scenario.

[17] Robert Gerber, "Adjustable-Rate Mortgages: Products, Markets, and Valuation," in Fabozzi, ed., *The Handbook of Mortgage-Backed Securities,* 3d ed.

14

The Future of Asset Securitization

The traditional system for financing the acquisition of assets called for one financial intermediary such as a commercial bank, thrift, or insurance company to: (1) originate a loan; (2) retain the loan in its portfolio of assets, thereby accepting the credit risk associated with the loan; (3) service the loan (i.e., collect payments and take legal action if payments were not made); and (4) obtain funds from the public with which to finance its assets (except for the small amount representing the institution's equity).

Times have changed. A new system has developed for lending capital in which more than one institution may be involved. Consider mortgage activities discussed in the earlier chapters. A lending scenario may look like this: (1) a thrift or commercial bank originates a mortgage loan; (2) the thrift or commercial bank sells its mortgages to an investment banking firm that creates a security backed by the pool of mortgages; (3) the investment banker obtains credit risk insurance for the pool of mortgages from a private insurance company; (4) the investment banker can sell the right to service the loans to another thrift or a company specializing in serving mortgages; and (5) the investment banking firm can sell the securities to individuals and institutional investors.

Besides the original bank or thrift, an investment bank, an insurance company, another thrift, an individual, and other institutional investors participate. The bank or thrift in our example does not have to absorb the credit risk, service the mortgage, or provide the funding. Also notice that there is no government agency involved in this process.

As we noted earlier, this system of lending is referred to as asset securitization because securities are created for which the collateral is the cash flow from the assets. By far the largest part of the market is the mortgage-backed securities market, where the assets collateralizing the securities are mortgage loans. Securitized assets backed by non–real estate mortgage loans are a small but growing part of the market. These securities are commonly referred to as *asset-backed securities*.

In this chapter we review several common asset-backed securities, explain how the structures that have developed are similar to those of passthroughs and CMOs, discuss the benefits of asset securitization for issuers, borrowers, and investors, as well as the far-ranging implications for the U.S. financial system. We conclude this chapter with some thoughts about the potential supply of mortgage-backed securities.

ASSET-BACKED SECURITIES

Asset-backed securities are securities collateralized by assets that are not mortgage loans. While the two most common types of asset-backed securities are those backed by automobile loans and credit card receivables, there are securities backed by home equity loans, boat loans, recreational vehicle loans, computer leases, senior bank loans,[1] accounts receivables, and Small Business Administration (SBA) loans.

As of September 1991, the cumulative issuance of asset-backed securities since 1985 was $142 billion. Table 14-1 shows the issuance by year and by collateral type. As can be seen, most of the issuance occurred in the most recent three-year period, 1989 to 1991. Securities backed by credit card

---

[1] Asset-backed securities collateralized by senior bank loans are called *collateralized loan obligations*. For a discussion of these securities, see Peter J. Carril Jr., and Frank J. Fabozzi, "Collateralized Loan Obligations," in Frank J. Fabozzi and John H. Carlson, eds., *Trading and Securitization of Senior Bank Loans* (Chicago: Probus Publishing, 1992).

Table 14-1

Asset-Backed Securities Issuance by Collateral Type, 1985 through September 1991

	Issuance Amount by Collateral ($ billions)				
	Collateral Type				
Year	Autos	Credit cards	Home equity	Other	Total
1985	$ 898.6	$ 0	$ 0	$ 338.3	$ 1,236.9
1986	9,473.0	0	0	617.6	10,090.6
1987	6,372.2	2,410.0	0	1,208.7	9,990.9
1988	5,497.8	7,420.0	0	2,276.1	15,193.9
1989	7,823.6	11,112.0	2,700.2	2,912.5	24,548.3
1990	11,632.6	22,731.0	5,499.9	1,963.9	41,827.4
1991*	11,240.5	16,342.0	8,820.5	2,928.4	39,331.4
Total	$52,938.3	$60,015.0	17,020.6	12,245.5	142,219.4

	Percent of Annual Issuance by Collateral ($ billions)				
	Collateral Type				
Year	Autos	Credit cards	Home equity	Other	Total
1985	73%	0%	0%	27%	100%
1986	94	0	0	6	100
1987	64	24	0	12	100
1988	36	49	0	15	100
1989	32	45	11	12	100
1990	28	54	13	5	100
1991*	29	42	22	7	100

*Through September 1991
Source: Data supplied by the First Boston Corporation.

loans are now the largest type of asset-backed security, followed by securities backed by automobile loans, and then home equity loans.[2]

In structuring an asset-backed security, issuers have drawn from the structures used in the mortgage-backed secu-

[2]The investment banking firms active in the asset-backed securities market compile their own data bases. The data furnished to us by Andrew Carron of First Boston, which is reported in Table 14-1, are consistent with the data provided to us by Paul Jablansky of Goldman, Sachs. According to the Goldman, Sachs data base, compiled through the end of November 1991, the next largest category of asset-backed securities after those backed by home equity loans is securities backed by mobile homes and recreational vehicles. As of November 1991, cumulative issuance with this collateral type was $4.3 billion, with just less than $0.8 billion issued in 1991.

rities market. Asset-backed securities have been structured as passthroughs and as structures with multiple-bond classes just like a CMO. This last structure is called an *asset-backed obligation*. Credit enhancement is provided by letters of credit, recourse to the issuer, overcollateralization, or senior/subordination (or A/B passthrough). All issues backed by automobile loans and credit card receivables have received ratings of at least double A.

Asset-Backed Securities Backed by Automobile Loans

The first public offering of an asset-backed security was in March 1985 by Sperry Lease Finance Corporation (now Unisys). The issue was collateralized by $192 million of lease-backed notes. Two months later, in May 1985, the first asset-backed securities backed by automobile loans were issued by Marine Midland. These issues are referred to as Certificates for Automobile Receivables (CARs).

The five largest issuers of automobile loan backed securities from 1985 to 1987 in order of the principal amount outstanding are General Motors Acceptance Corporation (16 issues, principal amount $11.4 billion), Chrysler Financial Corporation (three issues, principal amount $1.8 billion), Marine Midland Bank (three issues, principal amount $1.1 billion), Western Financial Savings Bank (four issues, principal amount $0.53 billion), and Bank of America (one issue, $0.51 billion).[3]

Cash flow for securities backed by automobile loans is either monthly or quarterly. Stated final maturities range from three to five years, but have average lives of one to three years.

The first asset-backed obligation was offered by Asset Backed Securities Corporation, a subsidiary of First Boston Corporation. This issue also goes down in the record book as the largest nongovernment debt issue in history: $4 billion. General Motors Acceptance Corporation originated the automobile loans used as collateral. The credit enhancement in-

[3]William Haley, "Securitizing Automobile Receivables," in Philip L. Zweig, ed., *The Asset Securitization Handbook* (Homewood, IL: Dow Jones-Irwin, 1989), pp. 60–90.

cluded a limited guarantee from GMAC, a letter of credit from Credit Suisse, and the equity of the issuer (Asset Backed Securities Corporation). There were three bond classes with average lives of 1.1, 2.2, and 3.0 years. Borrowers pay regularly scheduled monthly loan payments (interest and scheduled principal repayments) and may make prepayments. The uncertainty about the cash flow is due to prepayments. For securities backed by automobile loans, prepayments result from: (1) sales and trade-ins requiring full payoff of the loan, (2) repossession and subsequent sale of the automobile, (3) loss or destruction of the vehicle, (4) payoff of the loan with cash to save interest cost, and (5) refinancing of the loan at a lower interest cost.

While refinancings may be a major reason for prepayments of mortgage loans, they are of minor importance for automobile loans. Moreover, the interest rates for the automobile loans underlying several issues are substantially below market rates if they are offered by manufacturers as part of a sales promotion. There is good historical information on the other causes of prepayments. Therefore, the cash flow of securities backed by automobile loans does not have a great deal of uncertainty despite prepayments. Uncertainty is reduced even further in the asset-backed obligation structure.

Yields offered on these securities are typically higher than those on short-term corporate obligations with similar credit ratings, and liquidity in the secondary market is improving. There are several bellwether issues that market makers use as a pricing guide.[4]

Asset-Backed Securities Backed by Credit Card Receivables

The first two public issues of credit card asset-backed securities were by RepublicBank Delaware (a subsidiary of RepublicBank Corporation of Texas) and Bank of America in January and February 1987, respectively. The first offering was collateralized by $200 million of 227,000 Visa and Mas-

[4]Ibid., p. 84.

terCard accounts that were seasoned three months. The second offering by Bank of America (California Credit Card Trust 1987-A) was a $400 million issue backed by 840,000 Visa accounts. These issues were called CARDs (Certificates for Amortizing Revolving Debts). The first credit card-backed securities not collateralized by Visa and/or MasterCard accounts were issued in early 1988 by the retailers Sears, Montgomery Ward, and J.C. Penney.

The yield an investor realizes depends on the credit card borrowers' rate of repayment of the amount borrowed. Historical data on credit card borrower repayments indicate that repayments are high. For example, the Bank of America's $300 million California Credit Card Trust 1987-B had a projected cash flow of $2.05 million per month for the first 18 months and a constant monthly repayment rate of 18.5%.

Interest to holders of credit card backed issues is paid monthly. Most issues have a fixed interest rate, but there are floating-rate issues.

BENEFITS OF ASSET SECURITIZATION

Securitization of mortgage loans, consumer loans, and commercial loans can be beneficial to issuers, investors, and borrowers.

Benefits to Issuers

The most commonly cited benefits of securitization are (1) obtaining a lower cost of funds, (2) more efficient use of capital, (3) managing rapid portfolio growth, (4) better asset/liability management, (5) enhanced financial performance, and (6) diversification of funding sources.[5]

Obtaining a lower cost of funds. Segregating assets and using them as collateral for a security offering lets lower funding costs be obtained. The cost of funding for a mortgage-related entity such as a thrift, commercial bank, or home

---

[5] Ibid., p. 75.

builder depends on its credit rating. The lower the credit rating, the higher the cost of funding. By using mortgage loans as collateral and properly structuring a security, a mortgage-related institution can obtain a credit rating on the security that is higher than its own credit rating. This will result in a lower cost of funds.

This is also true in the asset-backed securities market, as can be seen in three examples. The Sperry Lease Financial Corporation asset-backed security backed by lease receivables was structured so that the cash flow from the underlying leases would be sufficient to satisfy the interest and principal payments; the security as a result received a triple-A rating. At the time, Sperry Lease Financial Corporation had a lower credit rating. Bank of America issued asset-backed securities backed by credit card receivables. The securities received a triple A rating, a rating higher than Bank of America's. It has been estimated that Bank of America saved at least 150 basis points over what it would have had to pay by issuing debt with a similar maturity.[6] More recently, while Chrysler Corporation has a quality rating of double B, it has been able to issue securities backed by automobile loans with a triple-A rating.

More efficient use of capital. For financial institutions that must meet capital guideline requirements, the sale of assets can free up capital. The recently established risk-based capital guidelines for banks, for example, require a certain percentage of capital for each asset a bank has. The percentage is supposed to reflect the credit risk associated with the asset. Often, however, the capital requirements are higher than the actual risks associated with the asset. If assets are securitized and the securities are sold, the capital required will reflect the actual risks associated with the assets. This will result in a reduction of excess capital requirements.[7]

Manufacturing corporations or their captive finance companies gain through securitization the opportunity to obtain greater leverage than the credit rating companies might

---

[6]Lowell L. Bryan, "Introduction," in Zweig, ed., *The Asset Securitization Handbook*, pp. 3–20.
[7]For a discussion of the role of asset securitization for asset/liability management of depository institutions, see Anand Bhattacharya and Krishnan Kandapani, "Asset Securitization: Prospects and Issues," in Frank J. Fabozzi and Atsuo Konishi, eds., *Asset/Liability Management for Depository Institutions* (Chicago: Probus Publishing, 1991), pp. 409–434.

judge acceptable otherwise. As an example, consider General Motors Acceptance Corporation or Chrysler Financial Corporation. These finance companies might have a ratio of automobile receivables-to-liabilities (a measure of financial leverage) of 8 or 10 to 1, acceptable for this industry according to the credit rating companies. Proper structure of an asset-backed security will allow reduction of credit risk exposure, so that the financing companies retain only a fraction of the credit risk associated with the assets.

Shifting the credit risk from the originator of the loan to another party reduces the issuers' return together with its risk. At the same time, the issuer may keep or sell the rights to service the loans. Earnings from the business thus come from fee income rather than interest rate spread income.

Managing rapid portfolio growth. As the business of a financial or nonfinancial entity grows, growth potential will be limited by capital constraints. Selling assets through securitization provides a means for quickly raising capital while keeping the asset, and hence the debt, off the balance sheet, avoiding capital requirements. The risk-based capital guidelines for banks encourage the practice of securitization of assets.

Better asset/liability management. Because mortgages and consumer installment loans expose financial institutions to prepayment risk, it can be difficult to establish a liability structure consistent with the structure of the uncertain cash flow of these assets. Securitization passes the prepayment risk to the investor. This gives the financial institution a means for funding assets in which maturity matches that of the asset.

Enhancing financial performance. When loans are sold via securitization at a yield lower than the interest rate on the loan, the originator realizes the spread. This spread partially reflects the fee for servicing the loans and partially reflects conversion of an illiquid loan into a more liquid security backed by loans and with credit enhancements. This is most obvious with the CMO structure. The issuer of the CMO owns the residual cash flow. If the issuer chooses not to sell the CMO residual, the cash flow will be received over time. Alternatively, the issuer can capture the spread immediately by selling the CMO residual. This source of spread over cost of transformation will of course tend to be eroded by competition, which will tend to reallocate the abnormal spread among final borrowers and final lenders.

Diversification of sources. Investors that ordinarily could not make mortgage loans, consumer loans, and/or commercial loans can invest in these securities. This provides more sources of capital for both financial and nonfinancial entities.

Benefits to Investors

Securitization converts illiquid loans into securities with greater liquidity and reduced credit risk. Credit risk is reduced because (1) it is backed by a diversified pool of loans, and (2) there is credit enhancement or, in the case of an agency mortgage passthrough, an agency guarantee. This permits investors to broaden their universe of investment opportunities. It also tends to improve returns through the reduction of the cost of intermediation.

Benefits to Borrowers

A financial or nonfinancial entity can securitize a loan it originates or sell the loan to some entity that will securitize it. A securitized loan is thus a more liquid asset than the loan itself, since it can be sold by the lender if capital is needed. The existence of securitized loans should reduce the spread between lending rates and safe assets such as Treasury securities. This has occurred in the mortgage market and, to some extent, in the automobile loan and credit card loan markets. As the market matures, competition among originators should produce lower lending rate spreads in other loan markets.

IMPLICATIONS OF SECURITIZATION FOR FINANCIAL MARKETS

Securitization has major implications for financial markets as well as for the structure of financial institutions such as banks and thrifts. Securitization eventually may replace the traditional system of indirect financing. To understand why, let's briefly review the role of financial intermediaries, particularly thrifts and banks.

Financial intermediaries act as conduits in bringing savers and borrowers together. They perform this function in several ways. First, banks and thrifts are in a better position than individual investors to assess credit risk. After evaluating credit risk, they may agree to grant a loan and hold the loan as an investment. Furthermore, being in a position to distribute their assets over many different borrowers and industries, they achieve risk reduction through diversification. The returns to investors are also made safer by government guaranteed liabilities (e.g., their insured certificates of deposit).

Second, the maturities of loans sought by borrowers may be different from those that investors want. Thrifts and banks acquire short-term funds and grant loans with longer maturities. This satisfies the objective of investors that may want shorter-term investments and borrowers that want longer-term funds; that is, banks and thrifts provide maturity intermediation. Finally, the amount of funds sought by borrowers is typically greater than any one individual investor would be willing to lend. Thrifts and banks make large denomination loans to borrowers and offer investors investments with smaller denominations. That is, they provide denomination intermediation, transforming very large assets into quite divisible ones.

Securitization provides direct financing between borrowers and investors, short-circuiting the traditional intermediaries. Pooling of assets reinforced by private credit enhancement reduces credit risk to more acceptable levels for investors. Recasting cash flows such as in CMOs and asset-backed obligations provides varying maturities acceptable to a wide range of investors. Thus, securitization serves a role similar to maturity intermediation. The availability of securities with smaller denominations than the underlying loans accomplishes denomination intermediation. All of this happens without the need for any government guarantees (although such guarantees may enhance the value of securitized instruments). The success of securitization indicates that it is a more efficient method for linking borrowers and investors than traditional financing through intermediaries. Consequently, the role of banks and thrifts may have to be reassessed.

The true innovations in this market are not really the securities themselves but (1) reduction of risk through pooling of assets and private credit enhancement, and (2) repackaging of the cash flows from assets in a way that relieves the intermediary of reliance on its own assets to finance the credit—i.e., that permits off–balance sheet financing. This is not an entirely new approach, as it underlies such instruments as bankers acceptances, mortgage bonds (popular in many foreign countries), and to some extent letters of credit. The current wave of applications, however, goes well beyond past practice in the magnitude and nature of innovative approaches, and it is already spreading to other countries.

CONCLUDING REMARKS ON THE POTENTIAL SUPPLY OF MORTGAGE-BACKED SECURITIES

In this book we have described the process of originating, servicing, insuring, pooling (to create passthroughs), and sculpturing cash flows to create derivative securities (collateralized mortgage obligations and stripped mortgage-backed securities). The creation of passthrough securities is motivated by the desire to enhance the characteristics of investing in individual loans. The attractiveness is further enhanced by creating certain derivative products. Some of these derivative products are useful in hedging the risks associated with servicing mortgage loans and hedging portfolios of passthrough securities.

The U.S. housing finance market is the best in the world, and it has achieved this status primarily through the securitization of mortgage loans. In this concluding section, we discuss the potential for increasing the supply of mortgage-backed securities. The potential supply can be seen by looking at the amount of real estate mortgage loans that remain unsecuritized and examining why they have not been securitized.

About 60% of the $2.74 trillion of 1-to-4 family mortgage loans outstanding as of March 31, 1991, is unsecuritized.[8] Most of the $476 billion of the FHA/VA-insured 1-to-4 family mortgage loans are securitized, but something less than one-third of conventional loans are not. Only 10% of the $3.03 trillion multifamily mortgage market is securitized. Thus, of the $2.77 trillion residential mortgage loans outstanding, $1.90 trillion remains to be securitized.

Multifamily housing is only one part of the market for income-producing real estate loans. The other part is commercial mortgages, which include loans for office buildings, shopping centers, industrial plants and warehouses, hotels, and restaurants. As with multifamily housing, no significant inroads have been made into the securitization of mortgage loans for these properties, which is more than $850 billion.[9]

Consequently, there is the potential to securitize outstanding loans with a par value of more than $2.7 trillion—an amount that is larger than the combined corporate bond market ($1.5 trillion) and municipal bond market ($852 billion).[10] For the reasons explained earlier in this chapter, regulated financial institutions will find it beneficial to securitize real estate mortgages they currently hold in their portfolio as well as newly originated ones. For example, under the risk-based capital guidelines for depository institutions, multifamily and commercial mortgages fall into the highest risk category and therefore have the highest capital requirements. By securitizing these loans, capital requirements can be reduced.

Barriers to Securitization

The barriers to securitization involve credit concerns, lack of standardization of documentation, and legal issues. These barriers are not mutually exclusive.

In the 1-to-4 family mortgage market, 87% of FHA/VA-insured mortgages are securitized, while only 26% of conventionals are. For conventional mortgages, Fannie Mae and Freddie Mac have accepted the credit risk by securitizing them. Of the $1.38 trillion of unsecuritized 1-to-4 family con-

[8] As reported in "Database," insert to *Secondary Mortgage Markets*, Summer 1991, Table 5.
[9] Source is the U.S. Flow of Funds Report, Federal Reserve Release Z.7.
[10] Based on December 31, 1990 par value as provided to the authors by Salomon Brothers.

ventional mortgage loans, not all can be securitized by these two agencies because of their underwriting standards. Specifically, these standards impose a maximum size on the loan and a restriction on the type of loan.

Loans that would not qualify for securitization because of their size are called jumbo loans. As of 1988, the amount of jumbo loans was estimated to be $500 billion, or roughly 25% of 1-to-4 family conventional mortgages outstanding.[11] Moreover, about a fourth of newly originated mortgages in 1988 would not have qualified for securitization by Fannie Mae or Freddie Mac because they were jumbo mortgages. Some of the jumbo loan market has been securitized by private issuers. The credit risk associated with mortgage pools that collateralize conventional passthrough securities has been reduced through the use of the credit enhancement techniques explained in Chapter 8. As issuers and investors become more comfortable with these credit-enhanced structures, the issuance of conventional passthroughs will increase.

Changes in the maximum size of a mortgage loan that Fannie Mae or Freddie Mac may securitize will also add to the potential supply of loans that may be securitized. Moreover, these agencies have been able to securitize more types of loans than they had previously. For example, shortly after tiered-payment mortgages became popular in 1989, they were used to back collateralized mortgage obligations issued by Freddie Mac. The creation of new mortgage designs suggested in Chapter 7 to overcome the drawbacks of existing mortgage products in the presence of inflation holds promise for securitization.

In the case of multifamily and commercial mortgages, credit concerns and lack of documentation remain major obstacles. Credit concerns are not present for the $51 billion FHA-insured multifamily mortgages, resulting in the securitization of 25% of these loans. For non-FHA-insured income producing real estate loans, Fannie Mae, Freddie Mac, and private issuers must develop experience in assessing the business risks associated with the property.

Commercial rating companies such as Moody's and

---

[11]Robert Gerber, "Introduction to Private Label Pass-Through Market," in Frank J. Fabozzi, ed., *The Handbook of Mortgage-Backed Securities* 3d ed. (Chicago: Probus Publishing, 1992).

Standard & Poor's now rate securities backed by mortgage pools of commercial and multifamily mortgages. The commercial rating companies will play a major role in securitization of income-producing property loans as they establish guidelines that issuers must adhere to in order to obtain the necessary credit enhancement to achieve a desired credit rating. Investors will then look to the credit rating as they now do with corporate and municipal debt obligations. The ability of the commercial rating companies to do an effective job of assessing the credit risk should improve over time as more historical information on defaults becomes available. Presently, there is limited historical data on defaults for multifamily and commercial mortgage loans, as well as other information such as prepayments that investors will require to value securities collateralized by these loans.

Standardization of documentation is a necessity for the securitization of loans, as well as for the transferring of servicing rights. This is no longer a problem for most 1-to-4 family mortgages. However, lack of standardization of documentation of multifamily and commercial mortgages will continue to remain an impediment to securitization since it is unlikely that complex commercial transactions can be standardized.

Securitizing Other Mortgage-Related Products

There are also second mortgages and home equity loans for residential property that can be securitized. This is not a small market. It is estimated that $300 billion of such debt is outstanding, with two-thirds being second mortgages and one-third home equity loans.[12] Moreover, the size of the home equity loan market should increase in the 1990s if the current tax law that limits the deductibility of interest paid by individual taxpayers on real estate loans is unchanged. As can be seen from Table 14-1, only $17 billion of home equity loans have been securitized. It is estimated that only $2 billion of second mortgages have been securitized.[13]

---

[12]Laura J. Swartz, "Securitizing Seconds," *Secondary Mortgage Markets* (Spring 1991), p. 12.
[13]Ibid.

Here, too, the risk-based capital guidelines for depository institutions will encourage the removal of these loans from their balance sheet via securitization. Generally, double the capital is required for second mortgages compared to first mortgages. Also, capital is required for unused lines of credit for home equity loans.

In Chapter 4 we mentioned the possibility of securitizing servicing fees. While attempts have been made to establish an asset-backed security collateralized by servicing fees, there are regulatory and legal obstacles that must be overcome. But as the experience with financial engineering in the 1980s has clearly demonstrated, no type of securitization should be considered insurmountable.

About the Authors

Frank J. Fabozzi is Visiting Professor of Finance at the Sloan School of Management at MIT where he has been a full-time faculty member since 1986. He is the editor of *The Journal of Portfolio Management* and associate editor of *The Journal of Fixed Income.* Professor Fabozzi has written and edited several widely acclaimed books in finance. He is on the board of directors of seven closed-end investment companies listed on the New York Stock Exchange and on the board of supervisory directors of three offshore funds, all specializing in mortgage-backed securities products. He received a doctorate in economics in 1972 from The Graduate Center of the City University of New York and is a Chartered Financial Analyst.

Franco Modigliani is Institute Professor and Professor of Finance and Economics at MIT. He is an Honorary President of the International Economic Association, a former President of the American Economic Association, the American Finance Association, and the Econometric Society. Professor Modigliani has written numerous books and articles in economics. In October 1985, he was awarded the Alfred Nobel Memorial Prize in Economic Sciences. He has served as a consultant to the Federal Reserve System, the U.S. Treasury Department, and a number of European banks. Professor Modigliani received a Doctor of Jurisprudence in 1939 from the University of Rome and a Doctor of Social Science in 1944 from the New School for Social Research, as well as several honorary doctorates.

Index

AA passthrough. *See* Conventional
  passthrough
A/B passthrough, 160–161
Accrual bonds, 220, 238–239
Adjustable-payment mortgages
  (APMs), 150
Adjustable-rate mortgage (ARM), 1,
  36, 44
  ARM passthroughs, 23, 103
  assessment of, 116–117
  benchmark indexes, 102, 105–109
  benefits of, 102
  characteristics of, 102–113
  convertible ARMs, 113–114
  cost of funds for thrifts indexes,
    105, 106–108
  features of, 109–113
  growth of ARM market, 103
  lifetime caps and floors, 112–113
  and mismatch problem, 101–102
  negative amortization, 110, 112
  payment caps, 109–112
  periodic caps, 109–112
  prepayment behavior, 210–211
  problems of, 118–119
  rate caps, 109–110
  reset period, 102, 107–108
  seasoning process, 210
  spread, 102, 106, 109
  teaser rate, 109
  from thrifts, problems of,
    104–105
  Treasury-based indexes, 105–106
Adjustable-rate preferred stock, 102
Agency mortgage-backed securities
  market. *See also* Agency passthroughs; *specific agencies*
  bid-ask spread, 29
  conforming mortgages, 30
  effect of FIRREA, 26–27

Fannie Mae, 21, 23–24, 27
Freddie Mac, 21–25, 27
Ginnie Mae, 21–22, 24
liquidity of, 22, 29
market making, 27–30
Agency passthroughs. *See also*
  Agency mortgage-backed securities market; *specific agencies*
  characteristics of loans in pool,
    148–149
  design of loans, 148
  features of, 147–149
  fully modified passthroughs, 147
  minimum pool size, 149
  modified passthroughs, 148
  number of lenders in pool, 148
  payment procedure, 149
  type of guarantee, 147–149
American Banker, 61
ARM. *See* Adjustable-rate mortgage
Askin, David J., 74
Asset-backed securities
  backed by automobile loans,
    312–315
  backed by credit card receiv-
    ables, 315–316
  definition, 312
  types of, 312
Asset Backed Securities Corporation, 314–315
Asset securitization, future of,
  311–325
  asset-backed securities, 312–316
  benefits to borrowers, 319
  benefits to investors, 319
  benefits to issuers, 316–319
  definition, 2
  implications for financial mar-
    kets, 319–321
  participants, 311

Asset securitization *(continued)*
  pooling of automobile loans,
    312–315
  pooling of credit card receiv-
    ables, 315–316
  traditional vs. new system, 311
Assumability of mortgages, 148,
  151, 154, 158

Balloon mortgages, 19, 81, 85
Balloon/reset mortgages, 115–116
Bank of America, 31, 314–317
Barmore, Gregory, 42
Basis risk, 54–55
Bear Stearns, 63, 212
Black-Scholes model, 279
Blind pools, 33
Blue sky laws, 33
Bonds. *See* Fixed-income analysis
"Boutique" securities, 157
Bullet payment, 236
Burnout, 198, 203, 208
Bush, George, 101

California Credit Card Trust, 316
Callable bonds, 255–260, 268–269
  decomposition of, 259–260, 278,
    285
  disadvantages of, 256–257
  price volatility of, 268–269
  price/yield relationship, 257–259
Call risk, 216
Capital Markets Assurance Corpo-
  ration (CAPMAC), 160
Caput, 60
CARDs (Certificates for Amortizing
  Revolving Debts), 316
Cash flow yield, 191–193, 271–272
Cash PCs, 152
Cash Program, 22, 152–153, 155,
  157
Certificates for Automobile Receiv-
  ables (CARs), 314
Chicago Board of Trade (CBOT),
  54, 166–167
Chrysler Financial Corporation,
  314, 317–318

Citicorp, 35, 160, 162
Clauretie, Terrence, 78
CMO residuals, 239–240
CMOs. *See* Collateralized mortgage
  obligations
CMT. *See* Constant maturity Treasury rate
Collateralized mortgage obligations, 3–4, 9–11, 125, 145, 318
  accrual bonds, 220, 224–225
  arbitrage profit, 223
  cash flow of, 221
  characteristics of classes, 224
  CMO classes, 10–11, 220,
    224–242
  CMO residuals, 239–240
  for commercial banks and thrifts,
    218
  companion or support classes,
    232
  companions with schedules,
    237–238
  considerations in structuring of,
    221–223
  coupon leverage, 227
  creation by Freddie Mac, 25
  credit risk, 224
  definition, 217
  floating-rate CMOs, 225–227, 237
  for insurance companies, 218
  inverse floater, 226–228, 237
  IOettes and PAC IOs, 240–242
  motivation for development of,
    218–219
  number of classes, 242
  PAC bonds, 231–237
  PAC I, II, and III level bonds, 238
  for pension funds, 218
  PO-collateralized CMOs, 246
  and prepayment risk, 10–11, 216,
    217–218
  REMIC CMO, 223
  resecuritization, 10
  risk/return pattern, 219
  sequential-pay CMOs, 220
  simultaneous-pay CMOs, 232
  structure of, 219–224

superfloater, 228–231
TAC bonds, 238
tax considerations, 223
two-tiered index bond, 228
VADM bonds, 238–239
yield/convexity characteristics, 276
Z-bonds, 220, 238–239
Companion classes, 232
Companions with schedules, 237–238
Competitive Equality Banking Act (1987), 112
Compound option (split-fee option)
back fee, 60
extension date, 60
front fee, 60
notification date, 60
Conduit, 50–52
Conforming mortgages, 30
Constant Maturity Treasury (CMT) rate, 106
Constant prepayment rate (CPR), 171–172, 173–175, 178, 190, 201, 208
Consumer Price Index (CPI), 126–127
Contraction risk, 216, 217–219, 238–239
Conventional Intermediate-Term MBSs, 158
Conventional Long-Term MBSs, 158
Conventional passthrough, 158–162. *See also* Private mortgage-backed securities market
A/B passthrough, 160–161
bond insurance, 160
corporate guarantees, 160
credit enhancement, 160
letters of credit, 160
mortgage design of loans, 162
senior/subordinated structure, 160/161
Convertible mortgages, 113–115
convertible ARMs, 113–114

reducible fixed-rate mortgates, 113–114
trigger rate, 114
Convexity, 217, 250, 257, 262, 264–267
effective, 267–268, 277, 301
formulas for, 267–268, 276–278
negative, 246, 259, 266, 269, 274–275
positive, 266
Coupon leverage, 227
CPR. *See* Constant prepayment rate
Credit life mortgage insurance, 69–70
Credit Suisse, 315
Cross-hedging risk, 53, 55
Custom pools, 150

Default, studies of, 74–77
Deficiency judgment, 77–78
Denomination intermediation, 320
Department of Housing and Urban Development (HUD), 27, 132. *See also* Federal Housing Administration
Derivative products. *See* Collateralized mortgage obligations; Stripped mortagage-backed securities
DiPasquale, Denise, 140–144
Discount, bond selling at, 251
Disintermediation, 18, 95
Dollar duration, 264, 266–267
Dollar roll agreement, 30, 164–165
DRM. *See* Dual-rate mortgage
Dual-rate mortgage (DRM), 14, 132–140
advantages of, 138–140
disadvantages of, 140–141
effective or debiting rate, 133
French mortgage, 137–141, 143
life of mortgage, 133
Mexican mortgage, 137–141, 143
negative amortization, 135
payment rate, 132–133
vs. PLAM, 132, 135–144

Dual-rate mortgage *(continued)*
  problems, opportunities in imple-
    mentation, 142–144
Duration, 265
  definition, 247
  dollar duration, 264, 266–267
  effective, 267, 277, 280, 301
  formulas for, 267–268, 276–278
  modified and Macaulay duration,
    262–264, 267
  and price volatility, 274–276
"Dwarfs," 158

Echo I Reuters, 45
Effective convexity, 267–268, 277–
    278, 280, 301
Effective duration, 267, 277, 280,
    301
11th Federal Home Loan Bank
    Board District Cost of Funds,
    107–108, 153, 157
Eurodollar floating-rate market,
    106
Expected cash flow, 249
Extension risk, 216, 217–219, 225,
    232, 237–239

Fallout risk, 46–48
  as option, 47–48
  sources of, 47
Fannie Mae, 2, 45, 59, 155–158, 203
  ARM passthroughs, 23
  balloon/reset mortgages, 115
  "boutique" securities, 157
  characteristics of loans in pool,
    157–158
  CMOs issued by, 224
  convertible ARMS, 114
  creation of, 19
  design of loans, 157
  division of, 20
  first mortgage-backed securities,
    23
  maximum size of loan, 323
  minimum pool size, 158
  number of lenders in pool, 157
  payment procedure, 158

pool of multifamily mortgages, 24
prepayment rate, 207–208
reverse mortgages, 98
seasoning, 195, 208–209
servicing fee, 65
stripped MBSs, 243
swap program, 23–24
type of guarantee, 157
underwriting standards, 322–323
Farmers Home Administration
    (FmHA), 20
  insurance for home mortgages,
    22, 151
Federal deposit insurance, 100
Federal Home Loan Bank Board
    (FHLBB), 103, 115
Federal Home Loan Bank Contract
    Rate, 107, 154
Federal Home Loan Banks, 18, 157
Federal Home Loan Mortgage Cor-
    poration (FHLMC). *See* Freddie
    Mac
Federal Housing Administration
    (FHA), 18–20, 82
  FHA-guaranteed vs. conventional
    loans, 207
  insurance for home mortgages,
    22, 69, 151, 207–208
  insurance for reverse mortgages,
    98
  prepayment experience as
    benchmark, 170–171
Federal National Mortgage Associa-
    tion (FNMA). *See* Fannie Mae
Federal Reserve Bank, 18, 93–94
  Regulation Q, 92
Federal Reserve Bank of New York
    Market Reports Division, 27
  Statistical Release H15, 106
Federal Reserve Board, Regulation
    T, 34
Federal Savings and Loan Insur-
    ance Corporation (FSLIC), 101
FHA. *See* Federal Housing Adminis-
    tration
FHLMC. *See* Freddie Mac
Financial Analyst Journal, 299

Financial Guarantee Insurance
 Corporation (FGIC), 160
Financial Institutions Reform, Recovery, and Enforcement Act,
 26–27, 62
Financial Security Assurance (FSA),
 160
FIRREA. *See* Financial Institutions
 Reform, Recovery, and Enforcement Act
First Boston Corporation, 314
First Nationwide, Certainly Affordable Mortgage Loans, 106
Fisher's Law, 100, 131, 135
Fixed-income analysis
 bond price volatility, 261–269
 bonds with embedded call options, 255–260
 convexity, 264–267
 coupon rate, yield, and price,
  250–251
 decomposition of callable bond,
  259–260
 disadvantages of callable bonds,
  256–257
 expected cash flow, 249
 formulas for duration and convexity, 267–268
 limitations of duration and convexity, 268
 measuring price volatility,
  262–267
 modified and Macaulay duration,
  262–264
 option-free bonds, 250–255, 261
 price compression, 257, 259
 price volatility of callable bonds,
  268–269
 price volatility properties,
  261–262
 price/yield relationship for callable bond, 257–259
 price/yield relationship for
  option-free bond, 250
 principle of valuation, 249–250
 required yield, 249–250
 sources of bond's return, 252

total return framework, 269–270
 yield to call, 256–257, 269
 yield to maturity, 252–255
Fixed-rate mortgage, 1, 44, 209–211
 reducible, 113–114
FLIP (flexible loan-insurance pro-
 gram), 124
FLIP Mortgage Corporation, 124
Float, 45, 65
Floating-rate certificates of deposit,
 102
Floating-rate CMOs, 225–226, 237
FmHA. *See* Farmers Home Administration
FNMA. *See* Fannie Mae
Foreclosure procedures, 77
Forward contracts, 49–51, 166–167
Franklin Savings Bank, 229
Freddie Mac, 2, 45, 203
 balloon/reset mortgages,
  115–116
 Cash PCs, 152
 Cash Program, 22, 51–52, 152–
  153, 155
 characteristics of loans in pool,
  154
 CMOs issued by, 25, 224
 convertible ARMS, 114
 creation of, 20
 default rate, 74–75
 design of loans, 153–154
 Gold PC, 152
 Guarantor/Swap Program, 23,
  152–153, 155
 maximum size of loan, 323
 minimum pool size, 155
 number of lenders in pool, 153
 participation certificate, first issue, 22
 payment procedure, 154–155
 pool of multifamily mortgages, 24
 prepayment rate, 207–208
 Regular PCs, 152
 reverse mortgages, 98
 seasoning, 195, 208–209
 servicing fee, 65
 Swap PC, 152

Freddie Mac *(continued)*
  TPMs, 124
  type of guarantee, 152–153
  underwriting standards, 322–323
French mortgage, 137–141, 143
Futures contracts
  basis, 54
  basis risk, 54
  cross-hedging risk, 53, 55
  disadvantages of, 53–54
  forward contracts vs., 53
  on passthrough securities,
    166–167
  risks of hedging with, 54–55
Futures options, 58–59, 167

GEM. *See* Growing equity mortgage
General Accounting Office (GAO),
  27
General Electric, 35
General Electric Capital Mortgage
  Insurance Corporation, 42
General Motors Acceptance Corporation (GMAC), 314–315, 318
Ginnie Mae, 2, 149–152, 203
  characteristics of loans in pool,
    150–151
  creation of, 20
  futures contract on, 166–167
  GNMA I, GNMA II, 150–151
  goals of, 22
  minimum pool size, 152
  mortgage design of loans, 150
  number of lenders in pool, 150
  payment procedure, 151–152
  prepayment rate, 207–208
  sales of servicing rights, 63
  seasoning, 195, 208–209
  servicing fee, 65
  type of guarantee, 150
  types of mortgages included, 22
GNMA. *See* Ginnie Mae
Goldman, Sachs, 287
Goldman, Sachs prepayment model,
  201, 203, 205, 214
Gold PC, 152
Government Long-Term MBSs, 158

Government National Mortgage As-
  sociation (GNMA). *See* Ginnie
  Mae
GPM. *See* Graduated-payment
  mortgage
Graduated-payment mortgage
  (GPM), 1, 14
  GPM plans, 121–123
  original version, 120
Grantor trust, 33
Great Depression, 18, 81–82, 92
Growing equity mortgage, 123–124
Guaranteed final maturity bonds,
  238
Guaranteed investment contract
  (GIC), 218
Guarantor/Swap Program, 23,
  152–153, 155, 157
Guttentag, Jack, 103

Harris, Steve, 63–64
Hayre, Lakhbir, 285
Herzog, Thomas N., 78
Hinkle, Hal, 63–64
Horizon return, 269–270
Housing finance market. *See* Mort-
  gage market
HUD. *See* Department of Housing
  and Urban Development
Hybrid mortgages
  convertible mortgages, 113–115
  reducible fixed-rate mortgages
    (FRM), 113–115

Impound balance, 65
Inflation problem, 1, 14, 69, 117–
  118, 120
Inflation-proof mortgage. *See*
  Dual-rate mortgage
Inside Mortgage Finance, 62
Interest on interest, 252–254
Interest only (IO)/principal only
  (PO) strips, 243–246
Interest rate risk, 253–254
Intermediation margin, 100
Internal Revenue Service regula-
  tions, 143, 162, 223
Inverse floater, 226–228, 237

Investment horizon, 269–270, 271, 302
IOette (interest only) class, 240–241, 247, 287

Jumbo loans, 30–31, 323
Jumbo pools, 150

Kling, Arnold, 114
KPMG Peat Marwick, Mortgage Servicing Performance Study, 66
Kutner, George W., 59

Lauterbach, Kenneth, 285
Level-payment mortgage
  amortization schedule, 84–85
  cash flow with servicing fee, 89–90
  formulas for cash flow, 86–89
  interest rate, 82
  mathematics of, 85–90
  maturity or term, 82
  monthly balance and interest, 87–89
  monthly payments, 83–87
  before 1970s, 92–95
  payment or annuity factor, 87
  prepayments and cash flow uncertainty, 90–92
LIBOR. *See* London Interbank Offered Rate
Liquidity of mortgages, 2, 22, 29, 146
Loan-to-value (LTV) ratio, 41–42, 69–70, 75–76, 142, 161
Loggins, Dick, 63–64
London Interbank Offered Rate (LIBOR), 106–107, 225–231
Long-term, self-amortizing mortgage, 19
LTV. *See* Loan-to-value ratio

Macaulay, Frederick, 263
Macaulay duration, 262–264, 272–273, 274
Mandatory contracts, 51–52

Marine Midland Bank, 314
MasterCard, 315–316
MBSs. *See* Mortgage-backed securities
MDC Mortgage Funding Corporation, 220, 231
Merrill Lynch, 35, 63
Mexican mortgage, 137–141, 143
Mismatch problem, 14, 99–102
  definition, 99–100
  face vs. market value, 100
  solutions to, 101
MIT mortgage, 14
Modified duration, 262–264, 267
Modigliani, Franco, 140–144
Monte Carlo simulation, 283–284
Montgomery Ward, 316
Monthly mortgage payment (MP), 86–87, 175, 190
Moody's Investor's Service, 71, 159, 161, 323
Mortgage-backed securities. *See also* Collateralized mortgage obligations; Passthroughs; Stripped mortgage-backed securities
  agency securities, 21–30
  components of cash flow, 4
  creation of, 2, 3–12
  foreign investors in, 2, 26
  government-guaranteed vs. private, 3
  private market, 30–35
Mortgage-backed securities, potential supply of
  barriers to securitization, 322–324
  commercial mortgages, 322–324
  multifamily housing, 322–324
  second mortgages, 324–325
  servicing fees, 325
  unsecuritized 1-to-4 family mortgages, 321–322
Mortgage banker, 17–18
Mortgage Bankers Association, 43, 45, 66
Mortgage broker, 17–18

Mortgage insurance, 69–78
  conditional default rate, 74
  default risks from underwriting,
      72–74
  expanding role of insurance in-
      dustry, 36, 71–72
  local economic risks, 74
  national economic risks, 74
  normal risks, 72–73
  originator underwriting risk, 73
  reasons for underwriting losses,
      71–72
  state foreclosure laws and default
      losses, 77–78
  studies of default, 74–77
Mortgage market (early)
  effect of inflation, 1, 14
  limitations of, 17–18
  recurrent crises in, 1
  size of, 1
  and thrift institutions, 1
Mortgage origination, 15
  alternatives for originator after
      closing, 44–46
  commitment letter, 43
  costs of, 42–43
  credit evaluation, 41–42
  fallout risk, 46–48
  fixed- vs. adjustable-rate mort-
      gage, 44
  forward contracts, 49–51
  futures contracts, 53–55
  hedging risk, 49–60
  mandatory contracts, 51–52
  option-type contracts, 49, 55–60
  origination process, 41–44
  originators, 39–40
  pipeline risk, 46–48, 56
  price risk, 46–48
  risks associated with, 46–49
  setting the contract rate, 43–44
  sources of revenue, 40–41
  symmetric and asymmetric risk,
      49, 51
  warehouse risk, 48–49
Mortgage passthrough securities.
    See Passthroughs

Mortgage servicing
  benefits of servicing rights, 65–66
  costs associated with, 66–67
  declining profit margins, 62
  excess servicing, 65
  the float, 65
  late fee, 65
  revenue from servicing, 64–66
  risks associated with, 67–69
  servicers, 61
  servicing fee, 64–65, 67
  servicing rights transfer market,
      62–64
  transfer brokerage industry,
      62–63
Mortgage Servicing Performance
    Study (KPMG Peat Marwick),
    66
Mortgage servicing rights, 12,
    62–69, 295
  benefits of, 65–66
  inflation and value of, 69
  interest rates and value of, 68
  prepayments and value of, 68
  transfer market, 62–64
MP. See Monthly mortgage payment

National Cost of Funds Index, 107,
    153
National Housing Act (1934), 18
Negative amortization, 110, 112,
    120, 130, 135, 142–144
Negative convexity, 246, 259, 266,
    269, 274–275, 278
New Deal reforms, 92
Nonconforming mortgages, 30

OAS. See Option-adjusted spread
Option-adjusted spread (OAS),
    282–285
Option-adjusted spread (OAS)
    methodology, 280–302
  application to passthroughs,
      285–287
  CMO applications, 287–294
  effective duration and convexity,
      301–302

industry acceptance of, 295,
299–301
limitations of, 301–302
Monte Carlo simulation, 283–284
option-adjusted spread, 282–285
option cost, 285
other applications, 294–295
procedure for calculation, 284
static spread, 281–282
Option-adjusted yield, 279–280
Options
call, 56
callable bonds, 255–260, 268–
269, 278, 285
caput, 60
compound options, 59–60
definition, 55
exchange-traded vs. OTC, 58
exercise or strike price, 56–57
expiration date, 56
vs. forward or futures contract,
56–57
futures options, 58 59, 167
optional delivery contracts, 59
option price or premium, 55
option pricing theory, 59
on passthrough securities, 167
put, 56–57
risk/reward characteristics, 56
split-fee option, 59–60
Origination fee, 40
Origination market, 15. *See also*
Mortgage origination
Oxford Acceptance Corporation III,
231

PAC (Planned amortization class)
bonds, 231–237, 246, 291
effective collar, 234
initial PAC collar, 234, 236
lockout, 237
PAC I, II, and III level bonds, 238
PAC window, 236
planned redemption obligation
(PRO) bonds, 232
predictability of cash flow, 232

simultaneous-pay CMOs, 232
stabilized mortgage reduction
term (SMRT) bonds, 231
Z-PAC bonds, 235–236
PAC IO (interest only) class,
240–242
PaineWebber, 229, 238
Pairoff fee, 52
Participation certificate (PC), 22,
152
Participation interests, 46
Passthroughs, 3, 10, 21. *See also*
Agency passthroughs; Conventional passthrough; Valuing
mortgage-backed securities
advantages of, 9
ARM passthroughs, 23, 103
cash flow characteristics,
146–147
cash flow uncertainty, 169, 216
features of, 145–167
forward, futures, and options on,
166–167
investor preference for, 145–146
liquidity, 146
negative convexity (price compression), 246
noncallable, 278–279
OAS applied to, 285–287
as securities with embedded call
options, 255–256
sources of total dollars, 302
synthetic coupon, 243
total return framework, 302–309
Passthroughs, price and yield conventions
bond equivalent yield, 191–193
cash flow yield, 191–193
constant prepayment rate as
benchmark, 171–172
constructing projected cash flow,
175–191
FHA experience as benchmark,
170–171
illustrations, 178–189
investor's cash flow, 177
need for caution, 194–195

Passthroughs, price and yield conventions *(continued)*
prepayment benchmark conventions, 169–175
price, 193–194
projected monthly mortgage interest and servicing, 176
projected monthly mortgage payment, 175
projected monthly scheduled
principal and prepayment,
176–177
PSA prepayment model, 172–175,
178
short-cut approach, 179, 190–191
Payment-to-income (PTI) ratio, 41,
77, 142
PC. *See* Participation certificate
Penney (J.C.), 316
Perfect hedge, 54
Peters, Helen F., 74
Pinkus, Scott M., 74
PLAM. *See* Price-level-adjusted
mortgage
Planned amortization bonds. *See*
PAC bonds
Planned redemption obligation
(PRO) bonds, 232
Pledged-account mortgage (PAM),
124
PO. *See* Principal only strips
PO-collateralized CMOs, 246
Points, 40
"Ponzi" technique, 100
Pool factor, 203, 205
Positive convexity, 266
Potential supply of mortgage-
backed securities. *See*
Mortgage-backed securities,
potential supply of
Premium, bond selling at, 251
Prepayment behavior, factors af-
fecting, 197–216
benefits from refinancing, 198,
200, 214
and cash flow uncertainty, 90–92,
169, 215–216

characteristics of underlying
loans, 205–212
contract rate vs. current mortgage rate, 198–201, 205
FHA/VA vs. conventional mortgages, 207–208
fixed-rate mortgage vs. ARM,
209–211
general economic activity, 213
level of mortgage rates, 205
location of underlying properties,
211–212
models and projections, 214–215
model using macroeconomic
variables, 213
path of mortgage rates, 201–205,
214
pool factor, 203, 205
prevailing mortgage rate,
198–205
reasons for prepayments, 90, 92,
197
refinancing burnout, 198, 203,
208, 214
risks associated with passthroughs, 215–216
seasonal factors, 212, 214
seasoning, 208–209, 214
trading up, 205
Prepayment risk, 3–4, 10–11, 145–
146, 215–216, 217–218
Presidential Commission on Housing, 31
Price and yield conventions for
passthroughs. *See* Pass-
throughs, price and yield conventions
Price compression, 246, 257, 259,
269
Price-level-adjusted mortgage
(PLAM), 14, 126–132
computing monthly payment,
126
Consumer Price Index and,
126–127
countries of use, 131
vs. DRM, 132, 135–144

problems of implementation,
143–144
real vs. nominal rate, 126, 131
risks, 130–131
Price risk, 46–48, 253–254
Primary mortgage market, 15
Principal only (PO) strips, 243–246,
308–309
Private-label passthrough. *See* Private mortgage-backed securities market
Private mortgage-backed securities
market, 30–35. *See also* Conventional passthrough
credit enhancement, 32, 45,
160–162
early problems, 31
government intervention, 31–34
the issuers, 34–35
margin requirements, 34
SEC registration regulations,
32–33
servicing fee, 65
state blue sky laws, 33
tax considerations, 33–34
Private mortgage insurance. *See*
Mortgage insurance
Prudential-Bache prepayment
model, 213, 285
PSA. *See* Public Securities Association
PSA prepayment model, 172–175,
178, 193–195, 208–209, 221,
285
PTI. *See* Payment-to-income ratio
Public Securities Association (PSA),
163–164
standard prepayment benchmark,
172–175, 178, 193–195, 208–
209, 221, 285

Real Estate Investment Conduit
(REMIC), 34, 223
Real indexation, 126, 132, 136
Refinancing burnout, 198, 203, 208
Regular PCs, 152

Reinvestment risk, 253–255
REMIC. *See* Real Estate Investment
Conduit
Repo, 29–30, 164–165
RepublicBank Delaware, 315
Repurchase agreement, 29–30,
164–165
Required net yield, 45
Required yield, 249–250
Resecuritization, 10, 11
Resolution Trust Corporation
(RTC), 35
Reverse mortgages
and the elderly, 95
illustration, 96
risks to lenders and borrowers, 97
secondary market for, 98
Reverse TAC bonds, 238–239
Richard, Scott, 287
RJR Nabisco, 231
Rollover mortgage, 115

Salomon Brothers, 35, 63
SAM. *See* Shared-appreciation
mortgage
San Francisco Development Fund,
98
Savings and loan associations, 1–2,
41
bailout problem, 3, 17, 27, 101
borrowing short, lending long,
93, 95
mismatch problem, 101
nonregulation of rates, 92–93
Sears, 316
Seasoning, 151, 208–209, 210, 214
definition, 148
effect on default rates, 76
patterns of, 194–195
Secondary Mortgage Market Enhancement Act (SMMEA),
32–33, 160
Secondary marketing profit, 40
Secondary mortgage market. *See
also* Agency-backed securities
market; Private mortgage-
backed securities market

Secondary mortgage market (con-
    tinued)
  development of, 2, 15–38
  dollar rolls, 164–165
  factors fostering, 28–29
  foundations for, 18–21
  government intervention in hous-
    ing market, 15–30
  pool prefix and number, 162
  required net yield, 45
  TBA trades, 163–164
  trading mechanics, 162–165
  whole loan market, 35–37
Securities and Exchange Commis-
    sion, 159
Securitization, 9, 21, 318. See also
    Asset securitization, future of
  barriers to, 322–324
Seifert, James A., 59
Senior/subordinated structure,
    160–161
Sequential-pay CMOs, 220
Servicing fees, 64–65, 67, 89–90,
    176, 325
Servicing rights, 12, 62–69, 295
Shared-appreciation mortgage
    (SAM), 125–126
Shearson Lehman Brothers, 225
Simultaneous-pay CMOs, 232
Single monthly mortality (SMM)
    rate, 171–175, 177–179, 190
S&Ls. See Savings and loan associa-
    tions
SMM. See Single monthly mortality
    rate
SMMEA. See Secondary Mortgage
    Market Enhancement Act
Sperry Lease Finance Corporation
    (Unisys), 314, 317
Split-fee option (compound option),
    59–60
Stabilized mortgage reduction term
    (SMRT) bonds, 231
Standard & Poor's, 159–161
Static spread, 281–282, 324
Statutory right of redemption,
    77–78
Strike rate, 228

Stripped mortgage-backed securi-
    ties, 4, 11–12, 145
  CMO strips, 246
  definition, 11
  hedging applications of, 246–247
  interest only (IO)/principal only
    (PO) strips, 243–246
  introduction by Fannie Mae, 242
  resecuritization, 11
  Super PO, 246
  synthetic coupon passthroughs,
    243
  types of, 242–246
Superfloater, 228–231
Super PO, 246
Support classes, 232
Synthetic coupon passthroughs, 243

TAC bonds. See Targeted Amortiza-
    tion Class bonds
Targeted Amortization Class (TAC)
    bonds, 238, 246, 291
Tax Reform Act of 1986, 33–34, 41,
    223
TBA trades, 163–164, 166
Teaser rate, 109
Telerate, 45
Tiered-payment mortgage (TPM),
    124–125, 323
  FLIP (flexible loan-insurance
    program), 124
  pledged-account mortgage
    (PAM), 124
Tilt problem, 14, 116, 117–119
  inflation and, 117–118, 120
Toevs, Alden, 299, 301
Total return framework, 271
  applications, 308–309
  bond equivalent yield basis,
    303–306
  calculating total monthly return,
    303–306
  effective annual yield, 303–306
  illustrations, 303–306
  OAS combined with, 306–308
  objections to, 270

for passthroughs, 302–309
specifications, 269
steps for computing, 269–270
TPM. *See* Tiered-payment mortgage
Traditional mortgage, 81–95. *See also* Level-payment mortgage
historical background, 81–82
level-payment mortgage, 82–95
prepayments and cash flow uncertainty, 90–92
Travelers, 35, 160
Treasury STRIP, 308–309
Two-tiered index bond, 228

VA. *See* Veterans Administration
VADM. *See* Very accurately defined maturity bonds
Valuing mortgage-backed securities
average life, 273–274
cash flow yield, 271–272
formulas for duration and convexity, 276–278
industry acceptance of OAS, 295, 299–301
limitations of OAS, 301–302
Macaulay duration, 272–273
OAS and Monte Carlo simulation, 283–284
OAS applied to CMOs, 287–294
OAS applied to passthroughs, 285–287
option-adjusted spread methodology, 280–302
option adjusted yield, 279–280
option cost, 285
option pricing methodology, 278–280
other applications of OAS, 294–295

price volatility: duration, 274–276
spread to Treasuries, 272–274
static cash-flow yield methodology, 271–278, 280–282, 302
static spread, 281–282
yield/convexity characteristics, 274–276
Van Order, Robert, 75–77
Variable-rate mortgage. *See* Adjustable-rate mortgage (ARM)
Very accurately defined maturity (VADM) bonds, 238–239
Veterans Administration (VA)
insurance for mortgage loans, 20, 22, 69, 151, 207–208
VA-guaranteed vs. conventional loans, 207
Visa, 315–316

Warehouse risk, 48–49
Western Financial Savings Bank, 314
Whole loan secondary market
dealers, 37
functions of, 35–36
relative illiquidity, 35–36
secondary market trading services, 36–37

Yield to call, 256–257, 269
Yield to maturity, 252–255, 269, 272

Z-bonds, 220, 238–239
accrual bonds, 220, 224–225
jump bonds, 235
Zero-coupon bonds, 262
Zero-coupon Treasuries, 281
Z-PAC bonds, 235–236